The Return of the Galon King

This series of publications on Africa, Latin America, Southeast Asia, and Global and Comparative Studies is designed to present significant research, translation, and opinion to area specialists and to a wide community of persons interested in world affairs. The editor seeks manuscripts of quality on any subject and can usually make a decision regarding publication within three months of receipt of the original work. Production methods generally permit a work to appear within one year of acceptance. The editor works closely with authors to produce a high-quality book. The series appears in a paperback format and is distributed worldwide. For more information, contact the executive editor at Ohio University Press, 19 Circle Drive, The Ridges, Athens, Ohio 45701.

Executive editor: Gillian Berchowitz
AREA CONSULTANTS
Africa: Diane M. Ciekawy
Latin America: Brad Jokisch, Patrick Barr-Melej, and Rafael Obregon
Southeast Asia: William H. Frederick

The Ohio University Research in International Studies series is published for the Center for International Studies by Ohio University Press. The views expressed in individual volumes are those of the authors and should not be considered to represent the policies or beliefs of the Center for International Studies, Ohio UniversityPress, or Ohio University.

The Return of the Galon King

History, Law, and Rebellion in Colonial Burma

Maitrii Aung-Thwin

OHIO UNIVERSITY RESEARCH IN INTERNATIONAL STUDIES
SOUTHEAST ASIA SERIES NO. 124
OHIO UNIVERSITY PRESS
ATHENS

NUS PRESS
SINGAPORE

© 2011 by the
Center for International Studies
Ohio University
www.ohioswallow.com

To obtain permission to quote, reprint, or otherwise reproduce or distribute material from Ohio University Press publications, please contact our rights and permissions department at (740) 593-1154 or (740) 593-4536 (fax).

Printed in the United States of America
All rights reserved

First published in Asia by:
NUS Press
AS3-01-02, 3 Arts Link
National University of Singapore
Singapore 117569

Fax: (65) 6774-0652
E-mail: nusbooks@nus.edu.sg
Website: http://www.nus.edu.sg/nuspress

ISBN: 978-9971-69-509-5

20 19 18 17 16 15 14 13 12 11   5 4 3 2 1

The books in the Ohio University Research in International Studies Series are printed on acid-free paper ∞ ™

Library of Congress Cataloging-in-Publication Data

Aung-Thwin, Maitrii.
  The return of the Galon king : history, law, and rebellion in colonial Burma / by Maitrii Aung-Thwin.
       p. cm. — (Ohio University research in international studies. Southeast Asia Series ; no. 124)
  Includes bibliographical references and index.
  ISBN 978-0-89680-276-6 (pb : alk. paper) — ISBN 978-0-89680-470-8 (electronic)
 1. Burma—History—Peasant Uprising, 1930. 2. Anti-imperialist movements—Burma—History—20th century. 3. San, Hsaya—Trials, litigation, etc. 4. Burma—Trials, litigation, etc.—History—20th century. I. Title.
  DS527.6.A86 2010
  959.1'04—dc22
                            2010033715

To Eileen

Contents

Preface   xi

Acknowledgments   xv

SECTION I: HISTORY
   ONE   Introduction   1
   TWO   Textualizing Rebellion
       *Remembering Kings and
       an Ethnology of Revolt*   47

SECTION II: LAW
   THREE   Legislating Rebellion
       *Ethnology and the Formation
       of Counter-Insurgency Law*   76
   FOUR   Adjudicating Rebellion
       The Trial of Saya San   106
   FIVE   Codifying Rebellion
       Origins of a Resistance Narrative   139

SECTION III: REBELLION
   SIX   Interpreting Rebellion
       Binary Structures and Colonial Remains   160
   SEVEN   Sanctifying Rebellion
       *Colonial Discourses and
       Southeast Asian Resistance*   191
   EIGHT   Remembering Rebellion
       Museums, Monks, and the Military   216

Bibliography   227

Index   243

Maps and Illustrations

1. Saya San c. 1920s — 5

2. Resistance activity in Lower Burma 1930–1932 — 7

3. British Burma in the 1930s — 15

4. Tharrawaddy District — 49

5. Rebellion clothing — 62

6. Defense lawyers — 114

7. Badges of rebellion displayed in "mocking" fashion — 124

8. Special Rebellion Tribunal — 129

9. Saya San exiting Tharrawaddy Jail — 140

10. Ne Win and Galon veterans, 1960s — 217

PREFACE

The *galon*, more popularly known as the *garuda*, is a well-recognized figure in the iconography and literature of Hindu-Buddhist Southeast Asia. Sometimes described as half-man and half-raptor, the *galon* is best known as the celestial vehicle of Vishnu, one of the three great deities of the Brahmanic universe. Embedded in the region's temple architecture, performance, astrology, literature, and ritual, this winged creature embodies the centuries of cultural exchange between India and Southeast Asia that contributed to the formation of the region's earliest civilizations. In regional folklore, the *galon* is also regarded as the eternal archenemy of the *naga* (snake/dragon). Driven by an ancient grievance, the *galon* hunts the *naga* from the skies in hope of devouring and defeating its traditional earthbound foe. This cosmic battle between *galon* and *naga* would come to represent ideas about the power of nature, the dualities of the world, and the challenges of the human condition.

While the symbol of the majestic *galon* had been circulating in the region for centuries, it was only in British Burma that this mythology was evoked as a metaphor for the colonial situation. In 1930, the *galon* came to represent the Burmese peasantry's aspirations to restore the banished monarchy by overthrowing the British (represented by the *naga*). By tattooing themselves with the *galon* symbol, rural cultivators exhibited their allegiance to Saya San, the rebellion leader who would be known as the *Galon King*. In time, the *galon* would become synonymous with the very notion of Burmese resistance. As such, the narrative that unfolds in this book might be seen as one chapter in a much longer story of the *galon* and its place in the cultural histories of Southeast Asia.

* * *

My initial encounter with the Saya San Rebellion and its historiography did not stem from an inherent interest in *galons*, *nagas*, or Burmese kings. At the time I began thinking about Saya San in 1995, I was only beginning to develop an ear for some of the ongoing discussions about empire, ethnohistory, and postcolonial studies that were permeating the graduate seminars and the Lane-Hall brown-bag lunch talks at the University of Michigan. Issues concerning the construction of knowledge, the history of anthropology, orientalism, and the postcolonial predicament were still very new to me, and I did not anticipate their potential for the study of Burmese history. Although the scholarship in the present book would eventually intersect with many of these conversations, these issues were not in play when I stumbled on what would become my focus for the next fifteen years of my academic life. As the book is primarily concerned with the epistemological construction of Burmese resistance in a particular time and space, it may be worthwhile to present a brief narrative about the context within which this study has taken place.

I "met" Saya San in Professor Rudolf Mrazek's exciting graduate seminar that explored the role of colonial scholar-administrators in the historiography of Southeast Asia. Our term paper required us to write an essay on a colonial scholar-official (loosely defined) of our choice and reflect upon the person's contributions to the field and perceptions about Southeast Asia. Having very little training in postcolonial methods but armed with Albert Memmi's *The Colonizer and the Colonized*,[1] I set out to read Dr. Ba Maw's autobiography (Ba Maw was the head of state in Burma during World War II) in order to study how an anglicized Burmese elite had defended the apparently traditional Saya San at his trial.[2] I had hoped to discover whether Ba Maw experienced the same internal conflict of identity that Memmi writes about in his portrait of the "colonized who accepts colonialism." I wondered whether I could detect in his defense of the famous peasant who personified the "last-gasp" of traditional Burma the internal conflict of identity that characterizes much of what Memmi termed the "colonial situation." I intended to explore the transcripts of the trial in order to reconstruct Ba Maw's impression of Saya San. I was disappointed, however, to find little with regard to the trial documents. After reading nearly everything available in the secondary literature, I realized that there were very few references to the trial at all, but nearly every scholar had cited the official blue-book report, *Origins and Causes of the Burma Rebellion, 1930-1932* (1934), as the foundational source to the historical narrative.

Thinking that my quest to find Ba Maw's voice was nearly over, I dove into the report only to discover that the entire narrative about the rebellion was actually based on findings derived from earlier trial judgments that were compiled by a Special Rebellion Tribunal who had overseen the majority of rebel hearings. Passages from these documents had been cut and pasted in order to supply much of the official report's text. To my surprise, the report presented only the legal positions, evidence, and contentions made by the prosecution team, led by (Sir) Arthur Eggar. The defense's case had not been recorded. I understood at once that the primary source that had been used by nearly every scholar on the Saya San Rebellion to authenticate the veracity of the event was not only a compilation of earlier legal documents but a record of only the prosecution's version of events. Realizing that such issues put into question nearly everything that we thought we understood about the Saya San Rebellion, I decided to shelve Ba Maw for the time being and devote at least the rest of the semester to this problem. I did not realize that fifteen years later, these initial encounters would result in the present book.

Notes

1. Albert Memmi, *The Colonizer and the Colonized*, New York: Orion Press, 1965.
2. Ba Maw, *Breakthrough in Burma: Memoirs of a Revolution, 1939-1946*, New Haven: Yale University Press, 1968.

ACKNOWLEDGMENTS

At its core, this book is interested in how histories are made and how circumstances affect the way pasts are remembered. Thinking about history from this perspective is the result of many intellectual and personal experiences that began in the heartland of the United States and has taken me—inevitably it now seems—back to the Southeast Asia of my roots. During this journey, there have been many individuals who have helped shape the way in which I have come to understand Southeast Asia in general and Burmese history in particular. Their friendship, guidance, and support cannot be appropriately recognized by a lifeless footnote or bibliography. It is impossible to demonstrate or qualify the undeniable influence that Mrs. Virginia Marsden had on me as a fifth grader or how Mr. Joe Locascio's high-school seminar on classical studies paved the way for an interest in history and classical Southeast Asia. Yet, they are part of this book's genealogy, all part of the processes that led to its shaping. Circumstances have been kind to me by bringing these people into my history, and without them this book and this scholar would not be possible.

One enormous influence on the texture of this study stems from the corridors of the University of Michigan's history department and the Center for Southeast Asian Studies. Professors Victor Lieberman, Thomas Trautmann, Rudolf Mrazek, John K. Whitmore, and Michael L. Ross were an amazing dissertation committee. They extended their patience, encouragement, and insight during my time in Ann Arbor. Vic's limitless knowledge, generosity, and critical eye gave me the time and confidence to find my own path to colonial Burma. I will always be thankful for the many times Vic and Sharon welcomed me into their home, where our dinner conversations took us (thankfully for Sharon) away from Burmese history to the other important things in life— "Law & Order," baseball, and family. I will always be grateful to Tom for urging me to select different books on the Indian past than what my father read for him; his advice led me to approach Burmese history from the broader story of colonial knowledge production. John's independent reading seminar introduced me to colonial scholarship on Southeast Asia and whetted my appetite for intellectual history and for Middle-Eastern food at our favorite restaurant on Maynard Street. (Auntie) Susan Go, head librarian of UM's Southeast Asia division, not only found key sources that are at the very heart of this book but made sure that every Thanksgiving I had enough turkey, *pancit*, and warm company, which were always good for the heart. I was fortunate during my time at Michigan to have the opportunity to speak with and learn from people such as Pete Gosling, Linda Lim, Diane Hughes, Eleanor Mannika, Judy Becker, Carla Sinopoli, Luis Gomez, Montatip Krishnamra, Nancy Florida, Martin S. Pernick, and Maria Montoya, while benefitting from the friendship and advice of fellow grad students Shah Alam Zaini, Laichen Sun, Kerry Ward, Sarah Womack, Michael Charney, Atsuko Naomo, Jennifer Gaynor, Parna Sengupta, Rama S. Mantena, Will Redfern, and Andrew M. Goss. The University of Michigan's deep commitment to interdisciplinary studies—especially in the fields of anthropology and history—has had a lasting impression on my work and I am grateful to these folks who took the time to share in and promote that unforgettable experience.

My friends and colleagues at the Department of History, the Asia Research Institute, and the Southeast Asian Studies Program at the National University of Singapore have offered me their expertise, funding, and collaborative opportunities, without which I would not have seen this project to completion. I am indebted to Lily Kong and Chua Beng Huat, who first considered my postdoctoral application to the SEASP and then forwarded it to what would be called the Asia Research Institute, setting into motion my "love affair" with Singapore. While there, Anthony Reid, James F. Warren, Geoff Wade, Ashley

Carruthers, Mark R. Frost, Maung Aung Myoe, Mika Toyota, and Tilman Frasch graciously offered their company and criticism, nurturing in me the incentive to think about the epistemology of rebellion from a broad, pan-Asian perspective. The Asia Research Institute was also instrumental in supporting my efforts to co-organize with Kyaw Yin Hlaing the 2006 International Burma Studies Conference, which pursued a perspective through which Burmese studies could be more inclusive and engaging. The conference papers and the rich discussions that ensued had a direct bearing on the perspective this book takes. Many thanks to Chelvi Krishnan, Valerie Yeo, Henry Kwan, Yati Hamsen, Verene Koh, Sharon Ong, and Alyson Rozells for their professionalism, friendship, and support of this and ongoing projects.

The following colleagues in the Department of History and the Southeast Asian Studies Program supported me in innumerable ways: Tan Tai Yong, Timothy Barnard, Mark Emmanuel, Michael Feener, Huang Jianli, Yong Mun Cheong, Albert Lau, Peter Borschberg, Thomas Dubois, Kwa Chong Guan, Derek Heng, Medha Kudaisya, Merle Ricklefs, Maurizio Peleggi, Michael Kelly, Lee Seung-Joon, Ian Gordon, Brian Farrell, Hong Lysa, Cheah Boon Kheng, John Miksic, Pattana Kitiarsa, Julius Bautista, Chie Ikea, Jan Mrazek, Michael Montesano, and Goh Beng Lan patiently listened to or unhesitatingly read drafts of early chapters; in no uncertain terms, they helped shape the intellectual substance of this book. Research assistants and future scholars Nurfadzilah Yahaya and Ho Chi Tim spent hours collecting and organizing legal documents, for which I am entirely grateful. But for taking me under their collective wings, I owe a special note of thanks to Paul Kratoska, Bruce Lockhart, and Reynaldo C. Ileto.

Through conferences, collaborative projects, and correspondence, I was fortunate to have James Scott, Eric Tagliacozzo, Jeff Hadley, Tamara Loos, Craig Reynolds, William Friedrich, Michael Adas, Barbara Andaya, Leonard Andaya, Webb Keane, Marc Gilbert, Carl Hefner, Peter Coclanis, Oscar Salemink, Parna Sengupta, and Charles Keyes comment on my work, which helped me think about how rebellion and resistance functioned as a discourse within Southeast Asian studies. Carol Tan, Eric Jones, Victor V. Ramraj, and

Arun K. Thiruvengadam gave me opportunities to situate rebellion more closely within the context of sociolegal studies through their panels and workshops. My colleagues in the larger Myanmar studies community have made a fundamental impression on me through their scholarship, mentoring, and friendship—U Saw Tun, Daw May Gyi Win, F. K. Lehman (U Chit Hlaing), Robert Taylor, Catherine Raymond, Mary Callahan, Patricia Herbert, Kyaw Yin Hlaing, Patrick Pranke, Alicia Turner, Elizabeth Moore, Jane Ferguson, Lily Handlin, Juliane Schober, Ward Keeler, Jacques Leider, D. Christian Lammerts, Mandy Sadan, Goh Geok Yian, Will B. Womack, and Alexey Kirichenko inspired me through their helpful criticisms, their politics, and their scholarship to consider the rebellion within the larger epistemological construction of "Myanmar" and Burmese Buddhism. The Burma Studies Group in particular has been so supportive, sponsoring my panels at the Association of Asian Studies conferences and agreeing in 2006 to allow Kyaw Yin Hlaing and me to convene the International Conference on Burma Studies in Southeast Asia for the first time.

Without a doubt, I am also indebted to my colleagues and *sayas* in Myanmar, especially those members and retired members of the Historical Commission who opened homes, archives, and memories to me without hesitation. I owe a deep debt of gratitude to Dr. Myo Myint, U Thaw Kaung, Dr. Khin Maung Nyunt, U Tun Aung Chain, U Toe Hla, U Sai Aung Tun, Daw Ni Ni Myint, Daw Kyan, U Hla Shain, U Aung Myo, U Win Maung, U Myint Aung, U Kyi Saw Tun, Troy Tun, U Than Ohn, U Tin Saung, Ko Soe Moe and Ma Win Win. Without their assistance I could not have grasped how Saya San the man and the rebellion in general were remembered in Myanmar in different and exciting ways. More importantly, my collaboration with this community of scholars has made a deep impression in how I eventually came to think about different renderings of rebellion as part of a larger discourse of agency, identity, and nation. To Dr. Thant Thaw Kaung I offer a special note of appreciation for all of his help in assisting me with my projects and for his continuous patience, hospitality, and flexibility.

Several institutions also made this book possible through funding, administrative, and publishing support. I am grateful to the U.S. Department of Education's Foreign Language and Area Studies Fellowships that the University of Michigan's Center for Southeast Asian Studies awarded me during my graduate years, along with the vital teaching assistantships that were offered by UM's Department of History. The Asia Research Institute generously awarded a postdoctoral fellowship, under which much of this book was revised. The faculty of Arts and Social Sciences of the National University of Singapore awarded crucial research funds that allowed me to visit Myanmar to complete my project, while my Department of History as a whole has enabled me to see this book to fruition by granting me two key semesters off from teaching. I am indebted to Gillian Berkowitz of Ohio University Press for belief in the project, her sensible mediation, and her steadfast navigation of the manuscript to its successful conclusion and to the anonymous referees whose careful suggestions and interventions improved the book's accessibility to a wider audience. A debt of gratitude goes out to Beth Pratt of Ohio Press and my copyeditor, Matthew Laughlin, for making this book more readable and accessible. Again, I am forever grateful to Paul Kratoska, whose guidance as a fellow historian, Southeast Asianist, and publisher made this book possible in the first place.

Perhaps the most important intellectual influence on me has been from Michael Aung-Thwin—scholar, teacher, soccer coach, and father. It is impossible for me to not see his historical insight, encouragement, and criticism within the pages of this book. Although we both learned our craft at Michigan (and sometimes under the same professors), we trained at different times with equally different scholarly priorities, political agendas, and disciplinary concerns. His earlier assessments of Saya San were, in fact, conceptually at odds with mine, but he gave me room as both a son and a colleague to explore my own suspicions for thinking this to be the case, engaging me at both the level of mentor and parent. Yet, his deep concern for articulating and delineating Southeast Asian experiences (especially those that we might define as "Burmese") is something that binds our lives and careers together.

It was his choice *not* to push me toward Southeast Asian history that was his greatest gift, allowing me to find my way back to a past and a culture that was thousands of miles away from the small towns in upstate-New York and Illinois that I grew up in. My father's surprise (and probable uncertainty) over my decision to tentatively follow in his footsteps is telling in itself, for it relieved the pressure of always having to work under his enormous shadow; and he allowed me to venture away from that shadow on my own. To this day, he still encourages me as he did when I was a boy, something that any son or scholar is truly lucky to have in his career and life.

I owe too much to my mother, Maria, to put into words. Her resilience, strength, innumerable sacrifices, and unconditional nurturing continue well into my adulthood. It was her support that kept me going through the more challenging episodes of life, along with her more-than-occasional "gifts" that found their way into my bank account that made graduate student-life manageable.

Amita—sister, friend, confidant, lawyer. She has been the one constant in my life that guaranteed that I would never be alone, even though the life of a historian is inherently lonely. Her determined journey to the law and beyond is one that I will never stop admiring.

My final thoughts of gratitude are reserved for my wife, Eileen, who took a chance that I might, just possibly, be "for real." Had it not been for her, had it not been for her endurance, had it not been for her warm and welcoming family, I would not be nearly the husband, father, and scholar that I am today. For her faith in me, Shan, and our future, I dedicate this book.

Chapter 1

INTRODUCTION

With Christmas celebrations nearly upon them, Rangoon officials were hardly prepared for the storm that was brewing in the Burmese countryside in late December 1930.

By all accounts, there was little reason to worry. The acting governor, Joseph Maung Gyi, was touring several rural districts and had even conducted a successful *durbar* (meeting) in Tharrawaddy—one of the more notoriously violent districts in recent years—without incident.[1] Although local village leaders and notables had petitioned him to postpone the collection of taxes, his refusal to do so did not appear to have any significant effect on the collection of village elders, notables, officials and headmen that were in attendance. Despite the recent economic downturn that was directly affecting the massive rice-economy in Irrawaddy delta region, British Burma was considered a success in the eyes of its administrators in Delhi and London. Yet the acting governor had no idea that a local headman, U Tun Hla, had recently warned the deputy commissioner and local superintendent of police that villagers throughout the district were preparing for a revolt in the area. One day later, on December 22, 1931, a police patrol that was sent to the village of Phashwegyaw would encounter and briefly engage two hundred men, mostly with *dahs* (knives) and a few guns.[2] District officers advised Rangoon that the outbreak was most likely local in nature and would settle almost as quickly as it began.[3] When the same police force returned to investigate, it was completely overwhelmed by nearly six hundred armed men, who killed the deputy-superintendant in charge. As events began to unfold, local officials would soon realize that they were witnessing something more than a random occurrence of rural unrest.

For what would emerge between the years 1930 and 1932 would be regarded by scholars as one of the largest anticolonial movements of Southeast Asia, spreading throughout the Lower Burma delta and into hills of the Shan States; involving numerous communities, thousands of villagers, and several thousand counter-insurgency troops. Officials would soon associate the name *Saya San* with the uprising in reference to the mysterious peasant leader who reportedly revived the ancient symbols of Burmese kingship in order to trigger the impressionable peasantry into action. Operating through a network of village cells that he and his lieutenants had established, Saya San promised supporters that as their new king, he would restore the authority of the Burmese monarchy, revitalize the Buddhist religion, and expel the British, who had completed the annexation of the kingdom as a province of British India in late 1885. Building his new "palace" on the hills east of Tharrawaddy, Saya San reportedly conducted a coronation ceremony, adorned himself with royal symbols of the Mandalay court, and assured his oath-bound followers that they would be protected by his magical amulets, incantations, and tattoos, which made one invulnerable to bullets. Rural cultivators, already frustrated by a severe drop in paddy prices, the privatization of communal forestry lands, high rental rates, the increasing burden of state taxes, and deepening credit-debt were quick to respond to Saya San's recruitment campaign that connected criticism of foreigners, taxes, and the hardships of the economic crisis to the erosion of tradional values and institutions. By resurrecting the monarchy, peasants were assured that the spirituality, predictability, and familiarity of precolonial, Buddhist Burma would be restored. In the coming weeks, individuals and institutions that represented the colonial state were attacked, resulting in the deaths of thirty-eight village headmen, a Forestry officer, and over a hundred cases of attack and injury.[4]

According to the official narrative,[5] Saya San would eventually adopt the title "Galon King" for signing his "royal" proclamations and encourage his followers to tattoo the Galon—the winged, man-raptor of Hindu mythology—on their bodies to display their commitment to him and to the rebellion. For while the Galon was known to be the celestial being who carries Lord Vishnu on his back, he is also known in Hindu-Buddhist Asia for his legendary battles with and imminent victory over the Naga (dragon/snake).[6] By adorning themselves with a tattoo depicting this scene, peasant rebels were associating their own struggle with the Galon's and ensuring his preordained victory with their own.

Colonial administrators interpreted the behavior of Saya San and his followers as simply another manifestation of the *minlaung* or "pretender-king" phenomenon of the nineteenth century that was based on a popular expectation that the king of Burma would one day return. Nationalist activists and historians would regard Saya San as a peasant hero who struggled and died for Burma's cultural heritage and political independence. To the majority of scholars in the latter half of the twentieth century, Saya San was more than a king—he was a millenarian prophet, a universal conqueror, and possibly a future Buddha—images that presented the rebellion and its leader as products of a resilient and enduring Southeast Asian resistance culture. Throughout the course of the twentieth and early twenty-first centuries, Saya San came to represent a variety of perspectives about Burmese political potential that would reflect historically a range of intersecting political and intellectual agendas in Burmese and Southeast Asian studies. With each new interpretative study, the Galon King would "return" as a historical subject, bound to an evidential record and interpretative paradigm (of returning kings) that remained surprisingly unchallenged, even as the epistemological context and scholarly priorities changed. This study explores the career of the Saya San Rebellion and in doing so presents how it became a pivotal event in the histories of Southeast Asia.

Origins of a Rebel King

The only actual connection that Saya San had to royalty was that he was born on October, 24, 1879 in Shwebo District, the same region in Upper Burma where King Alaungpaya founded the Konbaung

Dynasty (1752–1886). He was originally given the name Yar Kyaw by his parents, U Kyaye and Daw Hpet, who lived with their five children in the rural agricultural village of Thayetkan. Like many Burmese boys born in rural communities, young Yar Kyaw was exposed to Buddhist tenets at an early age by studying at the local village monastery, eventually extending his studies at the nearby Hpo Hmu monastery till he was nearly twenty years old. Yar Kyaw left for the village of Nga Kaung Inn soon after, in hope that he could make a better living selling mats and baskets as an alternative to working in the agricultural sector. He eventually met and married Ma Kay, with whom he raised two children, Ko Po Thin and Ma Sein. As economic conditions failed to improve, Yar Kyaw left for Moulmein in Lower Burma, where employment opportunities were better because of the expansion of the rice frontier. Earning his living as a carpenter for some time and then more successfully as a fortuneteller and traditional healer (*se saya*), he wrote two treatises on traditional healing practices that questioned the authority and efficacy of Western medical treatment.[7] It is perhaps during this period in his life as a medicinal healer (*se saya*), though it cannot be confirmed, that he took or was given the name Saya San.[8]

Exactly how Saya San made the transition from a practitioner of Burmese healing techniques to political activist is unclear, but colonial records and postindependence histories establish that Saya San joined the General Council of Burmese Associations (GCBA) in 1920.[9] Despite his rural upbringing, monastic training, and practice as a traditional healer, he was apparently able to understand and engage in the conversations, ideas, and goals of the more urban-oriented nationalist organization.[10] He began his political career as a representative of his village and soon progressed to lead his township and district branch of Moulmein. In 1924 at the annual congress of the GCBA, Saya San was elected to chair a commission to examine alleged abuses of villagers by government tax collectors. Between 1928 and 1930, Saya San and his lieutenants traveled the countryside, listening to peasant grievances and recruiting new members into his network of village associations. In 1929, Saya San attended the sixteenth conference of the GCBA

Saya San c. 1920s

where he proposed that collection of the capitation and *thathameda* taxes be resisted, that the restriction on free access to forest products be lifted in order to help alleviate the economic situation in the countryside, and that "defense associations" be formed to protect villagers from government abuses. His proposals were rejected by the GCBA membership, so Saya San decided to go and form his own network of Galon defense-organizations (*Galon Athin*) in order to empower rural communities to resist taxes and to protect themselves from aggressive police action. Using membership cards and tattooing, Saya San chose the symbol of the mythical Galon defeating its nemesis the Naga (dragon/serpent) in order to represent the imminent victory of the Burmese over the British. According to later accounts, members of the associations were encouraged by Saya San to have the Galon/Naga design tattooed on their bodies as a sign of their commitment to the cause and for protection from bullets. These village associations would allegedly provide the infrastructure and preparations for the rebellion and the "Galon" army in late 1930.

The Rebellion Spreads

In a few weeks it became clear that the violence that began in Tharrawaddy had escalated. Senior officials in New Delhi would soon be asked by their Rangoon counterparts to dispatch a considerable amount of men, money, and resources to the province in order to quell what was now being regarded as "the Burma Rebellion." By December 30, one hundred MPs, one hundred soldiers from the 2/15 Punjab, one hundred British infantry, and eventually the whole battalion of the 3/20th Burma Rifles were sent to the district. This escalation in military support did not produce immediate results, as outbreaks continued to spread in neighboring districts while the rebellion leadership continued to evade detection. Despite the capture of Saya San's "palace" in early January 1931, the rebellion spread to the districts of Pyapon, Henzada, Insein, Pegu, Toungoo, Prome, Thayetmyo, Naungcho Township, and the Northern Shan States. Other rebel leaders such as U Aung Hla, Bo Aung Shwe, and Bo Aung Pe led uprisings in neighboring districts to secure weapons, raid police stations, and attack government representatives. Official reports would soon connect the spread of the rebellion to tattooing ceremonies, which were regarded as recruitment drives, while the activities of *wunthanu athins* and wandering *pongyi* (Buddhist monks) were indicative of an imminent uprising.[11] Later that year, more distant districts such as Prome and Thayetmyo became rebellion hotspots, requiring concerted efforts by officials and troops to quell the violence.

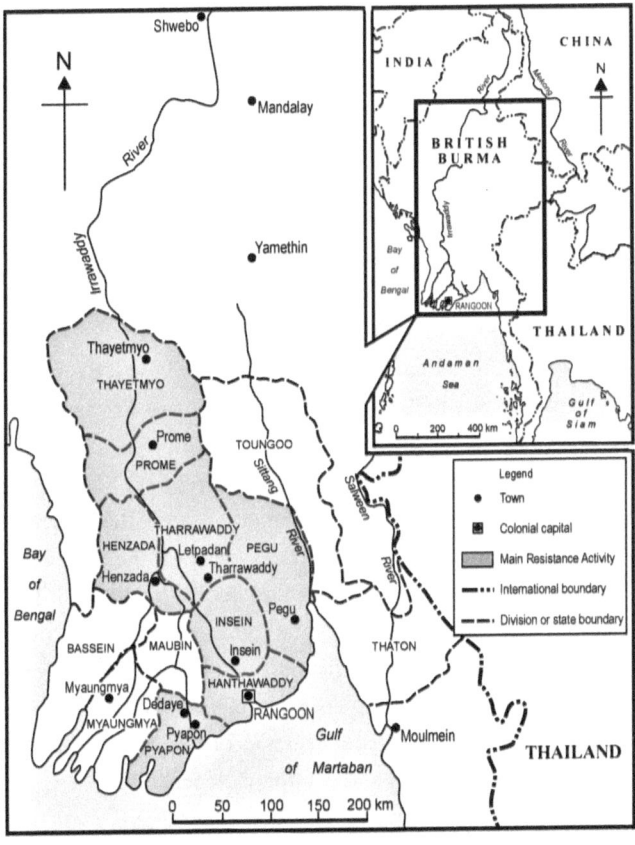

Resistance activity in Lower Burma 1930–1932

Within weeks of the first outbreak, Rangoon authorities responded by seeking special emergency powers from India to curb the movement of monks, political associations, and extend powers of arrest and seizure. By June 1931, a Special Rebellion Commissioner, Mr. Booth-Gravely, was appointed to manage affairs in districts that had been affected by rebellion. Measures were not always well coordinated as civil officials tried desperately to avoid declaring martial law, which would hand decision making over to military officers, with whom they shared many differences over rebellion matters. Meanwhile, legislators in the Burma Legislative Council held heated debates with government officials over the nature of special counter-insurgency legislation that would significantly curb protection from arbitrary arrest, search, and seizure. Over the ensuing months, political lines were drawn and deepened over the causes of the outbreaks, the measures taken by local government, and the rebellion's effect on the impending question of separation of Burma from India. These issues, along with concerns over the lingering economic crisis, were articulated through debates over the rebellion, marking it a key event through which other domestic concerns were engaged. By August 1931, Saya San was captured, tried, and sentenced by a Special Rebellion Tribunal, whose specific mandate was to preside over the abbreviated trials of arrested rebels. He would be defended by a group of lawyers, among them the fiery "Tharrawaddy" U Saw and the future premier of Burma, Dr. Ba Maw. The sensational trial of Saya San and many other rebels would draw mixed attention by the Burmese public—some sympathetic to what was seen as a futile, yet important, act of defiance while others more closely connected to the colonial authorities regarded the trial as an example of British legal order. Although Saya San was executed on November 28, 1931, the violence and disorder would continue for nearly two years, slowly degenerating (according to official accounts) into random acts of banditry and wanton violence.[12] By the end of 1932, thirteen hundred rebels had been killed, numerous were sentenced for transportation (exile) and up to nine thousand had surrendered.

Since 1934, this sequence of events—accepted universally as the official narrative of the Saya San Rebellion—has remained fundamentally the same for over seventy years.¹³ Numerous interpretations have been proposed to explain and debate the causes, characteristics, and motivations for the two-year uprising, but few have directly questioned the facts on which this narrative rests. A re-analysis of the legal history behind the making of the rebellion's key archival sources reveals that the entire narrative rests on an untenable evidential record, throwing into question many of the interpretations that have since relied on it. Recovering and reconstructing the origins of the rebellion narrative make it possible to study how a particular "history" of Burmese peasants and a particular argument about their political capabilities were made through the contributions of colonial ethnographers, counter-insurgency judges, nationalists, and area-studies scholars. In abstaining from interpreting the rebellion and remaining on the fringes of its epistemological legacy, this book is an exploration of the narrative's anatomy and career as a pivotal event in Burmese, Southeast Asian, and global history.

*Political Action in Precolonial and Colonial Burma:
The Historical Setting*

To colonial administrators at the time, Saya San's aspirations for the throne and the behavior of his supporters appeared to be consistent with traditional Burmese forms of political action. After all, the British had faced numerous outbreaks of resistance throughout the pacifications campaigns of 1886–1890, and Saya San's seemed to be much of the same sort. Historically, revolts were not unknown to precolonial Burmese polities, though many of these movements appear to have been mainly elite in nature, usually accompanying a succession dispute for the throne rather than those involving grass-root collective mobilization, communalism, or class-oriented motivations.¹⁴ Princes and younger brothers of the king would frequently jockey for positions of influence in anticipation that once the monarch was weakened or died, they would be able to step in and claim the throne for themselves. Court factionalism sometimes led to minor skirmishes, with followers of elite personalities bound by personal obligation to demonstrate their loyalty to their patron by supporting his claims to power. Very rarely would these uprisings include mass participation on the scale that would be seen during the high colonial period.

Other instances of contestation were connected to the periodic weakening of the state, allowing leaders of peripheral centers the opportunity to assert their autonomy through armed resistance or through refusal to supply the crown with men and resources.[15] The founder of Burma's last dynasty, King Alaungpaya, led one such "rebellion" against his regional overlord in Ava and then eventually against the Kingdom of Pegu, which by the mid-eighteenth century was in decline. He would later unify Upper and Lower Burma into the kingdom's last dynasty until the coming of the British. These movements were closely connected to the fluid nature of patron-client networks, the ongoing cycles of political integration and fragmentation that characterized the early-modern Burmese state, and to the dynamics of personal competition for power that structured the upper echelon of Burmese elite society.[16] As manpower was an important criterion for power in the pre-colonial Southeast Asian state, these regional governors could offer their allegiance (and their followers) to a competing center of authority for more attractive patronage or assert their own claim as a *cakkavartin* (universal conqueror) over their former liege lord. Right of succession was often justified through one's lineage in relationship to the king and through Buddhist notions of merit which could ultimately legitimize the successful usurpation of the throne. If contesting or claiming the throne, one would expect certain symbols and rituals of Burmese kingship to be displayed: the appearance of a royal umbrella, the wearing of royal clothing, the holding of an *abisheka* (coronation) ceremony, the establishment of a new capital according to specific Brahmanic specifications, the issuing of royal proclamations, and the adoption of prestigious titles that reflected their position as *cakkavartin* and as a protector of the Buddhist religion (*Dhamma-raja*).[17] Many of these elements of kingship would be connected to Saya San as part of a larger "Rebellion Ethnology," which provided the terms and concepts through which anticolonial resistance would be understood.

Many of these factors would continue to be relevant in the nineteenth century, as competition for manpower, prestige, and influence would factionalize the Konbaung Court. But the entry of an external source of power onto the frontier of the Burmese kingdom would introduce new social-political conditions that would threaten the abilities of the monarchy to maintain traditional sources of income, labor, and connections to maritime commerce. With the coming of the British, the Burmese court would attempt to resist the steady encroachment of annexation through formal, state-led military engagement. But as the Konbaung monarchs were overwhelmed by superior technology and the weaknesses of their own kingdom to muster an effective deterrent, older traditions of protest-banditry, flight, local risings, and communal violence would once again come into play.

Following a series of territorial disputes with British India's northeastern territories in Assam, the Kingdom of Ava found itself in a war with Britain from 1824 to 1826. The Treaty of Yandabo secured a relative peace between Amarapura and Calcutta but in essence created two territories out of one: Upper Burma would remain under control of the Konbaung Court while the western coast of Arakan, Tenasserim, Manipur, and Assam would now be under the authority of the British. Minor uprisings led by former officials, regional elites, local notables, and monks occurred infrequently following the first Anglo-Burmese war. Widespread local resistance and bandit attacks would intensify following the second war in 1852 as pressure on the Konbaung Court and remaining local provinces grew as the British annexed much of the Irrawaddy delta region. As with previous revolts, many of these were led by local notables and officials who were now marginalized under the new system of rule. Between 1860 and 1885, bands of men opposed to British rule continued to challenge authority, but armed police units were able to contain these incidents. In 1885, the kingdom was conquered, and King Thebaw, the last of the Konbaung kings, was deported to India.

Formal annexation in January 1886 may have signaled the end of the third Anglo-Burmese war, but the more difficult task of maintaining stability remained, as British authorities immediately faced a number of uprisings that erupted throughout the formal Burmese kingdom.[18] These opposition movements became more intensive and extensive as the removal of the monarchy unraveled much of the remaining network of institutions, like the Buddhist monkhood, which relied on the patronage of the throne. Some of these rebellions were led by former members of the court, like the Myinzaing Prince, who continued to wield considerable influence over troops and villagers in provincial centers that had once been in alliance with the throne. Other pockets of resistance were led by local headmen and monks but were limited by size and scope. These were often short-lived either due to lack of support or due to the overwhelming technical advantage of the British. Indian experiences with the "dacoit" (or bandit) informed many of these assessments. Even Indian terms were sometimes used in describing these encounters.[19] In any case, much of the knowledge related to Burmese-style resistance was first recorded in the context of pacification and military confrontation. Political officers accompanying these campaigns would write accounts of these skirmishes that would be preserved in later district gazetteers and reports. The nature of resistance and rebellion, at least as understood by colonial observers, would have their origins in these experiences.

By the 1890s, colonial officials had determined that the main pacification campaigns were successful, and they could concentrate on the business of building a social-economic infrastructure that could support their interests in the vast teak, mineral, and agricultural resources that their new colony provided. Attached as a province of India, British Burma would be subject to administrative policies established in New Delhi as well as the vast array of procedural structures that characterized the India Civil Service (ICS). The new territories were divided into districts and assigned a commissioner with a small support staff. Through the prism and experience of British India, Burmese peoples, cultures, languages, and histories were constructed by imperial surveys that now sought to map the new territories. Indigenous healing practices, rituals, folk tales, notions of authority and village life would be organized and categorized according to how well the district officer understood what he was observing. Just as surveyors represented the topography of the land and geologists identified the mineral composition of the soil, colonial ethnographers organized village life and worldviews through their surveys, producing a notion of culture that was immutable to change and history.[20] Elements of what would constitute "Burmese culture" were standardized through technologies of rule that would make behavior, ritual, values, and discourses not only recognizable to colonial anthropology, but appear as natural features of an unchanging social landscape.[21] Criminality and criminal tribes would be grafted on to this Burmese landscape as well, with Shwebo and Tharrawaddy drawing particular attention by the civil administration. As we will see in coming chapters, such administrative practices rendered an image of Burma that was not expected to change; inclinations towards restlessness and gullibility amongst rural populations were two ingredients that made outbreak in Burma predictable, if not expected. Thus, topographically and ethnographically, the communities of the Irrawaddy valley and its surrounding hill societies were merged into a single entity through these survey projects. Notions of rebellion would inform and be informed by these classifications, merging understandings of culture and resistance very closely.

The early twentieth century saw formal instruments of colonial rule being introduced through the extension of the Indian Civil Service (ICS) into Burma. Legal, educational, health, transportation, and economic structures were established with the migration of experienced Indian clerical staff, soldiers, and laborers. As a province of India, Burma was tied administratively, economically, and legally to the government of India, resulting in "Indian" forms of rule being extended to Burma as in other parts of the larger empire. These deep ties resulted in an understanding of Burmese society and culture through the lens and experience of British India. Civil servants trained at Fort William in the languages, histories, and ethnologies of India would then be posted to various assignments in the Empire.[22] Notions of martial races, banditry, criminality, and incarceration traveled with these officials, providing a frame of reference for interpreting and textualizing dissent and protest in Burma.[23] The idea that tattooing could represent criminality indicates shared notions of disciplining the body, punishment, and cultural production among officials in British India and Burma.[24] Burmese criminals would be shipped to the Andaman Islands while Indian criminals would be sent to prisons in Arakan, signaling Burma's incorporation into the management structures of the British Empire's criminals. Transportation was a punishment that was not limited to common criminals—the last Mughal Emperor was sent to Rangoon while Thebaw was exiled to Ratnagiri.

Law was as much an expression of British Indian culture as it was a frame of reference in the defining of Burmese culture. As a system of organization, terminology, mediation, disciplining, and punishment, law and its language contributed to the colonial ordering of Burmese society.[25] The legalization of nearly all aspects of society in the new colony closely followed models established in India, requiring a fresh generation of young Burmese lawyers to supplement Indian clerks and judicial officers who were practicing in Burma. Legal training provided opportunities in lucrative positions within the colonial state and also created an important portion of the middle-class who would be very well versed in the operations and functions of the Empire. A small few would be appointed or elected to the Burma Legislative Council, where the shaping of legislation pertaining to British Burma would take place. Dissent was now officially possible within the heart of the colonial administration by more of its outspoken members, like U Saw from Tharrawaddy, who would attempt to make rural concerns and perspectives a larger part of the discussions. Legal con-

British Burma in the 1930s

cepts, terminology, procedures, and paradigms would become an important language through which aspects of Burmese society and culture would be defined and conceptualized in British Burma.

Connections to India also resulted in similar ideas to how protest and resistance was articulated and pursued by the rise of new urban elites. Reform movements, ideologies, and strategies for mobilization would make their way to the colonial periphery as well. In the late 1890s, a small group of Buddhist associations with contemporary forms of organization and structure were founded by lay members in an effort to preserve the religion and its place in society.[26] Print media in the form of newspapers would grow in influence while book clubs, social improvement societies, and religious organizations would emerge as ways through which members of the growing middle class could engage in social reform. In 1906, political organizations such as the Young Men's Buddhist Association (YMBA) came into prominence within Rangoon, drawing young clerks and educated elites into working for changes in colonial society through accepted and approved channels. Focusing primarily on religious and cultural issues, it became an umbrella organization for the wide range of lay Buddhist groups that had emerged at the turn of the century. While the YMBA focused on improving social conditions and concentrating on educational reform during its earlier years of activity, following World War I it would adopt more direct means of engaging the colonial government on issues of cultural identity, education, and economic welfare. One famous incident included the YMBA's role in making the refusal of British to remove their shoes at pagodas and temples a public issue, by pointing to the indifference the colonizer had over important cultural behavior. By 1917, the YMBA would soon factionalize over its involvement in politics and specifically the question of its connections to India and measures that would lead to self-government. This would pave the way for the formation of the General Council of Burmese Associations (GCBA) which planned to participate more directly in political protest and demonstrations.[27]

The GCBA adopted many of the techniques employed by Gandhi's Indian National Congress in order to express its political aims more directly and publicly. One such tool was the use of the boycott, which was employed in the 1920 elections and in the more visible student boycott that began in Rangoon University and soon spread to other government schools. The GCBA began to campaign for national independence as a means of attracting a wide membership who held a wide range of interests and priorities. In order to engage rural communities, members of the GCBA would travel into the countryside conducting interviews, collecting data, and filing reports in order to establish lines of communication with emerging village activists. With branches numbering nearly twelve thousand, nationalist messages, symbols, and issues became part of the vocabulary for rural activists. Around the same time as the formation of the GCBA, the monkhood began to organize itself politically with the founding of the General Council of Sangha Sammeggi (GCSS) in 1920. Without the monarchy, the *sangha* saw the need to ensure discipline upon itself and to provide guidance for lay practioners, resulting in a more visible involvement with society. With the declining economic standards for villagers and monks alike, the GCSS began to address the need to improve social conditions more directly, creating factions between more conservative monks and its younger members who felt that campaigning for reform was commensurate with improving the religion. Under the leadership of monks such as U Oktama and U Wisara, groups of political monks called *dhammakatika* began to tour the countryside to help establish *Sangha Sammeggi Apwes*, small unions that complemented the secular-based *wunthanu athins* (patriot organizations) which became part of a vast nationalist network designed to provide a conduit through which village concerns could be articulated.[28] Peasant leaders saw in the *wunthanu athin* an organizational framework that could allow them to voice their grievances over issues such as taxes, rising costs, diminishing use of forestry products, and high rental rates while at the same time provide the structure to organize their own village networks of governance.

Taylor estimates that by 1924 there was *wunthanu athin* present in most villages.²⁹

As methods of articulating reform developed across the spectrum, so too did the colonial government adopt measures of social and political control. Numerous acts of legislation were enacted to curb the growing number of incidents and expressions of dissent. In 1919 the Anarchical Revolutionary Crimes Act and the Burma Habitual Offenders Restriction Act were introduced to deal with particular conditions while sections of the Indian Penal Code were frequently utilized to empower colonial authorities with the appropriate jurisdiction. In 1922 the Criminal Law Amendment Act, the 1923 Anti-Boycott Act, and the 1924 Criminal Tribes Act were invoked to disrupt the actions of individuals and *wunthanu athins*.³⁰ Many of these laws would deepen the commitment of radical nationalist groups and divide reformers who were willing to work with and through the government. At the same time, important legal precedence was established through the use of legislative measures as a response to security threats, an option that would be turned to with the outbreak of rebellion in 1930.

By the late 1920s and early 1930s, the political landscape contained many forms of resistance that were being tested, refitted, or discarded throughout Burmese society by different communities with equally different motivations and expectations. Political action could be expressed through a wide range of ideologies; some more culturally familiar through the application of recognizable symbols and rituals, while other forms of action were dependant upon newly imported concepts that relied on new forms of communication and public demonstrations. Youth organizations, quasi-military training corps (*tats*) and student organizations (All Burma Youth League) provided additional voices in an already volatile political scene.³¹ Armed resistance, banditry, and riots were available as expressions of dissent, but so too were street marches, sit-ins, newspaper editorials, clothing choices (wearing homespun cloth), and boycotts. The countryside was growing more integrated with urban centers due to the efforts of both secular and religious organizations to connect, educate, and immerse rural communities into the issues of the day. It is to no surprise that when the rebellion broke out in late December 1930, making sense of it within the immediate context of a strained economy, fissuring racial tensions, and a confrontational political climate would not be an easy task for officials.

Upon hearing about the events in Tharrawaddy, members of the Burma Legislative Council (BLC) expressed a range of views, some suggesting that the uprising stained the reputation of "modern" Burmese, prompting some representatives to condemn the violence as "sheer madness, worse than futile."[32] Other Burmese representatives in the BLC were more sympathetic to the conditions facing agricultural communities in the delta region and pointed to the worsening economic situation and the failure of government to respond to their needs in an appropriate manner as a causal factor. U Saw, the representative from Tharrawaddy District and eventual member of Saya San's legal team, frequently questioned the policies of the government in regard to how the rebellion and its underlying causes were being addressed.[33] His letter to a sympathetic member of Parliament caused an uproar in London and Delhi over a photo of decapitated heads of rebels on display at a local police headquarters who were killed by government forces.[34] Others began to see the actions of the peasants as an expression of latent pride for Burmese ethnicity and culture.[35] Members of the minority Karen ethnic group were frequently recruited by the police forces to suppress the rebellion and did not view the revolt or its participants in favorable terms. Former district magistrate Maurice Collis would remark that the peasants, "having no way except the traditional way of insurrection of showing their dissatisfaction" rose because "that was their way of expressing the national dislike of a foreign government."[36] Thus, the immediate interpretation of the peasant violence that spread throughout the country in the early 1930s was expressed through terms that were drawn primarily from the different experiences and encounters within colonial society that were connected to class structures, patronage networks, occupations, and political leanings. Even in its earliest stages, the Saya San Rebellion would come to mean different things to different people within Burmese society. In the years that followed, scholars would also interpret the rebellion to fit different intellectual concerns and priorities, eventually transforming an event that was anchored in the histories of Burma to an event that helped define the meaning and contours of Southeast Asian culture.

Interpreting Rebellion

The Saya San Rebellion has been interpreted by scholars from a number of intellectual, historical, and political perspectives that have characterized our understanding of Burma and Southeast Asia. One important feature of this scholarship has been the manner in which the event has been situated in and used to emphasize a variety of geopolitical contexts. Initially, the event was located in the history of Tharawaddy, as it was perceived to be only a local affair that would die a quick death. As the rebellion spread to include other districts, the event was soon positioned within the broader narrative history of British Burma, a perspective that was reinforced by nationalist scholarship that saw the peasant revolt as an expression of "Burmese" political identity in anticipation of the nation. Scholars interested in comparative nationalisms and development theory would include the rebellion in a broader conversation, but it was area-specialists that presented the uprisings as a reflection of a wider Southeast Asian cultural expression of resistance. The access to Burmese language sources, interdisciplinary approaches, and developments in the study of social movements shifted the event into the larger field of religion and resistance that took into account the ways in which Buddhist worldviews might have shaped the notion of revolt. Expanding this perspective further, the Saya San Rebellion has also been placed within a more global context that reflected an interest in the transnational experience of rebelling against the colonial order. The career of the Saya San Rebellion has thus come to map a wide range of intersecting intellectual conversations that have been closely linked by the persistence of a series of narrative conventions, approaches, and sources that exemplify what has been termed the "post-colonial predicament."[37]

One of the more enduring tropes in the existing scholarship has focused primarily on the causes and characteristics of the rebellion, no doubt influenced by the nature of the colonial sources, the purposes for which these documents were produced, and by their typical binary framings. With little exception, the historiography of the Saya San Rebellion has been guided by the following dichotomous structures that can be found throughout the evidential record: traditional/modern, political/economic, superstitious/rational, simple/complex, organized/spontaneous, and local/national. None of these studies were devoted primarily to the rebellion as historians were still establishing the narrative history of the country/nation. Writing in 1946, historian G. E. Harvey expressed what colonial reports had consistently asserted, that the rebellion was caused by "superstition, plain and simple."[38] D. G. E Hall noted that the rebellion was largely "anti-foreign," caused by "economic discontent," and led by a pretender to the throne.[39] Internal, post-independence histories also cast Saya San as the quintessential Burmese peasant, but did so more sympathetically in attempt to "write-back" against earlier perspectives and to appropriate the rebellion as evidence of an emerging nationalist consciousness in the countryside that was nonetheless disconnected with urban reformists.[40] John Cady's seminal *A History of Modern Burma* (1958) echoed this qualitative disjuncture by observing that the movement "paid little attention to the Indian National Congress program; it ignored the successive Round Table Conferences which were being held at London; it shut its eyes to the existence of regular and legal procedures for accomplishing political ends."[41] Although Cady's assessment that Burmese rural communities were constrained by cultural barriers that limited the range and form of political activism, he recognizes that local forms of political expression could be expressed through different, yet co-existing languages of reform or resistance. Lucian W. Pye's study of Burmese political identity also recognizes this framing of co-existing but mutually exclusive worldviews by describing the rebellion as "thriving on ignorance, superstition and readiness to accept a mystical and magical view of the universe," the opposite of what a contemporary modern Burmese politician strove to represent.[42] Taken together, both colonial-era and nationalist renderings of the rebellion used the event to establish a number of political claims regarding notions of authority and legitimacy in the context of Burmese colonial and postcolonial politics. In doing so, these interpretations also reified the boundaries and chronological narrative of British/Independent Burma by anchoring the Saya San Rebellion securely within the context of Burmese history.

Departing significantly from these earlier studies were key works that explored Buddhism's role in the history of Burmese state and society. By extending the chronological and cultural context within the political history of the country was interpreted, the Saya San Rebellion came to represent a nationalist response that was representative of these Buddhist worldviews. Donald E. Smith's recognition that Buddhist elements were historically prescriptive traits that informed an emerging national consciousness reversed earlier dismissals of these cultural overtures as superstition and marked a new integration of the religious with the national.[43] E. Michael Mendelson's *Sangha and State in Burma,* which was eventually published later in 1975, took this perspective much further by interpreting the Saya San Rebellion and its nationalist undertones in the context of the *sangha*'s institutional history and its attempts to negotiate its role with secular, lay organizations that were emerging in the earlier quarter of the twentieth century.[44] Arguing against the assumed historical unity of the Burmese *sangha,* Mendelson suggested provocatively that the Saya San Rebellion was most likely a series of personal uprisings rather than a coherent movement, a reflection of the sectarian nature of the *sangha* and the factionalism that chacterized lay organizations during this period. In other work, Mendelson suggested that the Saya

San Rebellion demonstrated characteristics that aligned it with *gaing*, religious communities that operated at the margins of Buddhist doctrinal behavior and at the intersection with indigenous spirit belief structures, acting as an alternative structure to the formal network maintained by the Buddhist *sangha*. His identification of the Saya San Rebellion as an expression of these social networks remains one of the most important (and often neglected) interpretations of the rebellion thus far and places its characteristics within its most precise context. Following closely Mendelson's insights were E. Manuel Sarkisyanz's *Buddhist Backgrounds of the Burmese Revolution* (1965), which situated the Saya San Rebellion squarely within the context of a much more deeply engrained millenarian tradition that provided the terms and perspectives through which colonialism and resistance to modernization could be understood and envisioned.[45] For Sarkisyanz, Saya San represented the Setyka-min (cakkavartin) or universal conqueror who would prepare or become the future-Buddha Maitreya, demonstrating that the cultural foundations that informed the peasant revolt in 1930s Burma were not "superstition plain and simple" but rich and complex expressions of a worldview under siege. Robert L. Solomon's article "Saya San and the Burmese Rebellion" (1969) attempted to synthesize the available interpretations at the time by suggesting that the rebellion was a reflection of the 1930s in that Saya San had contemporary organizational strategies available to him but chose a "traditional" collection of terms and symbols in order to appeal to his peasant constituency. In seeing the rebellion as an important stage in the formation of modern nationalism, Solomon followed earlier scholars by attempting to interpret the rebellion's unique characteristics as an expression of political action in Burma. In contrast to Sarkisyanz and the later (published) work of Mendelson, the emphasis on the agency of indigenous worldviews was downplayed in favor of more contemporary, pragmatic calculations on the part of Saya San.

Michael Adas's treatment of the Saya San Rebellion has provided some of the most significant insights into understanding the event, through two separate studies of the rebellion that reflect both a local and global interpretive framework. In *The Burma Delta,* his first study of the development of the colonial rice economy, the peasant uprisings are returned to the context of British Burma but focus more intensively on the institutions and patterns of the colonial economy as a contributing factor into the cause of the rebellion. Adas suggested that important shifts in the expectations of peasant cultivators contributed to the outbreak of rebellion by those who had once benefitted from the rice economy but were disappointed by the realities of the world market when the great depression hit.[46] Economic grievances made the promises of men like Saya San that much more attractive to rural cultivators who were trying to make sense of the social changes that were occurring around them at such a rapid pace and seemingly beyond anyone's control. Yet in including the discussion of the rebellion's character in his study of the rebellion, Adas clarified the relationship of the Buddhist traditions discussed by Sarkisyanz to the economic factors that contributed to the revolt. These millenarian traditions, he would argue later in 1979, would parallel the belief-systems and expectations of other colonized peoples, locating (for the first time) the history of the Saya San Rebellion in comparative and global context.[47]

The Burma Delta's important analysis of the economic conditions that contributed to the rise of rebellion in the 1930s intersected with approaches in peasant studies that wished to correct the perception that rural communities were passive actors in history. James Scott's *The Moral Economy of the Peasant* (1976) compared the Saya San Rebellion with the contemporaneous Nge Tinh Uprisings in French Indochina and argued that the colonial state had failed to meet traditional expectations that allowed peasants to maintain, in the very least, a subsistence existence in order to survive. The inability of the colonial governments to meet these "moral" standards that traditional states had recognized disrupted the social and conceptual agreement that peasant societies expected, resulting in the outbreak of rebellion. This approach became a significant part of an important, but problematic debate that attempted to define the causes of peasant protest as driven either by ideology or motivated primarily by pragmatic reasons.[48] At the same time, this seminal book reflected a concern emerging from both peasant and Southeast Asian studies; to correct for earlier images of peasants as passive, reactive, and simple by demonstrating agency, initiative, and complexity in these large resistance movements.[49] This priority to present the history of Southeast Asia from an internal or "autonomous" perspective (to be explored in greater detail later) intersected methodologically with scholars who sought to uncover the complexities of peasant mentalités that lay embedded, as it was thought, in large acts of violent protest. Michael Adas returned to the study of the Saya San Rebellion in 1979 with his stunning *Prophets of the Rebellion: Millenarian Protest Movements against the European Colonial Order* (1979), a groundbreaking work that exemplified precisely these concerns by bringing religious conceptions of millenarianism into the discussion about anticolonial movements in comparative perspective. For the first time in its narrative career, the Saya San Rebellion was presented alongside other rebellions beyond Burma and Southeast Asia, linking its cultural characteristics to what appeared to be a global trend of revitalization movements that responded in similar ways to the modernization processes of colonialism. The events concerning Saya San and other rural cultivators were now viewed as a significant chapter in the broader histories of peasants, resistance, and religion. This positive reinforcement in global studies affected the importance placed on studying peasant movements in Southeast Asia, as resistance and its connection to religion became a key theme through which enduring elements of a Southeast Asian culture could be uncovered.[50]

Studies that followed returned to many of the older questions and framings that had been posited earlier, with specific attention to the character of the rebellion remaining a dominant feature. Perhaps one of the most important interventions in the scholarship was Patricia Herbert's (1982) study that suggested that the research on Saya San had been operating from an understanding of the rebellion that limited it to a "royal" movement set on resurrecting the monarchy.[51] Her research suggested that the rebellion should be considered more closely (following arguments by Smith, Mendelson, and Solomon) within the political and religious context of the 1930s which saw new forms of mobilization and organization become a part of the political landscape. Arguing that scholars needed to study the role of the *wunthanu athin* networks more closely, Herbert regarded the rebellion as less a manifestation of traditional Burma and more a reflection of new, urban-based political networks that had entered the political scene. She suggested that the eruption of the rebellion in the forms that it took were actually a result of the inability of the *wunthanu athin* and the GCBA to facilitate any substantive change. Violent dissent was for Herbert not indicative of traditional political expectations, but the loss of faith in contemporary strategies that had been penetrating the countryside to no avail. Her work was the first to raise questions about the way in which crucial sources had been interpreted and how such readings misrepresented the nature of rural activism and political expression in colonial Burma. While emphasizing the need to explore more thoroughly the role of contemporaneous forms of political mobilization, Herbert provided a nuanced perspective of studying the rebellion through the role of local political institutions and networks. For the first time, scholars had an opportunity to think about the rebellion as a product of early-twentieth-century Burmese political developments rather than through the seemingly timeless categories of kingship and millenarianism.

Though providing an opening through her exciting research, few followed Herbert's lead as scholarly attention shifted to studying "everyday forms" of resistance and "avoidance protest" as potential alternatives to studying the types of large, direct, and often confrontational social movements to which the Saya San Rebellion was associated.[52] Oliver B. Pollack provided a review of most of the available literature on the Saya San Rebellion and asked whether the movement might be seen as a transitory hybrid form of political action that sought economic, spiritual, and political independence, but neglected to pursue (or reference) Herbert's findings any further.[53] Parimal Ghosh's useful *Brave Men of the Hills* (2000) returned the focus to colonial Burma by situating the Saya San Rebellion within the context of the nineteenth-century Anglo-Burmese wars, while Ian Brown's superb *A Colonial Economy in Crisis: Burmese Rice Cultivators and the World Depression of the 1930s* (2005), problematized the category of Burmese peasant-cultivators and the economic arguments that led to the outbreak of the rebellion. Michael Charney's treatment of the rebellion in his *A History of Modern Burma* (2008), represents how resilient the historical narrative remains despite several decades of debate. Cast within the narrative of Burma's encounter with the British, the events surrounding the series of uprisings are once again presented as a traditional response to the modernizing forces of the colonial project.[54]

Scholarship has thus come full circle in the way the rebellion has returned to its roots in colonial Burma. Despite the differences in interpretation over a half-century, a number of striking similarities are readily apparent. First, scholarship has concentrated on either interpreting the characteristics of the revolt and/or determining its likely motivations and causes. For many scholars at different times, the primary task was to study the facts of the rebellion in order to assess the impact of the rebellion, determine its meanings, or illuminating the worldview of its participants. Second, nearly all of the previous studies operated within a binary perspective that framed the analyses of the rebellion as a traditional/modern, political/economic, simple/complex or rational/irrational which led, as we will see, to an oversimplification of the rebellion as a single, coherent, and unified expression of Burmese resistance. Third and most crucial, current understandings of the rebellion were based on an archival record that remained unquestioned, no doubt a result of different political and intellectual priorities that urged us to think about the rebellion as an expression of Burmese identity and Southeast Asian culture. As a result of this interpretative agenda, the epistemological connections between the formation of the evidential record, the processes that shaped the narrative, and the categories that framed our understanding of rebellion in colonial Burma have been understandably overlooked. Emerging from the ongoing critique of colonialism since World War II, the intersection of anthropological-historical method, and developments in South Asian studies, these concerns provide several points through which the history and historiography of the Saya San Rebellion might be re-engaged.

Colonial Studies and Southeast-Asian Resistance

Scholarly interest in peasant militancy, protest, and other collective resistance movements has contributed to ongoing discussions about modernization, nationalism, local belief-systems, and the nature of change and continuity that emerged from the colonial encounter in Southeast Asia.[55] Emerging out of an early attempt in the 1930s and 1940s to rethink the region in its own terms, the study of resistance movements began to gain more currency at a time when the formation of area-studies programs required an internal perspective that addressed the problem of "Southeast Asian inertia," a perspective that presents local societies as entirely passive in history unless acted upon by an external force.[56] Some of the field's earliest efforts to assess continuity and change more accurately, establish our historical position more effectively, or recognize the politics of interpretation more sensitively, found cases of rebellion particularly useful in conveying these images of a Southeast Asian history.[57] Studying resistance provided a means of infusing indigenous agency into the region's story by showing that local actors were historically in charge of their own destinies, which was especially relevant in a time when the Domino Theory and French/American intervention in Vietnam continued to present Southeast Asia as lacking indigenous agency.[58] Resistance, especially in a colonial context, became equated with the very idea of an authentic Southeast Asia.

While the importance of resistance as a category in Southeast Asian studies owes much to the intellectual priorities that were particular to the defining of the field, many of the important questions pertaining to the study of protest emerged from developments in the sub-fields of peasant studies, cultural, literary, and colonial studies.[59] The critiques of colonialism that have examined the representation and construction of the Orient, connected colonial administrative projects to the construction of knowledge, and unveiled the relationships between the imperial project and academic disciplines, provide an important foreground to the type of analyses that will be attempted in this book.[60] Re-examining the epistemological construction of the region's identities and historicizing our categories of analysis has broadened and complicated what we accept to be an enduring "autonomous" culture of Southeast Asia.[61] Colonial categories, paradigms, and archives are now being considered for their role in the historical construction of Southeast Asia, an approach that has a direct bearing on understanding the role of resistance in the construction of Burma/Myanmar.

The collection of topics, methods, and approaches that we tend to refer to as "postcolonial" today has its origins in a wide range of intellectual conversations that have attempted to define and explore the colonial situation.[62] Frederick Cooper's account of the "rise, fall, and rise" of colonial studies demonstrates that thinking about the colonial encounter has been both at the margins and at the forefront of interdisciplinary scholarship, and this trend seems to be the case for Southeast Asian studies as well.[63] Following the decline and acceptance of colonial empires following World War

II, questions pertaining to modernization and economic development, understanding the psychology of colonialism, or finding new perspectives that provided the colonized with their own histories characterized the study of the colonial situation.[64] In doing so, the worlds of the colonized and the colonizer remained conceptually apart until scholars began to question the historically bounded nature of colonialism's influences.

Scholars today point to a reflexive turn in the 1970s and 1980s in the disciplines of anthropology, literature, and history that led many to take an interest in thinking about the methods, contexts, and priorities that produced what they knew about their subjects and how these ideas formed.[65] Talal Asad's *Anthropology and the Colonial Encounter* (1973) was a crucial intervention because it directed our attention to the ambiguities of the relationship between anthropologists and colonial regimes while raising interesting problems about the relationship of academic knowledge to the institutional (and historical) contexts in which it was produced.[66] The authority to represent knowledge, the "un-reciprocal quality of ethnographic interpretation," and the construction of writing of ethnographic texts were issues that raised questions about anthropology's isolation from its context and its subjects.[67] It was within this emerging discussion that Edward Said's seminal *Orientalism* raised important issues about how "the Orient" was constructed through particular images, histories, and categories that were consolidated into a single discourse or language of representation. Following Michel Foucault's concepts of power and discourse, Said set forth to demonstrate how our understanding of the Orient was constituted, how colonialism provided a particularly important context in which meanings were constructed, how this knowledge enabled and was a manifestation of power, and how these systems for thinking have come to define and order how we view the Orient today.[68] Upon scrutinizing the manner in which "Arab" and "Eastern" culture and history was produced, Said suggested that portraits of the Orient reflected a consistent pattern of articulating difference with European culture but were simultaneously self-referential located in the same analytical field. Today, we recognize that Orientalism can refer to Said's notion of an exotic East as well as a foundational body of scholarship that glorified the accomplishments of ancient civilizations through their archaeological, philological, anthropological, and historical research.[69] Said's treatment of Orientalism did not pursue how colonial representations were linked to administrative practices and structures, a relationship that has since been taken up by scholars of South Asia and one that will be explored in the present volume.[70]

The study of this relationship between administrative institutions and images of the colonized developed with Bernard Cohn, who (like Said) saw the critical potential in approaching the colonial situation from a single field. He suggested that the anthropological inquiry might be directed towards colonial culture that included an analysis of both the colonizer and the colonized. In directing these techniques towards the colonial administration and its structures, he showed not only how operational practices intersected with the ideologies of the British in India, but he showed how administrative categories influenced the way in which conceptions of the "Indian" and the "British" were frozen through these classifications. Cohn's work anticipated the techniques of combining anthropology and history into the study of colonial society, paving the way for future explorations of the way in which colonialism contributed to the historical constructions of crime, caste, sati, tribe, ethnicity and resistance.[71] This book draws much from this line of analysis by questioning the ways in which peasant resistance was produced through colonial ethnology and counter-insurgency law.

A third body of scholarship that this work is indebted to is that which emerged from the Subaltern Studies collective. Their project was both a methodological intervention and an attempt to liberate the historical voices of groups that had been marginalized or silenced by elite-based narratives. For scholars such as Ranajit Guha, David Hardiman, Shahid Amin, and Partha Chatterjee to name a few, the histories of peasant communities had consistently been appropriated, reconfigured, and represented to reflect the priorities and concerns of both colonial and nationalist elite narratives on the one hand and the politically passive image of the rural peasant on the other.[72] A critical reassessment, in a similar vein to John Smail's call for an autonomous history of modern Southeast Asia, was thus necessary to uncover the varying experiences of peasants within the context of colonial India and instill a more authentic agency that had yet to be written. Through studies that tracked the development of peasant political consciousness, expressions of peasant worldviews, and their complex relationships with elites, members of the collective attempted to construct the peasantry through the ways the subaltern saw itself.[73] Just as the study of indigenous belief systems supplied Southeast Asian scholars with important insight into re-conceptualizing resistance movements, so too did the wide range of religious cultural systems in South Asia provide the collective with new ways of reading peasant societies. The histories of peasant resistance movements in particular were topics that had been distorted by these elite perspectives, requiring both a different method of reading elite documentation and a different framework that would enable one to re-center the peasant within his own story.[74] Many of the tropes that Guha uses to explore peasant political action (negation, ambiguity, modality, solidarity, transmission, and territoriality) are readily apparent in the dominant narrative of the Saya San Rebellion, generating similar lines of critique. At the same time however, this study is concerned with showing how peasant consciousness in a Southeast Asian context (and by implication a South Asian context as well) was made and limited by the very categories of resistance found in colonial documents.

The Structure of Rebellion

Although this study explores the epistemology of resistance in Southeast Asia more generally, and the Saya San Rebellion more specifically, it is also an enquiry into the process of making "history" and the manner in which various actors, institutions, and disciplines produce narratives. Though situated in British Burma and within the

1930s, this study draws from more recent contributions and issues in postcolonial scholarship, sociolegal studies, and literary studies. It reconsiders the categories and ways of representation that are normally associated with "indigenous" Southeast Asia and investigates the relationships between the different forms of the colonial project and the production of culture. It considers how the criminalizing of culture and peoples were as much a part of the colonial ethnological project as it was an integral component of counter-insurgency policies.[75] Much of this story is connected to the construction of what I call "the Rebellion Archive," a collection of documents under the heading "Burma Rebellion General File" that represented and registered British conceptions of what Burmese rebellion was in its textual form.[76] Whereas the sources of this study pertain more directly to the issue of rebellion in Burma, much of what was delineated were notions of Burmese identity, memory, and place—revealing that culture both enabled and was enabled by categories of resistance, protest, and institutions of knowledge production.[77] In exploring this relationship, law's rhetorical functions, its narrative qualities, and its ability to dispense violence are also considered within the context of and as a means toward rendering these cultural features. For counter-insurgency law and the expansive parameters of emergency powers created the special conditions and language that enabled these ethnological categories to be authenticated and codified for the archive. The specificities of legal procedure and the rhetorical violence of its representations contributed significantly to the making of these narratives.[78] Thus, the story of the Saya San Rebellion is regarded to be the product of particular counter-insurgency policies, institutions, and priorities—revealing not the conceptions of a silenced Southeast Asian worldview, but the agendas and concerns of British counter-insurgency officials in Burma.

This exploration of narrative production involves Burmese, British, and scholarly commentators alike; implicates the contingency of archives; and problematizes historical conventions used by these contributors.[79] In recovering disparate and often conflicting narratives that were eventually submerged and consolidated into master narratives, this study draws from interventions in scholarship that recognize the legacy of the colonial in the postcolonial and the marginalization of historical voices.[80] Yet in demonstrating how colonial paradigms were submerged within the arguments and interpretations of postcolonial scholars, uncertainties with what we identify as "Southeast Asian" rise to the surface. Cultural symbols and profiles within the "Rebellion Ethnology" will be shown to have appeared as products of a counter-insurgency program that identified and criminalized elements of village life, revealing a particular colonial context in which these elements were drawn. Departing from numerous interventions made from within the Subaltern Studies collective, this study reconsiders the extent to which peasant voices remain embedded within colonial documents, and explores the ways in which the very categories for conceptualizing "the peasant" were constructed through these documentation projects. Along similar lines, reading "against the grain" may not be adequate for this line of enquiry as elements of a "Burmese culture" were first collected, defined, and typified within the context of resistance. For reasons that will be explained in these pages, rebellion, among many other categories associated with our field, was used to demonstrate that Southeast Asians (not merely Burmese) responded to colonial rule in similar ways, reifying the cultural boundaries and coherency of the region but at the same time simplifying political expression to neatly stereotypical norms. In this regard, colonial constructions of the Rebellion Ethnology that were originally designed to commit Burmese to a particular mode of political expression, were unintentionally adopted by scholars seeking "to liberate" Southeast Asians from these very shackles by employing their own version of the Rebellion Ethnology in order to explain what it was to be "Southeast Asian." In short, claims made for the autonomy of Southeast Asia were based on narratives and paradigms grounded in the colonial, making it exceedingly problematic to separate one from another. The story behind the making of the Saya San Rebellion narrative is not merely about the colonial construction of rebellion in Burma, it is about how an event was first identified, recorded, registered, and legitimated for the archive; how that archive preserved that narrative for historians to authenticate in their histories; and how that narrative served to support a much larger agenda about the character and definition of Southeast Asian societies.

Section I begins with the work of colonial ethnologists and their particular vision of Burmese history, which placed the region of Tharrawaddy within a particular context of culturally determined resistance. Political officers-cum-ethnologists amassed a corpus of knowledge based on their encounters during the pacification of the countryside following the overthrow of the Burmese monarchy in 1885. Many of the characteristics attributed specifically to the Saya San Rebellion were first identified and defined in district gazetteers and manuals produced during the consolidation of administrative rule in the late nineteenth and early twentieth centuries, but were appropriated by officials in the 1930s as explanations for the outbreak in Tharrawaddy. Most significant of these features was the idea of the *minlaung* (or incipient-king), a figure that represented the periodic rise of claimants to the throne that rallied followers around himself as the new King of Burma. This section explores how a "Rebellion Ethnology" was first developed by scholar-officials shortly after the pacification campaigns of the late nineteenth century and how colonial administrators produced a particular set of cultural features that would become entrenched in official documentation projects that were associated with the image of rural Burmese communities. One specific manual of 1914 would be of significant importance, as it provided the blueprint upon which all subsequent interpretations of the rebellion would be based by confirming Burmese kingship as an important image of peasant political expression.

Section II explores the role of law in the formation of the rebellion narrative and how legal institutions, procedures, and concerns made a lasting imprint in the formation of the evidential record most closely associated with the sources of the rebellion. Many of these sources came in the form of early situation reports that in turn provided the arguments behind the passage of several special legislative bills that expanded the emergency powers of the local government. Enacted as a response to the increasing spread of outbreaks throughout the Province, special rebellion legislation appropriated the Rebellion

Ethnology (and its images of Burmese culture) as a means of directing its policing powers. Most significantly, it called for the establishment of Special Rebellion Tribunals, which produced the evidential record and narrative structure that is associated with Saya San. Special counter-insurgency law was not merely a product of the particular historical context; it had an active role in the production of the arguments, paradigms, and analytical perspectives that would forever be attributed to the evidential record. The decisions made by the Special Tribunal were as much about reconstructing the past as they were about registering the memory of the rebellion for the future. The trial of Saya San is examined to demonstrate not only how the Rebellion Ethnology was infused into the events surrounding Tharrawaddy, but how Burmese culture was defined, criminalized, and conflated by law to produce a universal pattern of causality that could explain the insurrection. While special trial procedures dictated how Burmese culture would be presented and packaged, judgment summaries codified these constructions made by the prosecution, producing a particular narrative of the Saya San Rebellion for a particular audience. Thus, counter-insurgency law is demonstrated to be an active writer of the historical narrative, validating what earlier officials had reported in gazetteers while registering them for preservation in the archive.

Section III also explores the more recent phases of the story by examining the influence of the final blue-book report that served as the definitive assessment of the Saya San Rebellion. By first illustrating how legal sources predated and formed the basis for this report, the relationship between law and the making of a "historical" source is explored as this particular report has been treated by scholars as the primary source that establishes the "facts" of the rebellion. The report gave the narrative its formal structure, unifying the various outbreaks into a coherent movement. This section also studies the narrative scaffolding of the report, how a single narrative of rebellion was produced out of what was clearly an often disparate, conflicting, and varying series of outbreaks.[81] Through its narrative strategies, the report smoothed over these inconsistencies, producing a single vision of the rebellion for subsequent scholars to appropriate.

Following this discussion, scholarship on the rebellion is reexamined in Section III to illustrate the overarching influence of the official report and the manner in which scholars examined and interpreted the now-coherent "rebellion," drained of its earlier legal heritage. Scholars were drawn to the dichotomous structures of the report and continued to reinterpret within its discussions, never really questioning the categories, structures, and paradigms it espoused. As a result, specific themes emerged from this scholarship, taking them out of the context of Burma and into the context of Southeast Asian cultural studies, especially toward issues connecting "religion" to rebellion. Thus, out of the Rebellion Ethnology (and also in response to it) emerged the category of religious resistance in Southeast Asian studies, influencing our understanding of precolonial Southeast Asia as well as establishing a region-wide pattern of protest behavior reinforcing the place of indigenous agencies and identities in its historical narratives. In reconstructing this narrative process, the chapters within return colonial ethnology and law to the historical context that produced the Saya San narrative and to our visions of what constitutes an "autonomous" Southeast Asian history. Finally, the legacy of the Rebellion Ethnology is considered within the context of contemporary Myanmar and asks how urban and rural memories of Saya San continue to highlight different visions of the past while ideas of resistance and struggle—originally produced during the colonial period—are resurrected, appropriated, and redirected simultaneously by both the state and its detractors.

Rendering Southeast Asia

The contribution of postcolonial studies to the study of Southeast Asian rebellions has received relatively limited attention, especially since scholars devote much of their energy toward illustrating the nature of resistance in the region in all of its various forms and manifestations. The field has moved away from the study of large-scale rebellions to the "everyday" forms of resistance and "avoidance protest," broadening not how we might think about the Southeast Asian response to regimes of domination but how individual stories of the subaltern have been overshadowed by the grand narratives of revolution and dissent.[82] Although these alternative directions have redefined the study of resistance (and indeed contributed to Southeast Asian studies as a field), there are still angles of view that have not been explored in regard to earlier subjects whose cases were deemed closed. Furthermore, these departures are often contingent upon the acceptance that the "major" rebellions and the categories used to describe them are no longer problematic, which they can serve as stable historical points from which to engage new lines of enquiry. In this spirit, this study navigates among the following questions: (1) How were narratives about anticolonial rebellions connected to institutions of knowledge production and preservation (the archive, the court, or the museum)? (2) How did colonial scholar–officials come to know their subject? (3) What were the connections among colonial ethnography, law, and scholarship in the making of the Saya San Rebellion? and (4) How did the notion of Southeast Asian Rebellion come to define the region historiographically? In short, this work will explore the genealogy of the Saya San Rebellion in order to illustrate how a particular history was first produced and preserved through the intersection of ethnography, law, and history.

Thus, this story reconstructs the various contexts in which the facts of the Saya San Rebellion were first established. Rather than reinterpreting the content of the narrative, our attention will be drawn toward the career of this narrative; how it emerged as a product of colonial ethnography in British Burma; how this "Rebellion Ethnology" was appropriated by officials in early situation reports and condensed into a simple narrative; how it was politicized in legislative debates; how it was authenticated through the judicial system; and how it was codified and formalized by the official bluebook report. Part of the story retraces how the narrative was born out of conglomeration of several variant story lines, but unified into the single sequence of accepted "facts" and occurrences we accept today. By tracing the genealogy of this narrative, this book shifts the attention from interpreting the character of the Saya San Rebellion to exploring how various interpretations have constituted its very shape and understanding.

In addition, this study is concerned with how a particular "history" was made on the one hand and how categories constituting the field of Southeast Asian studies were established on the other. In doing so, this focus on the epistemology of a Burmese rebellion compels us to consider how such narratives both reflect and affect the way we define the field of Southeast Asia. Indirectly, the manner in which the rebellion was rendered in archival documents continued to influence attempts by later scholars to depart from colonial understandings of the rebellion, as categories such as kingship, tattooing, and superstition were recast within alternative frameworks (such as millenarianism) within which "autonomous" viewpoints were thought to represent the region's culture mentalities more acutely. In the discussions to follow, the problem of *the* Southeast Asian point of view will be considered through the making of rebellion in colonial Burma. The story of the Saya San Rebellion and its insertion into the region's history suggests that the very conceptual contours of the region—its epistemological characteristics—are implicated in and reliant upon the foundations established by colonial-scholar officials and the ongoing contributions of several communities of interpretation. Anticolonial rebellions (and resistance more generally), have played an important part in the rendering of Southeast Asia as a field of enquiry; *The Return of the Galon King* explores these and other epistemological intersections by situating the Saya San Rebellion within the context of its career—as a narrative of ethnology, a narrative of counter-insurgency law, and as a narrative of Southeast Asian cultural identity.

Notes

1. Government of Burma. "An Inquiry into the Causes of Crime in the Tharrawaddy District and a Search for Their Remedy," Annexure III, Letter No. 702T, May 25, 1916, Chief Secretary of the Government of Burma to the Commissioner of the Pegu Division.

2. Maung Maung, *From Sangha to Laity: Nationalist Movements of Burma, 1920–1940,* Australian National University Monographs on South Asia No. 4, (Columbia, MO: South Asia Books, 1980), 83–86.

3. Government of Burma. L/PJ/6/2020, Burma Rebellion General File (BRGF), Telegram. Government of India (G/I), Home Department

(H/D) to Secretary of State for India (SS/I), repeating telegram from Government of Burma (G/B), December 24, 1930.

4. Robert H. Taylor, *The State in Myanmar* (Singapore: NUS Press, 2009), 199–200.

5. The "rebellion narrative" refers to the facts and the series of events that first took shape in several preliminary reports that was eventually codified as the *Origins and Causes of the Burma Rebellion* (1930–1932). Later interpretations of the rebellion would use this document as their foundational source.

6. John Strong's *The Legend and Cult of Upagupta: Sanskrit Buddhism in North India and Southeast Asia* (Princeton: Princeton University Press, 1992) provides many versions of this eternal rivalry between the garuda and the naga in the context of Buddhist folk-tales and legends.

7. Saya San, *Let-hkanu-zu-kyan* (Moulmein: Myanma taing thadin-za pon-hneik-taik, 1927), *Weik-za theik-pan in-got-taya-kyan* (Nat-talin: Pyinna alin-bya, n.d.).

8. The majority of this account appears from investigations conducted in the early 1960s that culminated in the volume, Union of Burma, *Taungthu Lethama Ayedawpon* (Peasants Revolution) (Rangoon: Information Department, 1965). This source became foundational for many Burmese-language histories that followed its publication.

9. Union of Burma, *Taungthu Lethama Ayedawpon* (Account of the Peasants Revolution) (Rangoon: Information Department, 1965).

10. The complexity of the man is captured in one of the only remaining pictures taken prior to his incarceration that presents a middle-aged Saya San standing in Burmese formal attire with his left hand on a table and his right arm on a cane. This photo presents a well-dressed man who has the money and desire to take a portrait; a symbol of European bourgoise culture that contrasts with the traditional image of a peasant that nationalist historians have recorded. See the picture included in Saya San, *Let-hkanu-zu-kyan* (Moulmein: Myanma taing thadin-za pon-hneik-taik, 1927).

11. Government of Burma. L/PJ/6/2020. BRGF, Confidential. *The Rebellion in Burma, April 1931–March 1932* (Rangoon, 1932).

12. Government of Burma. L/PJ/6/2020. BRGF, Telegram, Government of Burma to Secretary of State for India, November 29, 1931. The day after Saya San was executed skirmishes continued to occur in the Pegu District.

13. Government of Burma. L/PJ/6/2020, BRGF, *Origins and Causes of the Burma Rebellion 1930–1932* (Rangoon, 1934).

14. Thant Myint U, *The Making of Modern Burma* (Cambridge: Cambridge University Press, 2001); Taylor, *The State in Myanmar,* 60–62.

15. Victor Lieberman, *Strange Parallels: Southeast Asia in Global Context, c. 800–1830* (Cambridge: Cambridge University Press, 2003).

16. Ibid.

17. Michael Aung-Thwin, *Pagan: The Origins of Modern Burma* (Honolulu: University of Hawaii Press, 1985), 30–68.

18. The establishment of British rule in Arakan, Tennasserim, and along the border with Siam did not create the same intensity of opposition as seen in other parts of the former kingdom for many of these territories contained communities that had resisted the state or held different notions of identity. See Taylor, *The State in Myanmar,* 154–58.

19. Parimal Ghosh, *Brave Men of the Hills: Resistance and Rebellion in Burma, 1825–1932* (London: Hurst, 2000), 45.

20. Nicholas B. Dirks, "Introduction: Colonialism and Culture," in Nicholas Dirks (ed.), *Colonialism and Culture* (Ann Arbor: University of Michigan Press, 1992), 3.

21. Dirks, "Introduction: Colonialism and Culture," 2–3.

22. Thomas Trautmann, *Aryans and British India* (Berkeley: University of California Press, 1997).

23. Clare Anderson, *Legible Bodies: Race, Criminality and Colonialism in South Asia* (Oxford: Berg, 2004).

24. Ibid.

25. Lawrence Rosen, *Law as Culture: An Invitation* (Princeton: Princeton University Press, 2006); Lauren Benton, *Law and Colonial Cultures: Legal Regimes in World History 1400–1900* (Cambridge: Cambridge University Press, 2002); Austin Sarat and Thomas R. Kearns (eds.), *Law in the Domains of Culture* (Ann Arbor: University of Michigan Press, 1998).

26. Maung Maung, *From Sangha to Laity: Nationalist Movements of Burma, 1920–1940* (Columbia, MO: South Asia Books, 1980).

27. Taylor, *The State in Myanmar,* 179–80.

28. Maung Maung, *From Sangha to Laity.*

29. Taylor, *The State in Myanmar,* 183–184, 193–197.

30. Maung Maung, *From Sangha to Laity,* 42–43.

31. Maung Maung, *From Sangha to Laity.*

32. John Cady, *A History of Modern Burma* (Ithaca: Cornell University Press, 1958), 317.

33. U Saw, The Burma Situation, (Rangoon: 1931).

34. Ibid.

35. Cady, *A History of Modern Burma,* 318.

36. Maurice Collis, *Trials in Burma* (London: Faber & Faber, 1938).
37. Carol A. Breckenridge and Peter van der Veer (eds.), *Orientalism and the Postcolonial Predicament* (Philadelphia: University of Pennsylvania Press, 1993); Peter Pels and Oscar Salemink (eds.), *Colonial Subjects: Essays on the Practical History of Anthropology* (Ann Arbor: University of Michigan Press, 2000).
38. G. E. Harvey, *British Rule in Burma 1824–1942* (London: Faber & Faber, 1946), 73–76.
39. D. G. E. Hall, *Burma* (London: Hutchingson's University Library, 1950), 158; idem, *A History of Southeast Asia* (London: Macmillan, 1964), 738.
40. Maung Htin Aung, *A History of Burma* (New York: Columbia University Press, 1967), 290–94; Bill Ashcroft, Gareth Griffiths, and Helen Tiffin, *The Empire Writes Back: Theory and Practice in Post-colonial Literatures*, 2nd edition, (London: Routledge, 2002).
41. Cady, *A History of Modern Burma*, 318–19.
42. Lucien W. Pye, *Politics, Personality, and Nation-Building: Burma's Search for Identity* (New Haven: Yale University Press, 1962), 259–60.
43. Donald Eugene Smith, *Religion and Politics in Burma* (Princeton: Princeton University Press, 1965), 107.
44. E. Michael Mendelson, *Sangha and State in Burma: A Study of Monastic Sectarianism and Leadership*, ed. John P. Ferguson (Ithaca: Cornell University Press, 1975).
45. E. Manuel Sarkisyanz, *Buddhist Backgrounds of the Burmese Revolution* (The Hague: Martinius Nijhoff, 1965).
46. Michael Adas, *The Burma Delta: Economic Development and Social Change on an Asian Frontier, 1852–1941* (Madison: University of Wisconsin Press, 1974), 200–205.
47. Michael Adas, *Prophets of Rebellion: Millenarian Protest Movements against the European Colonial Order* (Chapel Hill: University of North Carolina Press, 1979).
48. Michael Adas, "Comment," in Nicholas B. Dirks, *Colonialism and Culture*, 127–34.
49. John Smail, "On the Possibility of an Autonomous History of Modern Southeast Asia," *Journal of Southeast Asian History* 2 (1961): 72–102.
50. Reynaldo C. Ileto, "Religion and Anti-colonial Movements," in Nicholas Tarling (ed.), *The Cambridge History of Southeast Asia, Volume II, Part I* (Cambridge: Cambridge University Press, 1999), 193–244.
51. Patricia Herbert, *The Hsaya San Rebellion 1930–1932 Reappraised*

(Monash University Centre of Southeast Asian Studies Working Paper no. 27; Melbourne: Monash University, 1982).

52. Taylor's *The State in Myanmar* is a notable exception. For these alternative forms of resistance, see James Scott, *Weapons of the Weak* (New Haven: Yale University Press, 1985); Michael Adas, "From Avoidance to Confrontation: Peasant Protest in Precolonial and Colonial Southeast Asia," in Dirks (ed.), *Colonialism and Culture*, 89–126; idem, "From Footdragging to Flight: The Evasive History of Peasant Avoidance Protest in South and Southeast Asia," *Journal of Peasant Studies* 13, no. 2 (1986): 64–86; Michael Adas, "Comment" in Dirks, *Colonialism and Culture*, 127–34.

53. Oliver B. Pollack, "The Saya San Rebellion (1930–1932): Buddhism, Anti–colonialism and Nationalism in Burma," *Indo-British Review* 15, no. 1 (1988).

54. Michael Charney, *A History of Modern Burma* (Cambridge: Cambridge University Press, 2009).

55. Reynaldo C. Ileto's important contribution to *The Cambridge History of Southeast Asia* is an example of how influential the category of resistance has helped shape our understandings of Southeast Asian culture. See his "Religion and Anti-Colonial Movements," in Nicholas Tarling (ed.), *The Cambridge History of Southeast Asia, Volume II* (Cambridge: Cambridge University Press, 1992), 197–244. See also the seminal work of Michael Adas in *State, Market and Peasant in Colonial South and Southeast Asia* (Brookfield: Ashgate, 1998).

56. Mark T. Burger, "Decolonization, Modernisation, and Nation-Building: Political Development Theory and the Appeal of Communism in Southeast Asia, 1945–1975," *Journal of Southeast Asian Studies* 34, no. 3 (2003): 421–48; Lieberman, *Strange Parallels*, 6–15.

57. John Smail, "On the Possibility of an Autonomous History of Modern Southeast Asia," *Journal of Southeast Asian History* 2, no. 2 (1960): 72–102.

58. Lieberman, *Strange Parallels*, 6–15.

59. Frederick Cooper, *Colonialism in Question: Theory, Knowledge, History* (Berkeley: University of California Press, 2005), 33–55; Peter Pels and Oscar Salemink (eds.), *Colonial Subjects: Essays on the Practical History of Anthropology* (Ann Arbor: University of Michigan Press, 1999); Ann L. Stoler and Frederick Cooper, "Between Metropole and Colony: Rethinking a Research Agenda," in Ann L. Stoler and Frederick Cooper (eds.), *Tensions of Empire: Colonial Cultures in a Bourgeois World* (Berkeley: University of California Press, 1997), 1–56; Carol A. Breckenridge and

Peter van der Veer, "Orientalism and the Postcolonial Predicament," in Carol A. Breckenridge and Peter van der Veer, *Orientalism and the Postcolonial Predicament: Perspectives on South Asia* (Philadelphia: University of Pennsylvania Press, 1993), 1–19; Dirks, "Introduction: Colonialism and Culture," 1–25; Douglas Haynes and Gyan Prakash (eds.), *Contesting Power: Resistance and Everyday Social Relations in South Asia* (Oxford: Oxford University Press, 1991).

60. Breckenridge and van der Veer, *Orientalism and the Postcolonial Predicament: Perspectives on South Asia*, 1–19; Nicholas B. Dirks, *Castes of Mind: Colonialism and the Making of Modern India* (Princeton: Princeton University Press, 2001); Brian Axel (ed.), *From the Margins: Historical Anthropology and Its Futures* (Durham: Duke University Press, 2002); Jean Comaroff and John Comaroff, *Of Revelation and Revolution: Christianity, Colonialism, and Consciousness in South Africa, Volume I* (Chicago: University of Chicago Press, 1993).

61. John Pemberton, *On the Subject of Java* (Ithaca: Cornell University Press, 1994); Thongchai Winichakul, *Siam Mapped: A History of the Geo-Body of a Nation* (Honolulu: University of Hawaii Press, 1994); Timothy P. Barnard, *Contesting Malayness: Malay Identity Across Boundaries* (Singapore: NUS Press, 2004); Penny Edwards, *Cambodge: The Cultivation of a Nation, 1860–1945* (Honolulu: University of Hawaii Press, 2007).

62. Cooper, *Colonialism in Question;* Stoler and Cooper (eds.), *Tensions of Empire*; Breckenridge and van der Veer, *Orientalism and the Postcolonial Predicament*; Gyan Prakash, "Subaltern Studies as Postcolonial Criticism," *American Historical Review* 99, no. 5 (December 1994): 1475–90.

63. Cooper, *Colonialism in Question.*

64. Ibid.

65. "Orientalism and the Postcolonial Predicament," in Breckenridge and van der Veer, *Orientalism and the Postcolonial Predicament*, 1–19.

66. Cooper, *Colonialism in Question.*

67. James Clifford, *The Predicament of Culture: Twentieth Century Ethnography, Literature, and Art* (Cambridge: Harvard University Press, 1988).

68. Michel Foucault, *The Order of Things: An Archaeology of the Human Sciences,* trans. Alan Sheridan (New York: Vintage, 1970); idem, *The Archaeology of Knowledge* (New York: Pantheon, 1972); Edward Said, *Orientalism* (New York: Vintage Books, 1979); idem, *Culture and Imperialism* (New York: Vintage Books, 1994).

69. Thomas Trautmann, *Aryans and British India* (Berkeley: University of California Press, 1997); Dirks, "Introduction: Colonialism and Culture.".

70. Ibid.

71. Anand Yang, *Crime and Criminality in British India* (The Association for Asian Studies Mongraphs 42; Tucson: University of Arizona Press, 1985); Vicente L. Rafael (ed.), *Figures of Criminality in Indonesia, the Philippines and Colonial Vietnam* (Ithaca: Cornell University Southeast Asia Program Publications, 1999); Peter Zinoman, *The Colonial Bastille: A History of Imprisonment in Vietnam, 1862–1940* (Berkeley: University of California Press, 2001); Nicholas B. Dirks, *Castes of Mind*; Ann L. Stoler, "Rethinking Colonial Categories: European Communities and the Boundaries of Rule," in Dirks (ed.), *Colonialism and Culture*, 319–352.

72. Ranajit Guha, *Elementary Aspects of Peasant Insurgency in Colonial India* (Durham: Duke University Press, 1999); David Hardiman, *The Coming of the Devi: Adivasi Assertion in Western India* (Oxford: Oxford University Press, 1987); Shahid Amin, *Event, Metaphor, Memory: Chauri Chaura, 1922–1992* (Berkeley: University of California Press, 1995); Partha Chatterjee, *A Princely Imposter? The Strange and Universal History of the Kumar of Bhawal* (Princeton: Princeton University Press, 2002).

73. T. V. Sathyamurthy, "Indian Peasant Historiography: A Critical Perspective on Ranajit Guha's Work," *Journal of Peasant Studies* 18, no. 1 (1990): 92–144.

74. Ranajit Guha, "On Some Aspects of the Historiography of Colonial India," in Ranajit Guha (ed.), *Subaltern Studies* I (Delhi, 1983); idem, "The Prose of Counter-Insurgency," in Guha (ed.), *Subaltern Studies*, II (Delhi, 1983); Gyan Prakash, "Subaltern Studies as Postcolonial Criticism," *American Historical Review* 99, no. 5 (December 1994): 1475–90.

75. Vicente Rafael, ed., *Figures of Criminality in Indonesia, the Philippines, and Colonial Vietnam* (Ithaca: Cornell University Southeast Asian Studies Publication Series, 25, 1999); Anand Yang, *Crime and Criminality in British India* (Tucson: University of Arizona Press, 1985).

76. India Office Records. L/PJ/6/2020–2023, Burma Rebellion General Files.

77. Dirks, *Castes of Mind*.

78. Austin Sarat and Thomas Kearns, eds., *Law's Violence* (Ann Arbor: University of Michigan Press, 1995).

79. Francis X. Blouin Jr. and William G. Rosenberg, eds., *Archives, Documentation, and Institutions of Social Memory: Essays from the Sawyer Seminar* (Ann Arbor: University of Michigan Press, 2006).

80. Breckenridge and van der Veer, eds., *Orientalism and the Postcolonial Predicament*; Peter Pels and Oscar Salemink, eds., *Colonial Subjects:*

Essays on the Practical History of Anthropology (Ann Arbor: University of Michigan Press, 2000).

81. Peter J. Rabinowitz, *Before Reading: Narrative Conventions and the Politics of Interpretation* (Ithaca: Cornell University Press, 1987).

82. James C. Scott, *Weapons of the Weak: Everyday Forms of Peasant Resistance* (New Haven: Yale University Press, 1985).

Chapter 2

TEXTUALIZING REBELLION
Remembering Kings and an Ethnology of Revolt

As the first reports began to filter in from Tharrawaddy, a district three hours from Rangoon, it became clear that officials had underestimated the scope and breadth of the violence that had erupted just north of the capital.[1] Telegrams to Rangoon hastily stated that while the violence in Tharrawaddy District, "where outbreaks are not uncommon," was most likely a local disturbance, the intensification of violence in neighboring districts warranted close monitoring. With demands on local militia and police forces increasing, civil officers in Rangoon soon began to realize uncomfortably that additional military support from India would be necessary, along with special legal powers to curb the spread of violence and agitation in the affected areas. Such requests, however, would ultimately depend on whether approval from London (via New Delhi) could be secured, whether a convincing explanation on the part of the Rangoon administration could be offered, and whether or not such measures and recommendations would be sanctioned considering the heated relations within the local legislature. Such drastic changes in policy and administration warranted a consolidated view of the uprising and although two narratives would eventually emerge to explain the outbreak of violence in the countryside (one posited that Bengali revolutionaries were behind the rebellion), the version involving local monks, disgruntled medicine men, and pretender-kings would soon take precedent over the other, evolving into the familiar narrative involving Saya San that we know today.² Under considerable pressure from New Delhi and London to demonstrate control over the situation, officials in Rangoon looked desperately to find an explanation for the revolt and in doing so turned to a local gazetteer and to an obscure counter-insurgency manual, two key documents that would ultimately influence the manner in which the infamous Saya San Rebellion would come to be understood.

Locating Rebellion

As related in its official gazetteer of 1920, Tharrawaddy District appears like any other administrative unit on the colonial map of Burma—fixed to precise longitude and latitude coordinates like so many other districts that were carved and codified by the techniques of colonial surveyors and mapmakers, the district rests unassumingly between the Irrawaddy River and the Pegu Yoma.³ Derived from a feminized form of the Pali words *sara* (substance) and *vanta* (wealthy); *saravati* or *tharawadi* (as it is written in Burmese) means "of substantial wealth," leading colonial officials to speculate that the etymology of the term might have had something to do with the large amount of revenue that the region yielded during the reign of the Burmese monarchs. British officials regarded Tharrawaddy as a rather unremarkable district, describing it as a "dull monotony of the rice fields" marked by sporadic groves of fruit trees and the occasional toddy palm.⁴

Reading on however, one finds that this sleepy image shifts forebodingly as the physical features of the district camouflage a darker, criminalized, and more forsaken space in the lore of the region's popular history.⁵ One such history recounts a story of a King Myitkyanzwa who, while touring the region, decided to erect a pagoda and a palace in what would become present-day Tharrawaddy. As the location of the foundation posts were being laid, it was found that the ground was unable to support them due to swarms of ants that gave the ground an undesirable, entangled appearance of jungle vines. Advisers to the king interpreted the ants to represent the swarms of people that would populate this place in the future. Just as it was impossible

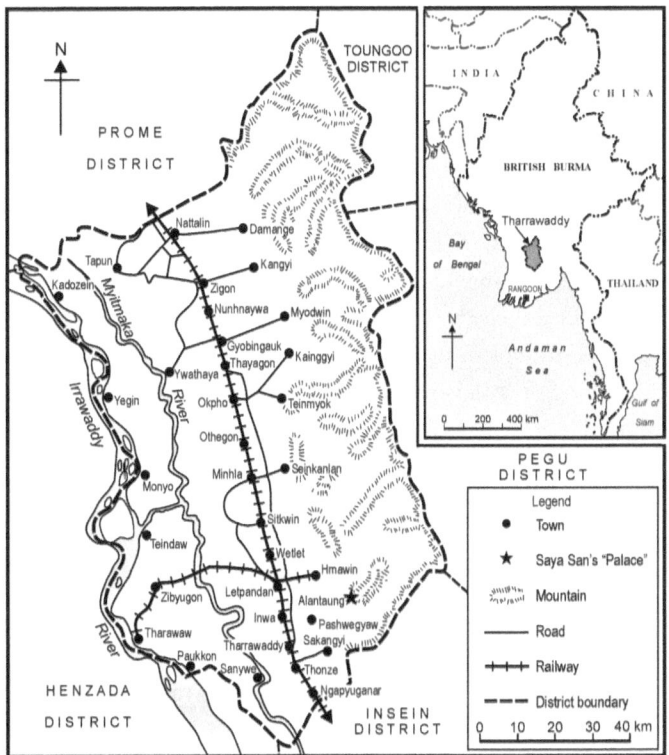

Tharrawaddy District

to disentangle the matted vines of the jungle upon which the palace would stand, so too would it be impossible to clear away the disorder that would exist among these peoples. To rectify this prophesy, the King was advised to kill four women to be buried at the corners as a sacrifice. One of these women, Ma Min Ban, prayed to the *nats* (spirits) to take witness of her curse by saying that no male child born in this area would be of good character. Although the area was eventually named after "a happy crow" who eats the fine fat earthworm to repletion, the "curse has lived ever since."[6]

Despite being compiled before the events of 1930–32, this local folktale and its inclusion in the opening pages of the gazetteer foreshadows the way in which rebellion and resistance would come to characterize Tharrawaddy District under British rule. Its potency as an ethnographic statement drew strength from the fact that it appeared to be an "indigenous" explanation for the region's criminal nature, reflecting the despotism of the Burmese monarchy on the one hand and the superstitious belief in spirits, sacrifices, and curses on the other.[7] Through the format of the district gazetteer, the civil-service manual, and other forms of colonial documentation, Burmese cultural elements such as these were constructed, collected, and codified to explain the district's tumultuous past while predicting the likelihood of an unstable future. As in India, land surveying and revenue collection was one administrative context in which this ethnography of Tharrawaddy was produced, though the annexation of the Burmese kingdom and the resistance movements it encountered also significantly informed the findings within this document. With rebellion and criminality as the overarching framework, the prescriptive nature of Ma Min Ban's curse was made to be binding not by the *nats* to whom she prayed, but by the way in which the story was ethnographically bound to the peoples of Tharrawaddy by colonial scholar-officials.

This image that presented Tharrawaddy as an inherently criminal region that bred unsavory characters would be reinforced in the pages that made up its official gazetteer, informing and enabling future narratives that would come to rely on its caricatures and categories. Comprehensive in nature, the document surveys the physical description, history, economic, ethnic, administration, education, public health, and social behavior of the Tharrawaddy people. Its section on history was organized by and recounted through the element of rebellion, as the narrative of the district was cast through descriptions of resistance movements, criminalized figures, and counter-insurgency tactics. Several key examples of resistance movements in the precolonial period and those that erupted during what would later be called the Anglo–Burmese Wars were provided in order to establish the general chronology of the region. One nineteenth-century king who took the name *Tharrawaddy* was "blamed for collecting bad characters in

Tharrawaddy District and the criminal taint which its inhabitants are reputed to possess has been described as a legacy from his followers."[8] Monks, princes, and self-declared kings like Gaung Gyi, Nga Aung, and the infamous U Thuriya were described as fulfilling and confirming the ethnographic character of the district. For instance, in raising "a golden umbrella" (a recognizable symbol of the monarchy), Nga Aung was said to have attracted several armed followers, while supporters of U Thuriya were drawn to his use of oaths and tattoos to signify allegiance to a restored monarchy and the invulnerability such measures would ensure. Palm-leaf membership tickets were prepared and distributed to the rank and file while proclamations of rebellion, issued by aspirants to the throne, demonstrated the overall *political* nature of these movements, a characterization that would remain entrenched for years to come.[9] By the time the document was published in 1920, several rebellions and outbreaks had already taken place in the district, adding weight to the impression that somehow the people of Tharrawaddy, as the curse ensured, were prone to disorder and crime.[10] In the words of a deputy commissioner in 1853, the unsettled state of Tharrawaddy arose from the "disposition of its inhabitants who from time immemorial, have been noted as a turbulent and lawless race."[11] Many of them, the gazetteer states, "still retained a superstitious reference for the king whom they regarded as a national sovereign."[12]

This particular ethnology, seemingly inscribed into the very essence of the district and the members of its community, would be remembered and reified through its application by colonial officials to the events later associated with Saya San. The Tharrawaddy reputation as a criminalized zone, complete with a criminalized mythology, was made to control the destiny of its communities, relegating them to determinable and predictably consistent behavior. Establishing Tharrawaddy's past enabled administrators to ensure assessments of its future by anchoring the district in an unchanging and essentialized history. As an official commented in 1853, "since long before the memory of man, the people [of Tharrawaddy] have been disorderly and rebellious; discontent, disunion, and anarchy have often prevailed there."[13] Registering that tradition textually demonstrated control over the district's past, reflecting the ability to reduce to words the chaos and uncertainty of armed insurrection. Furthermore, such assessments provided future officers with the appropriate explanation and working templates should uprisings occur under their watch. Years later, Tharrawaddy's Rebellion Ethnology would in fact reemerge in the documents pertaining to the largest series of peasant rebellions ever to occur in Burmese history. However, it would do so only after acquiring another layer of categories that made resistance and revolt the very substance of Burmese culture and the defining essence of the country's political potential. Rather than being limited to the history of the infamous district, these characteristics soon would be appropriated and applied to the majority of rural communities throughout the country.

A Rebellion Manual

Before Saya San became known to scholars as a millenarian prophet, before he was anointed a peasant martyr by nationalist scholars, and even before his name was connected to the Burma Rebellion in the first place, British officers had in their possession a working template of how future rebellions in the Province would be rendered administratively. Compiled in 1914 by Bertram S. Carey, Commissioner of Sagaing District near Mandalay, "Hints to the Guidance of Civil Officers in the Event of Outbreak of Disturbance in Burma" was meant to serve as a reference to younger British officials who had not taken part in the earlier pacification campaigns of Upper Burma by providing civil officers with an overview of how Burmese resistance emerged historically and how they might expect future disturbances to occur. Though similar in form and content to many instructional documents used by the colonial administration, this particular manual would establish the conceptual foundations linking the criminalized history of Tharrawaddy to the template employed for the original rendering of the Saya San Rebellion.

At one level, the manual might be regarded as a standard security brief, as it recommended measures that would ensure an aggressive military presence in the Province, a position that was deemed necessary to the maintenance of security and stability. Current dossiers on the enemy were deemed outdated and Carey identified certain shortcomings in the availability and relevancy of existing manuals that could provide new officials with information should "grave disorder" present itself. Earlier documents like "The General Rules for Jungle Warfare in Burma" (1886) were released well before considerable intelligence and experience could be gathered and recorded during subsequent pacification campaigns that followed annexation and the banishment of the monarchy. Carey's manual was based on his duties as political officer in the pacification of the Chin communities in the 1890s and designed to provide current information on "what is likely to happen, what is the accepted method of dealing with the situation, and how to take the vigorous offensive against the enemy."[14]

At another level of analysis, this document provides an opportunity to explore the ways in which Burmese rebellion was produced, defined, and registered by British administrative officers for future administrative and operational needs. The notion of rebellion (in Carey's terms) was essentially predictable and preventable if one understood the environmental, historical, and cultural context in which it emerged. As such, the manual was exactly that—it was an ethnographic statement that claimed authoritative knowledge over the very ingredients that fostered rebellion in Burma. In doing so, rebellion was taken by him to be something distinctly "Burmese" and therefore required a template that might make this profile more easily understandable. His typology cast Burmese rebellion in particular cultural terms, made discursive statements about peasant political potential, and fashioned what might be called a "Rebellion Ethnology"; it denoted a series of prescriptive representations that would eventually be relied upon by colonial officials, legal officers, and scholars in their epistemological rendering of the Saya San Rebellion. Whereas the document provided civil officers with a detailed account of how resistance would occur in Burma and instructions on how to respond to potential outbreaks, it also revealed insight into the character, disposition, and memories of rural peasants that made the prospect of rebellion an intrinsic part of being Burmese. It was as if resistance epitomized the very notion of "Burmeseness" while simultaneously freezing "natives" into essential modes of behavior.[15] Central to this profile was the idea that Burmese were always receptive to memories involving the monarchy, which automatically stirred and fostered notions of revolt. This memory enabled, and was enabled by, the potential threat of *minlaung* (king-to-be) movements—outbreaks by aspirants to the throne that embodied the character and the quintessential form of the Rebellion Ethnology. Thus, rebellions in the future would "be very much what happened in the past" for Burmese political expression was confined and defined through the symbols, rhetoric, and pageantry of the late Konbaung dynasty.

The Rebellion Ethnology

As an ethnographic statement, the manual delves into the nature of Burmese identity, psychology, and a disposition toward resistance. Readers are made aware that certain signs of impending trouble are certainly detectable as the "Burman, when excited, both acts and talks recklessly."[16] Rumors and warnings (an oddly persistent "Burmese" caricature that is still found in use today) would usually precede such events, and civil officers were cautioned to take seriously the "knave" who is seemingly "talking the wildest nonsense." Although officers could take heart in the fact that reliable intelligence networks could reveal the earliest stages of a revolt, the manual also warned that "attacks on police-stations and districts have suddenly rebelled with absolute secrecy and without warning," since in "political affairs Burmans can be very secretive if they wish."[17] Interestingly, this element of surprise (though in a sense, predicted by the manual) would be a significant component of the legal case against Saya San and the historical narrative associated with him in his role in organizing the revolt. The suddenness of the rebellion and the inability to foresee the eruption of violence in late 1930 "fit" into the model proposed by Carey while providing the perception that Rangoon officials did indeed have a degree of control over the situation. Thus, the early signs of a rebellion were made readable if officers were provided the right ethnographic text—rumors and prophesies were inextricably connected to the outbreak of disturbances, while patterns of behavior, to be examined below, were equally predictable as they were embodied and embedded in the history and culture of the Burmese.

Carey's manual posited that every few years, a Burmese *Saya* (teacher/elder) will envision himself as the prophesized king, a *minlaung* that would restore the monarchy to its former glory.[18] Seeking to enlist ignorant and expectant peasants to his calling, this "pretender-king" (the British translation for the term *minlaung)*[19] would follow a prescribed pattern: he would be expected to lead isolated attacks on outposts; he might attract followers with his promises of protective tattooing and powerful amulets; and he undoubtedly would set up his headquarters at traditionally sacred spaces or historically meaningful locations.[20] Buddhist monks were also thought to be a threat in connection to this *minlaung* pattern as experience during the pacification of Upper Burma in the late nineteenth century saw certain monks, like the movement associated with U Thuriya, taking to arms in battle in support of such a figure. Commenting on the declining role of the monkhood's ecclesiastical authority (the *Thathanabaing),* "pongyis (monks) were becoming more undisciplined" and "openly flouted and denied" the former directives, which warranted the cultivation of relations between civil officers and monks. Officials were advised to listen carefully and to take seriously rumors of "soothsayers," "charm-givers," or other men claiming "supernatural powers" for if these figures were left alone, they would "get such a hold on the imagination of the people that they will first shelter and then follow him."[21]

In short, particular institutions, figures, and symbols of precolonial Burma—not just Tharrawaddy—were criminalized under Carey's ethnology, registering new meanings into elements of Burmese culture that were stripped of their former historical and social significance. More significantly, "Burmese Culture" was itself being constituted and codified through the prism of rebellion as many of its features were textualized within the aftermath of pacification and under the threat of future rebellions. Monks and indigenous medicine men were deemed potential fomenters of rebellion, while rituals, religion, and modes of adornment (such as tattooing and amulet wearing) were identified, transformed, and reconfigured to convey resistance and difference. Burmese kingship, a truly significant and complex institution in Burmese history, was reduced and redefined to becoming the very symbol of revolt. Rebellion and "the traditional" became mutually reinforcing through colonialism's role in the production of knowledge, leaving little room for alternative forms of protest or debate to be recognized outside of the parameters established by Carey's ethnology. Future officials using the manual would read that Burmese peasants were limited in their ability to engage and work within the administrative apparatus of the colonial state because their inherent disposition toward the traditional and their nostalgia for past kings forever prevented their participation in the colonial-defined modern world. Remembering the monarchy and rejecting the British Raj placed the Burmese on a different stage of development from their Indian counterparts, a sentiment that would influence the way in which the events of 1930–32 would be presented by colonial authorities.

Colonizing Memory

A central component to Carey's manual was the underlying assumption about Burmese memory and its effect upon the ways in which Burmese would rebel in the future. As part of the Rebellion Ethnology, particular memories represented and bound Burmese to a traditional past that would forever compel them to see the world through those visions. It argued that for the most part that "what will happen in the future will be very much the same as what happened in the past," regulating the way in which Burmese remembered monarchy (the symbol of traditionalism) and their inability to engage the technologies and progressive ideologies of the modern (British) world.[22] This formula cast Burmese as "imaginative," prone to "credulity," and by nature "restless," whose "history is a record of sudden and successful rebellions resulting in the seizure of the throne."[23] It was as if the act of rebelling (especially on behalf of the defunct monarchy) was a preoccupation that imprisoned Burmese from pursuing any alternative form of political expression, a culturally determined trait that reified colonial rule on the one hand while cleverly delegitimizing potential resistance to it on the other. Carey recounts when a former *minlaung* promised that his amulets would protect his followers from bullets; it was his fantastic claims and extraordinary character—not particular political, social, or economic grievances—that actually attracted his followers.[24] Such sentiment would be echoed by later colonial historians such as G. E. Harvey, who would later blame the 1930 rebellions on "superstition, plain and simple," effectively entrenching the ethnographic character established by colonial documentation and compelling professional scholars in the 1970s and 1980s to respond by amplifying the complexity and importance of these indigenous mentalities (a subject to be engaged later).[25] As such, officials were advised to expect and even anticipate rebellion, for it was not a reflection of British policy that might contribute to future uprisings but the superstitious nature of the Burmese that went hand in hand with their willingness and innate hope that monarchy and state-protected Buddhism would once again be restored in Upper Burma. Thus, kingship was writ within the context of pacification and rebellion, as both a cause of, and motivation for, resistance movements in Burma. By extension, Burmese culture was cast as being bounded to and defined by this institution, unable to free itself from the legacy of despotism even as British modernity had sought to emancipate Burma from itself. The possibility of *"minlaung* pretenders" rising up against authorities was emblematic of the minds and memories of Burmese peasants whose image of authority was the defiant, arrogant, and isolated monarchs of Mandalay—unable to draw upon, comprehend, or negotiate a path toward the modern as kings in Thailand and India had supposedly demonstrated. Carey's rebellion manual reshaped and confined Burmese memory to one seminal moment—the fall of the Burmese monarchy to the British in 1885. In doing so Carey restricted any possibility of adaptation, appropriation, or even assimilation on the part of the Burmese peasant by rendering him or her incapable of remembering much else and unable to comprehend the future through alternative symbols or ideas. The colonizing of Burmese memory and the rendering of the Rebellion Ethnology as unequivocally linked to kingship enabled British officials to predict how Burmese would remember and how they would act upon those memories.

If memory of the Burmese monarchy was emblematic of the Rebellion Ethnology, registering that memory in the archive was emblematic of colonial ethnological projects. Recent scholarship on archives, law, and the production of knowledge has convincingly demonstrated how documents inform, predict, and implicate the nature and direction of scholarship that drew from it. Scholars hailing from Subaltern Studies, sociolegal studies, and ethnohistory have all explored the way in which documents refer to each other as much as they invoke the past to authorize the present and future.[26] More importantly, archives serve to materialize memory, by providing textual representations of remembering while operating on the basis of preserving and prescribing memory for future reference. Documents placed in what would be called the Burma Rebellion General Files would ensure and produce particular memories about the rebellion for the future, as much as the content within represented particular memories of the past. Even under a cursory review of the sources, we can actually see how Carey's "*minlaung* model" was adopted and projected into the events of the 1930s in order to cast the movement in its traditional coloring.[27] Historians have relied on crucial documents such as *The Origins and Causes of the Burma Rebellion 1930–1932*, which refers to the "prophetic observations" of Carey's manual that "rebellions would recur from time to time."[28] The result of this memory production, both textually and ethnographically, can be found among the earliest telegrams and reports at the onset of the rebellion. Carey's model was almost immediately adopted mere weeks into the fighting, and familiar ideas about Burmese memory began to appear in the telegrams and situation reports of early 1931. This relationship between Carey's rebellion manual and subsequent reports also reveals an interesting function in that it enabled future officials to secure their policies by anchoring their assessments to the document. Establishing documentary precedence was as important to officials looking to the past as it was to officials hoping to register their observations for the future.

Memory was thus both the subject and the administrative mechanism underlying the epistemological rendering of the Saya San Rebellion.

The textualization of Burmese memory and the projection of the Rebellion Ethnology into the events of late 1930 can be detected in the earliest situation reports concerning the outbreak of violence in Tharrawaddy District. For the first two weeks, communication among district officials, Rangoon authorities, and New Delhi reveal that officers did not have a clear idea of what was happening in the suburbs of Rangoon. Initial assessments dismissed the attack on a Forestry official as a local uprising that was immediately retracted once disorder began to spread in neighboring districts. On December 29, 1930, officers on the ground reported that little was known about the causes of the skirmish or the whereabouts of the leader, though suspicion remained that it was organized.[29] However, little explanation was offered by local officials until the arrival of troops into the affected districts, nearly two weeks after the original outbreak. It was during a military operation against a group of rebels gathered near a hill called Alantaung that the first traces of Carey's Rebellion Ethnology could be detected.

Though the original descriptions of Saya San's alleged mountain headquarters called it "a bamboo stockade with a flag," this event would later be refashioned as Saya San's "palace," considered by officials (and later by scholars) to be evidence of his attempt to resurrect the Burmese monarchy along traditional lines.[30] On January 1, 1930, the military officer in charge of the Alantaung operations reported that he had found "ten dead and five wounded, of whom two are important leaders. One red flag and other trophies seized and large quantities rebels' stores found and burned [sic]."[31] The very next day, Rangoon officials reported to the Secretary of State for India that the "rebel headquarters" and "palace" had been burned and of the seventeen killed, several of the principle leaders had been killed.[32] "One red flag" had been transformed into the throne of a *minlaung* king. Though the uprising in Tharrawaddy was barely ten days old, Carey's ethnology was already beginning to emerge.

The evidential basis for rendering the events surrounding the Battle of *Alantaung* through the prism of kingship is actually very thin, though several provocative assessments have suggested that this example fits a paradigm for Southeast Asian conceptions of revolt and resistance, not unlike Carey's model for Burmese rebellion.[33] By inscribing in the memories of peasants a nostalgia for the monarchy, officials created an ethnographic understanding of rebellion that cast Burmese peasants as forever rooted to the past and unable to move beyond the symbols, rituals, and authority of kingship. Establishing the battle for, and discovery of the encampment as, "the Palace" of Saya San also rendered rural peasant protest as qualitatively different from the nationalist movements in the cities, which by 1930 had already developed a sophisticated network of parties and associations that were concerned with a variety of political issues. British administrators were resurrecting the memory of kings on behalf of the Burmese peasantry for counter-insurgency purposes by relegating peasant political dissent to "superstition" while making it difficult for urban-based nationalists within the Burmese Legislative Council to associate themselves with peasant concerns.[34] These peasant combatants, kept silent by the categories of reports and telegrams, were also muted by the memories that were being attributed to them by officials. To British sensibilities, rendering rebellion in these terms not only relegated the Burmese to certain modes of political expression, but using the memory of past kings helped to justify and enable counter-insurgency policy.

These initial projections would find their way into the earliest documents that would provide the textual basis for the special tribunal hearings and official reports that would subsequently follow that year.[35] In short, British officials hoped to establish that Burmese memories for the return of the king could explain the rebellion, while at the same time, administrators wanted to document the basis for that assessment by republishing Carey's manual. Carey's model of future rebellions depended on remembering his predictions, as much as it depended on the Burmese rebelling. In some ways, the manual provided documentary evidence that administrators knew such disturbances were possible as suggested in the final blue-book report.[36] Drawing upon Carey's manual provided Rangoon officials with a template that could be inserted whatever the circumstances, for the document established clear operational strategies for dealing with new outbreaks, but at the same time it kindled the memory of rebellions during the pacification. For administrators in Rangoon, remembering rebellions in the past influenced the way that they engaged and represented rebellions in the present. The early documents closest to the outbreak of the Saya San Rebellion reveal how easily the models established by Carey and others were inserted into the events of early 1931 at a very early stage. For police and civil administrators, the outbreak in Tharrawaddy and administrative pressures from London and New Delhi, which demanded clear situation assessments, would require them to remember quickly.

Registering Memory

In the week following the disturbances of December 22, 1930, records reveal that Rangoon officials appeared to make quick use of the characterizations associated with the Tharrawaddy region that had been established two decades earlier. In a series of confidential letters between the Government of Burma and the Government of India (documents that constitute the earliest attempts to assess the outbreak in Tharrawaddy), one can trace Burma government efforts to make sense of the outbreaks within the context of Carey's template and those codified by the gazetteer.[37] The earliest of the letters, dated December 29, outlined in five sections the details of the "outbreak," reporting that it had started "without any warning" in villages about eight miles outside of Tharrawaddy town in the area of Pashewgyaw, in the southeast corner of the district. In the course of the skirmishes, two village headmen and a deputy forest ranger were killed, prompting a small civil-police party to investigate, which eventually encountered a large force of rebels nearing four-to-five hundred in number. Upon contact, the deputy commissioner requested a further one hundred military police be dispatched to reinforce and secure the area. The letter went on to describe steps taken to secure neighboring

Rebellion clothing

districts while summarizing details of related skirmishes involving village headmen, mild disruption of rail services, and attacks on police patrols that resulted in the dispatch of a Company of "Buffs" from Rangoon, the 15th Punjabis, and eventually a whole battalion of the Burma Rifles from Maymyo being sent to the district.[38]

By the fifth section, the influence of Tharrawaddy's criminalized ethnology began to reappear as descriptions of the "outbreak" were characterized in line with the district's official gazetteer and the predictions within Carey's manual. The findings were said to be consistent "in keeping with the usual Burmese risings" as the "favourite place for such risings in Lower Burma is the Tharrawaddy District and in Upper Burma the Shwebo District."[39] The letter stated that the disturbances had to be "carefully and skilfully [sic] organized for a considerable time" as a "large number of men wear a definite uniform and they are nearly all tattooed as is the custom among Burmans to make them invulnerable."[40] Following Carey's warnings about the potential secrecy surrounding such outbreaks, the letter commented that it was "remarkable" that the manufacture of these uniforms and the tattooing had proceeded without detection, as it must have been carried out "so secretly that no rumour of it reached the authorities." However, rumors were now beginning to circulate that a "mysterious Sayagyi" was supposed to have organized these preparations and of a *"minlaung* or pretender" who had built a palace in the forest. The familiar characterizations of rumor, kingship, and rebellion had once again found its way into Tharrawaddy.

Though the identity of the *minlaung* had not yet been reported, his profile was already being established, one that would eventually be extended and developed in weeks to come. More importantly, certain key elements, presented in binary terms, would be registered and recorded in a manner that would frame future discourses about the Rebellion. For example, the outbreak was characterized as being traditional (not modern) in character, an organized (not spontaneous) affair, political (not economic) in motivation, and local (not urban) in scope, despite speculation that nationalists' associations were being implicated in the violence. Ascribing these crucial features with the events of late 1930 would not only preserve Tharrawaddy's criminalized ethnology, but documenting the outbreak provided precedence for future assessments; allowing correspondences, memos, and police records to become the textual basis for more comprehensive official reports that would come to represent the sanctioned view of the rebellion.

Indeed by January 5, 1931, a new assessment had already been formulated, which proceeded to clarify and further establish what had been introduced only a week earlier but was now being called "the Tharrawaddy Rebellion." Adding four new sections to the previous letter of December 29, 1930, the new document proceeded to discuss more confidently the character and nature of the outbreak while seeking to retain troops that had been sent via India. Responding to reports in the press that the outbreak was the result of economic pressures on rural communities, the document stated that a proclamation had been found on a dead rebel, which demonstrated "conclusively" that the risings were "of the ordinary type of rebellion under a pretender or minlaung."[41] Although the rebellion was barely two weeks old, debate had already emerged surrounding the origins and facts of the rising, one small example of the contested circumstances within which the historical narrative would come to light. This written proclamation, along with description of events surrounding the battle at Alantaung, would further entrench the Rebellion Ethnology and the memory of kings into the context of events associated with Saya San. While officials confidently reported that a rebel encampment had been destroyed on Alantuang Hill, the way in which the event was presented would establish and transform the terms through which the future Saya San Rebellion would come to be known.

The sources pertaining to the Battle of Alantaung Hill reveal the ambiguity surrounding what actually happened, but they remain important for how they connect the event with Tharrawaddy's criminalized past. Through a comparison of official telegrams with the letter sent to India on January 5, 1931, it is possible to trace when officials began to impregnate their reports with elements from the Rebellion Ethnology. For example, telegrams dated December 30, 1931, state that preparations for a major operation against a rebel encampment on Alantaung Hill were being made, but by the time the battle was over on January 1, 1931, what had been earlier described as a bamboo thatch with "one red flag and other trophies" became, on January 2, 1931, the rebels' headquarters and "burnt Palace" reinforcing the idea that this rising was of the traditional kind involving Burmese kingship. The subsequent letter of January 5, 1931, amplified this caricature by noting that "the most fantastic stories were current about this palace, which was said not only to be impregnable, but even to be invisible to the ordinary human eye, presumably with the exception of the rebels themselves." For officials, establishing that the restoration of the monarchy was directly connected to the "credulity of the jungle Burman" was at the very heart of the Rebellion Ethnology.[42]

The battle for the "palace" was actually very quick, resulting in seventeen rebel casualties and the eventual burning of the structure, which was said to have contained large quantities of petrol, kerosene, and gunpowder. Of the rebels that were killed, it is curious to note that that reporting officer stated that "there is very good reason to believe that a man who was killed while being carried away on a litter was 'the King,'" as his "description agrees with a photograph which has since been discovered."[43] He was described as conceiving the idea, "so common to Burma, of starting a rebellion with himself as King," an idea that "rapidly took hold of the imagination of the superstitious Burmans." Identified as Saya San, the letter proceeded to describe him as a "Shan" or "Taungthu" who had declared himself king on December 22, 1930, and took the title "Thupannaka Galon Raza Mingyi" (Great Galon King) and called his capital "Buddha Raza Myo." Members were tattooed with the Galon (Garuda), given enlistment cards with numbers, and organized into companies, seemingly following the pattern of earlier movements in the district. The successful recruitment of followers, beyond the weakened economic situation, was attributed to the way in which Burmese interpreted unusually heavy rains in December and an earthquake as omens, once again returning to the types of characterizations found in Carey's manual and the district gazetteer.

Curiously, the government of Burma's official letter seemed to have trouble reconciling whether the rising was purely an "insurrection of the usual Burmese type" or one that was connected to the political context of the 1930s, a binary framing that would mark rebellion discourse well after the uprisings were over. For whereas officials maintained that the rebellion was connected with resurrecting the monarchy, the letter also revealed that recruitment was most likely connected to the growth of village associations *(wunthanus)* that were affiliated with urban-nationalist organizations, like the Soe Thein General Council of Burmese Associations, which was eventually censored for its alleged involvement with the rising and outspoken declaration for complete independence from Britain.[44] These political connections, in addition to rumors in the press that the initial successes of the rebels were due to ex-army service men being closely connected to the rising, suggest that the clear boundaries between traditional and modern Burma were not easily conflated by British officials as much as they attempted to make it so. Yet the first official reports, which would draw on these early correspondences between India and Burma, would attempt to do just that: where there might have been hints of ambiguity, speculation, and contestation present in the earliest records of the rising, these subsequent reports, which constitute a major component of the rebellion archive, demonstrate the attempt to slowly erase and smooth over traces of contradiction as the official narrative began to take its more confident and assured shape. The rising would continue to be regarded as of a traditional type, described and inscribed as a fundamental trait of the Tharrawaddy people who were made to be distinctively separate from the life and world of the cities. Urban nationalists and their organizations were implicated in the Rebellion as having stoked the fire of resistance by attempting to take advantage of this culturally determined disposition for resistance in the countryside. In essence, officials tried to separate rural village worldviews from urban-nationalist agendas, new technologies, and progressive ideas that were permeating within and without the Empire. Efforts to control the rebellion textually were never entirely successful, as the variety, unpredictability, and unevenness of the uprisings stretched the totalizing measures of colonial documentation projects. Even the figure of Saya San seemed to confound the categories of counter-insurgency as his education, background, and apparent political participation contradicted the profile that was being made for him. By the time the first official report was published in March 1931, there would already be visible attempts to reduce these varying patterns to the simplicity found in the Rebellion Ethnology.

Codifying Rebellion

Ralph Clarence Morris's "Causes of the Tharrawaddy Rebellion," one of the earliest comprehensive reports on the rebellion, was the first document to present an attempt to synthesize information on it. On the one hand, the report was a product of a colonial administration that was under pressure from New Delhi and London to provide a coherent picture of events in early 1931. On the other hand, the document also represents another manifestation of the Rebellion Ethnology that emerged during Anglo–Burman wars that were textually extended to the history and character of the Tharrawaddy people. Resurrecting key elements from Carey's formula for rebellion and Tharrawaddy's criminalized history, Morris's report continued where the 1920 gazetteer left off by relating a history of opposition through the many political figures and movements that had drawn considerable attention throughout the province since 1917. Interestingly, the report provides a summary of the rise of national-opposition parities, urban-political activism, and the spread of these networks into the countryside via village organizations called *athins*. Saya San's connections to these nationalist interests and organizational infrastructure were made in an attempt to establish the political motivations for the rebellion while differentiating urban-political expression from that in the countryside. Tharrawaddy's propensity for rebellion was well known, a characteristic Saya San allegedly used to his advantage.

The report delineated how Saya San planned the Rebellion, by focusing on the alleged leader's recruitment practices, his promises to resurrect the Burmese monarchy, and the general sociohistorical conditions that made such entreaties attractive to peasants. Thus, the document reflects the perception of events in early 1931 and the older perceptions of the district that were codified in the 1920 gazetteer. Following Carey's profile and the types of rebellions associated with the district, Saya San's alleged lieutenants recruited followers by promising them protection from bullets through the use of tattooing and amulet wearing. Specifically, these members were instructed to inscribe on their bodies the figure of the Galon (Garuda) in reference to the mythical bird that is the archenemy of the Naga (dragon).[45] The Galon is often depicted holding, biting, or ensnaring the Naga to submission, a curious image when one remembers the supposed etymology of the name *Tharrawaddy,* which is said to refer to crows eating earthworms until satisfied. In the context of the events in 1930–31 however, this symbol would be argued in the trial of Saya San as representing the very idea of "rebellion" in Burma, as the Galon supposedly represented the Burmese while the Naga denoted the British.[46] These assertions, coupled with claims that he would build a palace at Alantaung and call himself "the Galon King" completed the profile of kingship and its connections to this prescribed past. Saya San's emergence was not only a characteristic of the Tharrawaddy past; it was a sign that Burmese peasants were hopelessly bound to a tradition that was deeply imbedded in the memory of an exiled monarchy. In the words of the original gazetteer, which was repeated verbatim in the report of 1931, "the unsettled state of the district arose from the disposition of its inhabitants who from time immemorial had been noted as a turbulent and lawless race."[47]

Not only was Tharrawaddy made responsible for the emergence of another claimant to the throne, but the district was renewed as a criminal region, full of bandits, rebels, and pretenders who had "always been a thorn in the sides of kings and Governments."[48] Arguing that "this same disposition to disorder and anarchy continued," Morris sought to reestablish that rebellion was a common feature of the district and that the memory of that tradition continued, exemplified by the numerous rebellions that broke out following the dismantling of the monarchy. Whereas the gazetteer had provided two sections of "history" that explored resistance during the pacification period, Morris's report continued with a history of nationalist activities in the region, detailing the growth of the Young Men's Buddhist Association, its evolution into the General Council of Burmese Associations, and the activities of specific nationalist leaders. All these nationalist leaders utilized more contemporary "Western" forms of political expression and mobilization; they were also associated with the "rebellious" and criminalized pasts of this district, complicating and blurring the distinctions between local activist, criminals, and pretender-kings. Thus, the criminalization of the Tharrawaddy District conflated the memory of British pacification with the memory of lawlessness in the region. The ethnographic construction of Burmese memory during the Rebellion would serve as a significant feature of the official narrative involving Saya San.

The thrust of this early report sought to establish the causes of the revolt in Tharrawaddy, which drew attention to the district's local history of engagement with the colonial state. In doing so, the report reintroduced a template of how rebellions were conducted in the past, continuing a framework through which the current disturbance would be evaluated. In effect, Morris hoped to establish that the propensity for revolt in the Tharrawaddy district was culturally inscribed among the people and communities of the area, if not for the entire province. Pointing to disturbances and "dacoities" in the 1880s, the report recounted how monks attracted peasants to their causes through oaths, royal proclamations, and protective tattooing.[49] Similarly, politically active monks of the 1920s were successfully woven into the memory of resistance movements in the Tharrawaddy district in an attempt to establish a symmetrical line between nationalist organizations, the immediate events surrounding the rebellion, and the individuals being held responsible for them.[50] In doing so, the report cast the recent memory of events in early 1931 into an older memory of rebellions dating back to the pacification campaigns of the 1880s. Not only was the rebellion in Tharrawaddy being connected to a different historical context (which froze Burmese peasant memory in the context of kingship) but it also diverted the events associated with Saya San from their connection with current domestic issues (worldwide depression, capitation taxes, privatization of public forests, and the Separation Issue) to one of timeless nostalgia. As much as the memory of early 1931 was being recast along traditional lines, Morris's report authenticated that memory and preserved it for future remembering, signaling the birth of an archive that would come to represent the very idea of Burmese rebellion.[51]

Taken together, B. S. Carey's manual, the Tharrawaddy District Gazetteer, and R.C. Morris's "Causes of the Tharrawaddy Rebellion" represent the foundation of what would later become a much larger archive of resistance under the category of the Burma Rebellion General Files, British colonialism's construction of the Saya San Rebellion in its textualized form. Comprising legislative records, trial records, telegrams, reports, memos, and newspaper clippings, the

Burma Rebellion General File extends the scope and reach of documents covering the uprisings as it spread beyond Tharrawaddy into several other districts throughout Lower Burma. Read in this manner, the archive marks the development of the rebellion both spatially and chronologically as it grew out of Tharrawaddy and extended to other districts, faithfully captured and contained in the records and registers of the Burma Rebellion Files. Following Brian Axel, colonial ethnology not only supplied the archive with texts, it was responsible for the growth of the archive itself.[52] As such, one can trace the genealogy of the rebellion's narrative as it was first recorded in late 1930 and continued well into 1934, outliving its roots in Tharrawaddy and even its supposed founder, Saya San. The Rebellion Files act not as a repository of facts but as sources to a particular telling of that story, infused with the priorities and concerns of scholar–officials whose focus was in containing and controlling that narrative. While the settings, actors, and events eventually would change through the tumultuous years of 1930–32, the fundamental elements of the Rebellion Ethnology that were first articulated through the case of Tharrawaddy would soon be projected conceptually and textually into nearly the whole of Burma, resulting in what would now be called "the Burma Rebellion." Despite the increasing variance in the types of uprisings, officials would continue to hold on to the basic elements of the Tharrawaddy narrative, attributing the spread of the rebellion to the movement of Saya San and his "lieutenants." Though clearly no longer a "local" disturbance (as it was first reported), officials continued to apply Tharrawaddy's framework to the whole of Burma and in doing so, projected the role of Saya San into the whole of the rebellion.

Yet recording this story would require more than what the Rangoon administration had at their disposal for controlling the dissemination of information, requiring a whole new set of narrative tools. Through the acquisition of special powers, new legislation would be enacted that would give the Burma government the ability to write the story of the Rebellion into history by creating the terms, institutions, and procedures through which the Burma Rebellion Files would be created. Special legislation would provide the authorities not only with the prescriptive powers to define and codify what rebellion might be in a Burmese context, but it also ensured that special rebellion tribunals be created to authorize those constructions. Moreover, what began as generalizations about the history and culture of Tharrawaddy district or the unruly disposition of the Burmese peasant would continue to permeate the rhetoric, language, and substance of counter-insurgency policy. Carey's *minlaung* model and the criminal nature of the Tharrawaddy district would become firmly associated with Saya San; but it would also be projected into other cases of rebellion throughout the province, effectively consolidating the rebel network in history and in space. Like gene strands in DNA, the Rebellion Ethnology was born in the context of pacification and would continue to be passed on to its descendants: from the earliest gazetteers to situation reports, from correspondences to legislative proceedings, from amendments to court cases, and finally from judicial summaries to the official blue-book report on the rebellion which would enter into the bibliographies of postcolonial scholars as the most primary of primary sources. In short, the particular ethnology that made Burmese kingship criminal and central to the notion of rebellion has several stories and contexts of its own. It is toward these stories and their relationship to the rendering of the Saya San Rebellion that we now turn.

Notes

1. For around two weeks there was no clear understanding as to the nature of the rebellion and its possible causes according to telegrams detailing the immediate events. See Government of Burma, L/PJ/6/2020, Burma Rebellion General File (BRGF). Copy of telegram, Government of India (G/I), Home Department (H/D), to Secretary of State for India (SS/I), repeating telegram from Burma Government (G/B), from December 24, 1930, to January 2, 1931.

2. Government of Burma, L/PJ/6/2020, BRGF. Copy of letter no. C30, December 29, 1930, from G/B to G/I, H/D. One of the earliest comprehensive reports that developed into the series of official reports on the rebellion can be found nearly one week after the first outbreak in Tharrawaddy.

3. Matthew H. Edney, *Mapping an Empire: The Geographical*

Construction of British India, 1765–1843 (Chicago: University of Chicago Press, 1997).

4. *Burma Gazetteer*, Tharrawaddy District Volume A. (Rangoon: Superintendent, Government Printing and Stationary, Union of Burma, 1959, reprint from 1920) pp. 1–3.

5. Ibid.

6. *Burma Gazetteer*, 1959, pp. 1–3. It is striking how a later image associated with rebellion in the region, that of the Galon (mythical bird) defeating the Naga (snake), resembles this crow–earthworm dichotomy.

7. Compilers of the volume include Mr. S. G. Grantham (ICS Asst. Settlement Officer), Mr. R. G. McDowall (ICS Asst. Settlement Officer), and Mr. B. W. Swithinbank (ICS Asst. Settlement Officer).

8. *Burma Gazetteer, Tharrawaddy District*, pp. 25–26. Interestingly, this explanation is also taken with caution, as "the people had this reputation before his time and other explanations are available."

9. *Burma Gazetteer, Tharrawaddy District*, p. 39.

10. The document focuses on instances involving resistance to pacification, including U Thuriya's Rebellion and the movement led by the elusive Gaung Gyi. *Burma Gazetteer*, pp. 26–41, 88–96.

11. *Burma Gazetteer*, p. 91.

12. *Burma Gazetteer*, p. 88.

13. Ibid.

14. Government of Burma. General Files, L/PJ/6/2020, BRGF, B. S. Carey, "Hints for the Guidance of Civil Officers in the Event of Outbreak of Disturbances in Burma," 1914 (reprinted April 1931).

15. James Clifford, *Routes: Travel and Translation in the Late Twentieth Century* (Cambridge: Harvard University Press, 1997), p. 24.

16. Carey, "Hints for the Guidance,"p. 2.

17. Ibid.

18. Ibid., p. 3.

19. The etymology of this word is unclear and warrants attention, as it may actually have been created by the British.

20. Carey, "Hints for the Guidance," p.4.

21. Ibid., p.6.

22. Ibid., p.2.

23. Ibid., p.3.

24. Ibid.

25. G. E. Harvey, *British Rule in Burma, 1824–1942*, (London: Faber, 1946); Michael Adas, *Prophets of Rebellion: Millenarian Protest Movements*

against the European Colonial Order (Chapel Hill: University of North Carolina Press, 1979).

26. Austin Sarat and Thomas Kearns (eds.), *History, Memory, and the Law*, Ann Arbor: University of Michigan Press, 1999, 2–14; Gyan Prakesh, "Subaltern Studies as Postcolonial Critique," *American Historical Review*, vol. 99, no. 5, 1994; Brian Axel (ed.) *At the Margins: Historical Anthropology and Its Futures* (Durham: Duke University Press, 2002).

27. Government of Burma, L/PJ/6/2020, BRGF, copy of telegram, Government of India (G/I) to Secretary of State for India (SS/I) repeating from Government of Burma (G/B), January 2, and 4, 1931. Roughly two weeks after the initial outbreak, reports that a *minlaung* and his "palace" were soon reported to have been killed and burned. Two days later, the *minlaung* was prematurely said to have been Saya San.

28. Government of Burma, L/PJ/2020, BRGF, March 1, 1934.

29. Government of Burma, L/PJ/6/2020, BRGF, G/I, H/D, to SS/I, rpt. from G/B, December 29, 1931.

30. See Michael Adas, *Prophets of Rebellion: Millenarian Protest Movements against European Colonialism* (Chapel Hill: University of North Carolina Press, 1979); Patricia Herbert, *The Saya San Rebellion Reappraised 1930–1932* (Melbourne: Monash, 1982); Robert Solomon, "Saya San and the Burmese Rebellion," *Modern Asian Studies*, vol. 3, no. 3, 1969, pp. 209–23; Emanuel Sarkysianz, *Buddhist Backgrounds of the Burmese Revolution* (The Hague, 1965); and Maitrii Aung-Thwin, "Genealogy of a Rebellion Narrative," *Journal of Southeast Asian Studies*, V. 34, 2003.

31. Government of Burma, L/PJ/6/2020, BRGF, copy of telegram, G/I H/D, to SS/I rpt. from G/B, January 1, 1931.

32. Government of Burma, L/PJ/6/2020, BRGF, copy of telegram, G/I H/D, to SS/I rpt. from G/B, January 2, 1931.

33. See Ileto and Adas. This is not to suggest that either scholar had the same intentions as B. S. Carey. The point is to establish an epistemological link between colonial points of view and scholarship that followed.

34. John Cady, *A History of Modern Burma* (Ithaca: Cornell University Press, 1958). Scholars have suggested that urban elites were reluctant to associate themselves with the "superstitious" peasantry. A closer look at Burma Legislative Proceedings reveal that several Burmese legislators were actually sympathetic to the conditions in the villages and argued on their behalf throughout the course of the rebellion but were often criticized by government representatives for seemingly siding with the suggested goals of the uprising.

35. Government of Burma, L/PJ/6/2020, BRGF, letter no. C30, F. B. Leach, G/B to S/SI, G/I, H/D, December 29, 1930, January 5, 1931, and January 12, 1931; see also L/PJ/6/2020, BRGF, Ralph Clarence Morris, "Causes of the Tharrawaddy Rebellion," March 1931.

36. Government of Burma, L/PJ/6/2020, BRGF, *Origins and Causes of the Burma Rebellion 1930–1934*, March 1934.

37. Government of Burma, L/PJ/6/2020, BRGF, copy of letter no. C30, December 29, 1930, from the G/B (F. B. Leach) to the G/I, HD; government of Burma, L/PJ/6/2020, BRGF, copy of letter no. 429C30, January 5, 1931, from the G/B (F. B. Leach) to H/D, G/I; and Government of Burma, L/PJ/6/2020, letter no. 429C30, January 12, 1931, from the G/B (F. B. Leach) to H/D, GI.

38. Government of Burma, L/PJ/6/2020, BRGF, copy of letter, no. C30, December 29, 1930, from the G/B to the G/I.

39. Ibid. It is important to note that at the time, Saya San had not been mentioned by name, though the town of his birth was already being codified in the record.

40. Ibid. The issue of a standard uniform of the rebels is murky at best. The letter states that one rebel's body appeared to have a blue uniform on him "of a type of which a large number have since been discovered."

41. Government of Burma, L/PJ/6/2020, BRGF, copy of letter, no. 429C30, January 5, 1931, G/B to H/D, GI.

42. Ibid.

43. Ibid.

44. Government of Burma. L/PJ/6/2020, BRGF, Press Communiqué, 1931.

45. Government of Burma, L/PJ/6/2020, BRGF, *Causes of the Tharrawaddy Rebellion*, Criminal Investigation Department, compiled by Ralph Clarence Morris (deputy inspector-general of police for railways and CI) March 26, 1931.

46. See the arguments in Maitrii Aung-Thwin, "Genealogy of a Rebellion Narrative" (2003) and *British Counter-insurgency Narratives and the Construction of a 20th Century Burmese Rebel* (2001).

47. *Causes of the Tharrawaddy Rebellion.*

48. Ibid.

49. *Causes of the Tharrawaddy Rebellion.*

50. Specifically, the Soe Thein branch of the General Council of Burmese Associations was being connected to anti-tax collection campaigns in the 1920s and 1930s in an effort to connect their activities with Saya San, who was once a member of this group. Ironically, the view of the report

on this issue tends to contradict later assessments that later presented Saya San as a pretender to the throne who was concerned with reviving the monarchy along traditional lines. His anti-tax rhetoric and methods seem, as Patricia Hebert argues, more in line with contemporary forms of political mobilization rather than a more nostalgic traditional platform.

51. Government of Burma, L/PJ/6/2020, BRGF, *Origins and Causes of the Burma Rebellion 1930–1932*, 1934. This report serves as the final statement on the events associated with Saya San and tends to be more comprehensive in scope as the rebellion extended to other districts in British Burma. However, a closer examination of the report indicates that a majority of its content and prose was drawn from Morris's *Causes of the Tharrawaddy Rebellion*, suggesting that the Tharrawaddy paradigm, which was based on Carey's *minlaung* model, continued to frame the way the Saya San Rebellion was understood.

52. Brian Keith Axel, "Introduction: Historical Anthropology and Its Vicissitudes," in Axel (ed.), *From the Margins: Historical Anthropology and Its Futures* (Durham: Duke University Press, 2002), pp. 1–44.

Chapter 3

LEGISLATING REBELLION
Ethnology and the Formation of Counter-Insurgency Law

If one were to focus exclusively on the series of telegrams, letters, and reports that have been associated with the earliest accounts of the Rebellion, it would appear that notions of Burmese kingship were informing the character of the uprising in Tharrawaddy, reconfirming the template established earlier by administrative gazetteers and Bertram Carey's 1914 manual on Burmese uprisings. Drawn primarily from the Burma Rebellion General File and specifically within the Public and Judicial records of the India Office (L/PJ/6/2020), the bulk of these sources delineate the official story of the Rebellion, beginning with the initial outbreak in December 1930 and ending with the question of releasing imprisoned rebels in 1935. Although it was clear that officials were somewhat uncertain as to what the causes of the uprising might be in its earliest stages, such disparities were soon offset by documents such as "The Tharrawaddy Outbreak" and "Causes of the Tharrawaddy Rebellion," which definitively cast the *minlaung* model as the explanation for the outbreak of violence in December 1930.[1] At face value, the files within L/PJ/6/2020 appear to present the official perspective on the Rebellion as being more or less consistent; officials seem to have unanimously attributed the uprising to the periodic rise of a pretender king who captured the imagination and support of a receptive peasantry. What might arguably have been interpreted as a series of spontaneous and diverse expressions of peasant activism was effectively contained by the idea of a single movement, centrally organized around the persuasive influences and manipulative designs of a dynamic leader. R. C. Morris's "Causes of the Tharrawaddy Rebellion" fostered coherency among the earliest series of archival materials (January–March 1930) by providing a consistent argument that unified the disparate documents that marked the first representation of the uprisings in the files under the L/PJ/6/2020 designation.

Archival coherency reinforced the notion that a set of uniform cultural traits characterized the uprisings, effectively smoothing over the possibility of variation and difference in the record by establishing the *minlaung* model within official explanations. Political, legislative, and judicial priorities not only informed the organization of these documents within the archive, but reflected the lens through which the rebellion was conceived and constructed in order to meet this demand. Legislative procedure, legal precedent, and the institutional relationships between administrations in New Delhi and Rangoon prescribed the way in which knowledge about the Rebellion would be produced, documented, and archived for the Province of Burma. Attempts to establish coherency in official documentation was as much an expression of administrative consolidation within counter-insurgency policy as it was a reflection of British India's prescriptive influence over Burma.

One might presume then, given the manner in which the Rebellion Files were organized within the Public and Judicial records, that Saya San had been connected to the event surrounding the uprisings from its earliest stages and beyond. A broader examination of the sources suggests that Burma officials were actually presenting several narratives at one time, addressing a range of theories to meet administrative demands related to the acquisition of emergency powers. Focusing on these stories reveals not only the uncertainty (on the part of officials) surrounding the events associated with the Tharrawaddy outbreak, but the way in which counter-insurgency legislation condensed and conflated the series of outbreaks into a single rebellion and a single narrative. The existence of multiple narratives in the history of the Saya San Rebellion can be detected within official "British" and "Burmese" discourses.

In the process of projecting Tharrawaddy's criminalized past into the events of 1930–31, administrative officials in Rangoon moved to secure special legislation in order to provide local government with more effective counter-insurgency measures. This process required constant communication and coordination with the government of India, which oversaw affairs in British Burma and acted as a liaison between Rangoon and London. In addition, discussion was allowed in regard to counter-insurgency policy in the Burma Legislative Council, drawing heated debate over these ordinances and subsequent bills. Notions about the nature of Burmese peasant beliefs and behavior were recorded, regularized, and rehearsed within the context of legislative debate and discussion that pertained to their passage. Particular characteristics of Burmese peasant life were identified as, and translated into, a counter-insurgency prose that presented tattooing, wondering monks, and various aspects of spirit worship as subjects understandable within the context of terrorism. By introducing these proposals through the procedural infrastructure of the Burmese Legislative Council, Carey's ethnology was effectively authenticated and maintained in official debates, proceedings, and related documentation.

Between January and April 1931, officials in Burma and New Delhi negotiated the promulgation of two rebellion-specific ordinances that provided the legal flexibility and authority deemed necessary to launch a comprehensive counter-insurgency campaign. Drawing on a model provided by the Bengal Criminal Law Amendment Act of 1925, Burma officials sought a single ordinance that would enable police to detain without trial those "persons suspected of offences" and provide legal officers with special tribunals that could try "terrorists" and "revolutionaries" under certain sections of the India Penal Code.[2] Among other demands, local government also sought power to control the press, arrest without warrant suspected rebels, and prohibit "drilling" among village associations, in an attempt to curb the growing influence of these organizations in rural locales.

Whereas on paper these powers were directed toward restoring social stability, these ordinances would also affect the way in which the situation in Burma was conceptualized as elements of rural life began to be evaluated in reference to counter-terrorism policies. Requests to make "tattooing and the distribution of charms...a penal offence" reinforced the notion that particular Burmese practices could be read as warning signs indicative of rebellion. Despite New Delhi rejecting such profiling as being of "doubtful legality," trial records would in fact reveal that tattooing and the distribution of amulets would remain dominant characteristics of the Rebellion. Colonial ethnology informed the way in which legislation would be constructed, signaling an important intersection of colonial ethnography and law.

Counter-insurgency law was represented by two temporary pieces of legislation: the Burma Rebellion Trials Ordinance (BRTO) and the Burma Criminal Law Amendment Ordinance (BCLAO).[3] Rangoon officials hoped to secure powers quickly and molded their proposals along the model of the Bengal Criminal Amendment Act of 1925. The BCLAO was promulgated on January 31, 1931, to enable government to control the movement of suspected rebels and provide the administrative means to process the inordinate number of rebels that were being held under detention. By creating a tribunal with special procedural provisions that were designed to "stop the activity of leaders of whose guilt they are convinced but of which they cannot produce sufficient evidence to secure conviction in the courts," Rangoon officials "seized on an Ordinance which would meet their immediate needs."[4] By merely appearing before these courts, suspects had already been targeted and identified as "rebels."

At the time of their enactment however, separate narratives of resistance (beyond the framework of the Rebellion Ethnology) were being rendered for the situation in Burma since particular security conditions on the ground were required to demonstrate the need to secure extra powers from London. The passing of the Ordinance/Bill depended on Burma officials persuading both their Indian and London superiors that such extraordinary judicial and policing powers were warranted to respond to extraordinary circumstances. These alleged circumstances, involving terrorist cells from Bengal, were eventually overshadowed by the Rebellion Ethnology and the figure of Saya San, but the story behind the securing of special-rebellion legislation reveals an important stage in producing the conditions within which the rebellion narrative was written.

Legislating Rebellion

On the evening of January 12, 1931, the secretary of state for India received a secret telegram from New Delhi, conveying information about the rebellion in Burma. It described how quickly Burma officials were able to ascertain the origins of the rebellion, despite the uprising being barely three weeks old. Important documentary evidence had been discovered demonstrating that the rebellion had been in planning for two years, under the silent patronage of the General Council of Burmese Associations, the most outspoken political opposition party of the colonial government.[5] More sinister however, was the revelation that the Council had been in touch with the Bengal Revolutionary Party, a terrorist organization that felt that insurrection in Burma was "more suited to Burmese temperament than assassination on Bengal line[s]."[6] Bengali terrorists allegedly believed that arms were available in Rangoon and that the organization of dacoit cells in rural areas was instigated in order to obtain funds for weapon purchases.[7] Due to this recent intelligence and the continuing violence in the Tharrawaddy district, the secretary of state learned that Burma officials were requesting permission to enact a special ordinance that would expand the policing and prosecutorial powers of the local government. Rangoon officials were seeking the inclusion of sections 121–123 of the Indian Penal Code (which pertained to waging war against the government of the king-emperor) because it was believed that the terrorist activities of the Bengal Revolutionary Party were involved with the open rebellion occurring in Lower Burma.[8]

One hour later, the Secretary of State received another telegram describing the details of the legislative provisions being sought by Rangoon and their plan for implementation. Specifically, Burma officials sought provisions for the establishment of special tribunals in order to try the large number of offenders that had been arrested in relation to the rebellion.[9] Additionally, they urged the immediate issue of a policing ordinance following exactly the provisions of the Bengal Criminal Law Amendment Act (1925), due to the connection being established between the Bengal Revolutionary Party and the uprisings in the countryside. Although by the fall of 1931 these two separate requests would eventually be combined under the Burma Criminal Law Amendment Act, India officials recommended that their counterparts in Burma keep the matters distinct because they were concerned that securing two objects in a single ordinance left the potential for overall rejection by London.[10] In addition, if the decision to establish special courts for trial of the rebels was approved, Rangoon felt that there would be "ample justification for inclusion to that end of sections 121 to 123 of the Indian Penal Code."[11] Even though officials initially used an external terrorist threat as a reason for securing these sections, it would be Saya San, not the Bengal Revolutionaries, who would end up being charged with waging war against the king-emperor.

New Delhi officials were somewhat reluctant to allow "immediate" action as proposed by their Burma subordinates. One issue in particular was using the expansive powers to arrest alleged rebels since experiences in Bengal suggested that keeping a large number of revolutionaries together tended to allow for better communication among them.[12] New Delhi preferred that the legislation be used only in select cases, even suggesting shortening procedures for trials and curtailing the right of appeal.[13] Although Rangoon initially resisted reducing the numbers to be tried under ordinary courts, officials eventually modified their view and said that arrests (using the regulations stated in the proposed legislation) would be limited and based on "individual cases."[14] This pattern of placating New Delhi and London would continue throughout the year in order to secure the administrative powers Rangoon officials wanted. In fact, forty minutes later the Secretary of State read that the local government "would definitely prefer effective action should be taken against a comparatively few than ineffective action against a considerable number."[15] In the end, Burma officials managed to persuade London to approve temporarily the Act against terrorism on January 31, 1931. Although the use of Regulation iii (sections 121–123 of the Indian Penal Code) would only be allowed through a New Delhi review of individual cases, the matter of creating a special tribunal was to be addressed separately.

Despite assurances that Burma's newly acquired policing parameters would be applied on a limited scale, officials in London learned that Rangoon authorities were stressing the need for courts with large powers and summary procedure in order to "dispose" of "the not less than three-hundred" accused rebels.[16] Citing the recommendations of their Chief Justice of the High Court, the Burma Government suggested that the special tribunal be modeled along the lines described in a typical Martial Law Ordinance. In an included extract from the said Ordinance, the structure, authority, and procedures of the special tribunal were described along with the relationship between the local government and the tribunal. Although the powers and provisions of this tribunal were supposed to be implemented if martial law were declared, Rangoon civil officials essentially proposed a military-tribunal structure in the guise of a civilian court.[17]

The proposed ordinance gave authority to the local government to form a special tribunal and appoint any member at its discretion, provided that those appointees had at least two years experience in the session courts. In addition, the local government could direct the special tribunal to try offenses as ordered in writing, essentially giving Burma officials the power to tell the tribunal what crime a defendant committed and which law he might be tried under. The local government was also granted the right to make rules providing for "the times and places at which Special Tribunals may sit and the procedure of Special Tribunals, including the powers of the President."[18] Since it was the intention of the Burma government to secure these powers in order to process captured rebels, local officials would be in the comfortable position of appointing the tribunal, defining court procedures, and managing the record all at the same time. By the time this legislation was passed under the new title of Burma Rebellion Trials Ordinance, defendants did not have a chance since prosecution, judges, and local government were working in tandem. But these so-called special provisions were not the only reasons why the proceedings would go quickly.

Within the proposed ordinance were very unusual procedures guiding the deliberation of the tribunal.[19] Section 14 of the document allowed the court to "take cognizance of offenses without the accused being committed to it for trial," effectively forgoing proceedings that decided whether a case had the merit of going on to trial or not. This acceleration of the proceedings operated on the assumption that the prosecution had a case and that the role of detainees was already established. As Burmese defense lawyers would find out in the course of the special tribunal tenure, omitting committal hearings also gave the prosecution an advantage by not permitting the defense to examine evidence before the trial, thereby reducing the opportunity for developing more comprehensive arguments. Yet, the provision allowing the special tribunal to make only a memorandum of "the substance of the evidence" would have far greater implications to the case of Saya San and his place in history than any other factor discussed thus far. Eliminating the requirement to compile a complete and thorough recording of the evidence may have decreased the amount of time spent on each case, but it surely obstructed the ability for defense lawyers to prepare adequately for appeal since all the evidence was not necessarily recorded.[20] These court documents would not be complete because it was up to the judge—who was under the jurisdiction of the interests represented by the prosecution—to record only what was deemed pertinent to the proceedings. Legal sources pertaining to the trial of Saya San would include only the evidence and arguments of the prosecution and those comments offered by the judges. Worse still, *The Origins and Causes of the Burma Rebellion (1930–1932)*, as noted, considered the definitive source to the Rebellion narrative, relied exclusively on these very documents, illustrating how legislative, legal, and documentation offices were all involved in the production of what would become an unreliable historical source.

The Secretary of State was still unsure by February 12 whether to grant Rangoon officials these expansive powers, preferring they use "the ordinary courts or that, failing that, the Burma Govt. [sic] should do what was necessary by local legislation."²¹ In addition, London authorities were reluctant to put the matter to the Indian Legislature when Rangoon stated that the matter could not be handled locally because "they must let the Council depart by a certain date."²² Yet, it was not so much an issue of passing the work on to the Indian Legislature as much as it was the attempt by the local government to avoid letting the matter be settled by the Burma Legislative Council, which was already resisting passage of the proposed Ordinance.²³ Members identified several concerns in the content of the Ordinance and were quick to voice their dissent.²⁴

Although the official position by F. B. Leach and others within the Council attempted to reassure their colleagues that the measures in the Ordinance were directed toward Bengali terrorists, a separate communiqué two days earlier clearly indicated that Saya San was the leader and planner of the rebellion, revealing that this story was the official explanation currently being formed.²⁵ Authorities in London, however, did not hear this version until two weeks later, and after receiving continuous reports blaming the uprising on the Bengal Revolutionary Party.²⁶ On the one hand, Rangoon officials needed to secure the Ordinance, relying upon the story of Bengal terrorists to secure approval. On the other, a local explanation was needed in order to deal with participants of the Rebellion who were obviously not Bengali. Thus, two stories were being used by the local government in order to cover all possible avenues for repacification.

Since opposition in the Burma Legislative Council was fairly robust, government officials concentrated on obtaining permission from their superiors in New Delhi and London, on the assumption that the governor's power of certification could ultimately override any blockage from the Legislature. By February 18, Rangoon unexpectedly found itself in the difficult situation of facing resistance from colleagues in the colonial administration. London was continuously uncomfortable with the large numbers of defendants who would potentially come under the jurisdiction of the Ordinance, and encouraged the use of usual judiciary processes. In addition, the curtailment of procedure as proposed by the local government was also unsettling. Local officials responded by stating that there was a precedent for using speedy trials in cases of disturbances in the Moplah rebellion and Punjab disturbances of 1919.[27] Furthermore, full rights of appeal were allowed in cases of sentences exceeding five years. The local government was sure that the Ordinance would not rouse "much feeling in Burma."[28]

Thus, on March 12, 1931, the Burma Rebellion Trials Ordinance was promulgated under the permission of the Governor-General of India.[29] In his statement regarding the legislation, the viceroy adopted Rangoon's argument that the special judiciary structure would prevent "serious congestion in the courts" and would "materially assist restoration of normal conditions."[30] To the consternation of Burmese members of the Legislative Council, the Ordinance was ambiguously directed to "provide for the speedy trial of persons accused of offences connected with the recent rebellion in Burma."[31] Unknown to the legislature, legal advisers were already planning for the renewal of the Ordinance, which was set to expire September 12, 1931.[32] Indeed, the numbers of arrested persons believed to have taken part in the Rebellion exceeded one thousand and, although more than half were eventually released, about three hundred and fifty persons were still held under Section 121 and 121A of the Indian Penal Code, which amounted to waging war against the king emperor.

In fact, by May, fifteen defendants from the inaugural trial had already been sentenced to death under these two laws, surprising even the Secretary of State for India at the swiftness of the proceedings. The accused were assumed to be "ringleaders" by New Delhi officials, but internal documents suggest that these rebels were supposedly connected with the original uprising in Tharrawaddy.[33] Sensing perhaps possible irregularities in these procedures, the Secretary of State ordered a review of all the cases involving executions before they took place, stating:

> I should be glad to learn whether the circumstances in which these fifteen persons were found guilty and sentenced to death . . . were such as to have made them responsible for the death of Government servants or supporters or otherwise made them amenable to death penalty apart from being in opposition to Government.[34]

This procedure was delayed, however, by a combination of bureaucratic foot-dragging and redtape that pervaded the New Delhi administration. Indian officials were reluctant to carry out the prescribed order by the Secretary of State since they were responsible for scrutinizing and processing anything that would eventually be sent to the secretary of state. This would become a problem, an Indian official commented, "if the Government of Burma maintains what is apparently a present practice of imposing no sentences other than death or transportation."[35]

The passage of the Rebellion Trials Ordinance was one component of the government's comprehensive counter-insurgency program. Whereas it addressed the issue of processing large numbers of accused rebels, it was directly responsible for the creation of the Special Rebellion Tribunal and the authorial context within which the official narrative of the rebellion would be produced. The various trials that would fall under the jurisdiction of the tribunal would operate under the guidelines and prescriptive procedures of the ordinance, directly affecting the way in which evidence would be introduced, recorded, and authenticated by and within the judicial system. Legal authority invested in these ordinances cast the findings established by the tribunals as historically credible, a perception that would eventually be reified by official reports covering the rebellion. Counter-insurgency legislation produced the legal authority and context in which knowledge about the rebellion could be made ready for the archive while providing the language, terms, and interpretive coherency necessary for its textualization. This ordinance, along with the soon-to-be-passed Burma Criminal Law Amendment Ordinance, reconstituted the Rebellion Ethnology and established the profile of the Burmese rebel within the discourse of the 1930s.

The Burma Criminal Law Amendment Ordinance

While efforts were being made to secure the Trials Ordinance, Rangoon officials were maneuvering to secure the BCLAO, regarding it as "a bill to supplement the ordinary criminal law in Burma." The ordinance was intended to be a reproduction of the BCLAO originally enacted in 1925 in the province of Bengal to deal with the threat of revolutionary activities that had risen toward the end of 1922.[36] Officials had in fact proposed its enactment as early as December 15, 1930 (a week before the Tharrawaddy outbreak), in order to deal with "the terrorist movement" in Burma.[37] Burma officials sought permission from the government of India to arrest and detain without trial revolutionaries suspected of committing terrorist acts. Interestingly, in warning that "gullible" and "excitable" university students might be attracted to the agenda of the Bengali terrorist, authorities revealed that Carey's Rebellion Ethnology could be easily applied to urban Burmese as much as peasants.[38]

The outbreak in Tharrawaddy, which occurred a few weeks later, was determined to be a continuation of these Bengali operations, even as the *minlaung* model was being communicated simultaneously through other official channels.[39] As noted above, the dominant narrative regarding the role of Burmese kingship involved sources collected within L/PJ/6/2020 designation of the India Office Records. In contrast, those sources pertaining to the role of the Bengali revolutionaries were collected under the L/PJ/5/2022 designation, a separate group of sources for a seemingly separate rebellion narrative. To this date, scholars have concentrated on the files concerning the *minlaung* narrative, whereas the Bengali narrative has remained conspicuously absent in the study of the rebellion. The history around the securing of BCLAO reveals how this alternative explanation involving Bengalis revolutionaries is connected to the *minlaung* model on the one hand, while simultaneously excluded from the dominant narrative on the other. In addition, while the ordinance was passed in order to curb the influence of foreign terrorists, the ordinance also reveals how this legislation used ethnology to define the profile of a Burmese Rebel. For as this section will demonstrate, BCLAO expanded not only the ability to arrest, detain, search, and seize, but it established what would be considered "rebellious acts" against the crown. The criminalization of Burmese ritual, the movement of nonstate authorities, and in particular the criminalization of tattooing became an important part of Rangoon's counter-insurgency program. Just as the enactment of the

Trials Ordinance has shown, counter-insurgency legislation was the key phase that brought earlier ethnographic constructions of Burmese rebellion into the orbit of colonial legal culture.

At 11:45 A.M., January 8, 1931, the Secretary of State for India received a letter from India (on behalf of the Burma government), seeking special legislation to deal with terrorism in Burma that had occurred in Tharrawaddy district.[40] Although several situation reports had already identified Saya San as the prime suspect to British authorities, an entirely different story was being constructed for legislative purposes. At noon, the Secretary of State began to receive detailed information that the outbreak was the result of Bengali terrorists that were attempting to smuggle "arms into Bengal from Singapore and the Far East," but were now assuming "terrorist activities in Burma."[41] These terrorists, functioning under the Bengali Revolutionary Party, were said to be "mainly Bengali" and numbering around three hundred members.[42] Officials attributed recent reports of "political dacoity" in Rangoon, and an attempted derailment of a train in September and October of 1930 on this terrorist organizaiton.[43] By 2:30 P.M., information from an informer provided government officials with new intelligence that indicated a slightly different story. According to this version, "Burman monks were connected with the movement and involved in the importation of revolvers and ammunition from the Chinese border."[44] Tattooing had occurred in several districts as the rebellion spread, indicating (according to officials) signs of "excitement" and "disaffection."[45] This arrangement was apparently the "definite plan" of "the notorious revolutionary absconder" Rash Bihari Bose, the General Council of Burmese Associations (GCBA, the most outspoken and well-organized opposition organization in Burma), and U Oktama (political activist–monk) who had ties to the Bengal Revolutionary Party.[46] He was well known to British officials as "a revolutionary firebrand" who had been imprisoned more than once for his activities.[47] A 1929 report described U Otktama as "exceedingly excitable," "intelligent," "endowed with great energy and driving power...and is hand in glove with the most extreme Indian agitators."[48] The spreading of the rebellion to neighboring districts was attributed to visits by U Oktama and his subordinates, making it "impossible not to associate these risings with him" and its connection to the Bengali Revolutionary Party.[49] Due to the rapid expanding of the outbreak, the Burma government requested permission to search the headquarters of the Soe Thein General Council of Burma Associations, in order to "arrest leaders and declare the Association and its most important branches illegal."[50] However, it was "uncertain whether sufficient evidence will be obtained to convict leaders under ordinary law" and therefore a more favorable set of laws in the form of the Ordinance was desired.[51] In short, the securing of new counter-insurgency legislation was based on a completely separate narrative from the *minlaung* explanation involving Saya San; British administrators identified another monk (U Oktama), the GCBA, and the Bengali Revolutionary Party as having planned and instigated the growing number of outbreaks in rural Lower Burma.[52]

By January 11, 1931 the Burma government recommended immediate promulgation of the Criminal Law Ordinance through the executive powers of the Governor General. They reported that the rebellion was more widespread than originally believed, partly based on speculation that the GCBA and its affiliates had penetrated the local countryside and won the support of the monkhood.[53] U Oktama's involvement was further embellished, describing his meetings with Rash Bihari Ghose, his contact with other Bengali revolutionaries, and his membership with the Executive Committee of General Council of Buddhist Associations.[54] Curiously, the telegram closes with the statement

> information independently obtained received from Bengal Government to which reference was made in previous telegram, definitely states armed rising as object of *Burmese* Revolutionary Party acting in conjunction with Buddhist monks and other Burmans.[55]

In effect, three days after the telegrams of January 8, 1931, the view that the Bengali Revolution Party, the GCBA, and sympathetic monks were connected to the recent outbreak, it was suddenly revealed that a coherent entity known as the *Burmese Revolutionary Party* was running the show. Later documentation would eventually confirm that the legislation was meant not for some external terrorist group, but for Burmese accused of rebellion. For the moment, Rangoon officials were satisfied with the contrived Bengali connection since any delay in securing these extended powers would allow the party "to gravely embarrass Local government" even if it were found (as it was admitted) that the party was "not directly connected with the rebellion."[56]

Internal documents on January 11, 1931 indicate that the use of the Bengali narrative was crucial to guaranteeing the requested Ordinances, even though officials quietly admitted that it "was a little out of date."[57] By creating the impression that the situation in Burma was as serious as it was in Bengal, Rangoon would be able to seek special provisions at least comparable to those imposed in Bengal.[58] In fact, advisers saw the situation in Burma as more precarious since it was thought that the Revolutionary Party in Bengal was "comparatively small in numbers" and that an organization in Burma that had the administrative apparatus of the GCBA posed a much more serious threat.[59] Dealing with an organization as politically experienced as the GCBA and one that had penetrated the countryside demanded quick and thorough action. Extended powers, such as the authority to detain without trial, the denial of habeas corpus, the creation of special tribunals, and provisions stated in the Bengal Criminal Law Amendment Act of 1925 were all deemed necessary by both the India and Burma governments. On January 16, the government made clear what it needed: one Ordinance to deal with Bengal revolutionaries and one to give special powers for trials of rebels.

Thus, on January 31st, the BCLAO was issued, along with a statement from the governor-general explaining his actions:

> It has been known to Government for some years that there is a terrorist party in Burma which is closely associated with terrorist movement in Bengal. This party has of late engaged in commission of terrorist outrages and there is reason to believe that it was responsible for a political dacoity in Rangoon Town in September, 1930, and for derailment of a mail train in October, 1930, at Nyaungchidauk in Toungoo District, in which high officials of Government were traveling [sic]. A recent feature of its activities has been wide

distribution among students and others of revolutionary pamphlets directly inciting violence. There is good ground for belief that it is privy to rebellion in Tharrawaddy District and that it was intention of those responsible for that rebellion to organize [sic] risings in different parts of Burma with a view to overthrow of Government as established by law.[60]

In other words, the Burma Criminal Amendment Law Ordinance was a response to the perceived connection between the rebellion and Bengali terrorists. The powers conferred by the Ordinance were to be used only against "those in regard to whom there is reason to believe that they are members of terrorist party in Burma or are acting in furtherance of terrorist movement [sic]."[61] In short, the Tharrawaddy Rebellion was being conceptualized as part of a Bengali narrative of resistance, thereby allowing action against it as prescribed by the Ordinance. Although the Governor-General of India issued the Ordinance as a supplement to "ordinary Criminal Law" in Burma, its subsequent introduction as a bill in the Legislative Council would soon draw heavy criticism from its Burmese members, who also saw several problems in the government's narrative.[62]

Debating the Ordinance

In the February 14, 1931, meeting of the Burma Legislative Council, Sir Joseph Maung Gyi, former acting Governor-General, under whose brief tenure in office was the outbreak of rebellion in Tharrawaddy, introduced the Criminal Law Amendment Bill and urged for it to be formally considered.[63] Repeating the words from the current Governor-General's statement, which was also included as "the objects and reasons" section of the bill, Maung Gyi reiterated the need to extend the duration of the Ordinance as it was only a temporary measure with a limited period of operation. His argument attempted to convey much of the views that officials had sent on to London: namely, that the Government had always been well aware of the presence of the terrorists in Burma but certain jurisdictional obstacles required a more substantive and concrete amendment. He states,

> The Government has been aware since 1922 of the existence of a section of the Bengal Revolutionary Party in Burma, but hitherto they have contented themselves in keeping a careful watch on the activities of these men....Now when those members of the Association came to Rangoon the Police were aware of their arrival and they were not met at the wharf, but to all appearances and purposes these revolutionaries who were fugitives looked harmless people [sic], and as the Police had nothing to show against them, they could not take any steps to prevent these revolutionaries from carrying on their nefarious work. We have no law with which to deal with these revolutionaries. Until they acted overtly we could do nothing to them[64]

Even more curious than describing the police's extraordinary powers of detecting terrorists was Maungi Gyi's explanation as to how the Indian social body determined these terrorist qualities:

> The Hindus believe, Sir, that the Brahmins proceed from the mouth of Brahma and therefore they are the most intellectual people because they are the teachers of the people. They are known as Brahmins, but the Kshatriyas and the fighting classes proceed from the arms and chest of Brahma. Now if you take the map of India, you will see that Bengal is the head of India, that the North-West Province of Punjab, where the fighting races come from, are the arms and chest of India. The Bengalis are efficient people and very highly intellectual. They are a mild mannered people and well disposed as a rule, but out of all the different districts in Bengal, there is one that lies right to the east nearest to the hills where the wild tribes go in for head hunting and that is Chittagong, and it is in the district of Chittagong that the Bengal Revolutionary Association had its birth and the majority of the members of the Association come from Chittagong.[65].

In objection to these and other statements made by Maung Gyi, several members of the Legislature attacked the content of the proposed bill or the interpretation of events that led to the Ordinance's promulgation on the basis of its legality and whether an emergency situation existed that warranted such extraordinary judicial powers.

Although the impression has been made by some scholars that urban elites were unimpressed and embarrassed by the rebellion, significant debate was raised by opposition members as to how the rebellion was being portrayed and responded to by the local government. Local members of the Burma Legislative Council were deeply engaged in considering the powers delineated by counter-insurgency legislation.[66] One example can be found in section six, paragraph two, of the bill, which was raised by U Kun from Bassein. The section is as follows:

> If in any trial under this Act it is found that the accused person has committed any offence, whether such offence is or is not an offence specified in the First Schedule, the commissioners may convict such person of such offence and pass any sentence authorized [sic] by law for the punishment thereof.[67]

Although U Kun's discomfort with this section was based on the grounds that one could be punished, "even if a person accused under this sub-section of this law be not found guilty," his focus was actually misplaced because the real teeth of the section were in the passage that allowed the government to convict someone for a crime that may not have been *specified* in the first schedule. Burmese members sensed, quite correctly, that this bill might be used against citizens in the name of anti-terrorism. Proponents, such as chief secretary F. B. Leach, assured them,

> this bill was not aimed at anyone except revolutionaries who commit all sorts of frightfulness, such as assassination, throwing of bombs and so on, and honorable members will see that this bill is not intended to be used against any other persons *such as those who have risen in Tharrawaddy, Pyapon and elsewhere*, because if you turn to the First Schedule after section 121, Indian Penal Code, the taking up of arms against the King is not mentioned.[68]

Indeed, an examination of the bill's First Schedule (a listing of offenses that the bill covers) did not contain section 121, the crime of waging war against the king-emperor. But the disputed section allowed for a conviction *"whether such offense is or is not an offense specified in the First Schedule."* In other words, Maung Gyi's assurances that the bill would not be used against Burmese thought to be involved in the rebellion were deceptive, because even though 121 was not listed, the clause allowed the government to convict the accused on any law it saw fit. Even Secretary Leach, hoped to placate doubting members of the Council by stating that "it is obvious, I think, that if the Local Government had intended it to be used against the rebellion, it would have put the sections of waging war against the King into the Schedule."[69] What opposition members in the council did not realize initially was that Rangoon officials had intended to use the bill and specifically sections 121–123 against the rebellion from very early on, since "actual offences have been committed by the rebels under these sections."[70]

Although it would be another month until the full policing powers of the bill would be realized, members of the Legislative Council were already suspicious of the reasons used to justify the legislation. The two narratives, one involving Saya San and the other the Bengal Revolutionary Party, had not been separated for the Burma Legislative Council members as it had been for historians, but combined to form a somewhat confusing position on the rebellion. One member, U Ni, complained that

> The Government is pursuing a chimera when, among its objects and reasons, it tries to draw a connection between the Tharrawaddy rebellion, the U Soe Thein GCBA, and the Bengal Revolutionaries. Ever since the rebellion started Government issued communiques from time to time. From the beginning no mention was made that this rebellion was the result of revolutionary activities. The first information was that it was due to economic depression. Later on it was changed into the statement that a pretender was aspiring to the throne of Burma. Subsequently, when Government thought fit to introduce this bill, they were ingeniously tried to connect two outrages that occurred in Burma [sic] with the rebellion.[71]

Along the same lines, Mr. Rafi from Moulmein found it hard to believe that any of the rebels in Tharrawaddy "had even heard of Bengal and know anything about it."[72] This statement was followed by another observation by E. P. Pillay, who on commenting on the government's position that it had the Bengali organization under observance since 1922, stated that

> There had been a careful watch, and yet they were not in a position to discover the connection of these revolutionaries with the rebellion long before this! It is only to-day they open their mouths and say, "Oh, these revolutionaries are connected with the rebellion"! Could it, by any stretch of the imagination, be said that persons unacquainted with the language, custom, and manners of the people of this country would have gone and influenced the villagers who are now taking part in this rebellion?...It strikes me that the Bengal revolutionaries were thrown into the scale in order to hoodwink the Viceroy into granting permission to introduce this Bill.[73]

In fact, Burma officials had simultaneously reported two versions as to the cause of the rebellion although only one was receiving attention in the papers. While the indigenously led uprising by Saya San was publicly receiving the most official attention, the Bengali explanation was being privately used to secure special legislative, judicial, and municipal powers for Rangoon. These extended powers would provide the government with the authority to create the tribunals system that would eventually produce the legal sources connected to the rebellion narrative. Local opposition members were more than aware of the legal ramifications found in counter-insurgency legislation, and resisted their passage aggressively.

After continued heated debates over particulars in the bill, the bill was narrowly defeated in a vote of 46–39.[74] Despite this defeat in the legislature, Governor Charles Innes invoked his powers of certification to override the Council decision, which for all intents and purposes signaled the transformation of the Ordinance into a longer-lasting Bill. Although the Criminal Law Amendment Ordinance was not officially directed toward the Rebellion, it gave special powers to create other legislation that was specifically aimed to deal with the uprising. One such example is the Burma Emergency Powers Ordinance which was later secured in order to confer powers to the local government to suppress and prevent rebellion in Burma.[75] Not only would this third ordinance extend the powers of the British counter-insurgency plan, but it would define more directly against whom these provisions would be used. One noticeable feature was that the government sought to apply specific powers throughout the whole of Burma (rather than in limited "affected areas"), in order to curb the movement of political monks who were associated with tattooing and recruitment of rebels.[76] Though these specific measures were regarded by London as of "doubtful legality" and despite instructions that no further proposals would make reference to tattooing or supernatural charm use, future tribunal records would demonstrate that arrests, detainment, and association with the rebellion were in fact based on the arrest of these "agents" of Burmese rebellion culture.[77] In essence, the new Ordinance extended counter-insurgency attention from Tharrawaddy and neighboring districts to include the entire province while simultaneously narrowing the ethnographic profiles associated with rebellion. In a single stroke, measures against wandering monks (reflecting the role of U Oktama and his connection to rural nationalist associations) and *minlaung* pretenders (in reference to the Rebellion Ethnology) were combined to form an image of the rebellion that labeled monks as recruiters, village associations as terrorist cells, and the resurrection of the Burmese monarchy as the ideological platform upon which peasants were motivated to participate. Just as official reports began to conceptualize the rebellion as a single, coherent expression of Burmese resistance, so too did counter-insurgency legislation reflect and enable this change in perspective. Essential to this shift from the external Bengali threat and a reemphasis on Burmese rebellion culture was the criminalization of tattooing.

Criminalizing Tattooing

The interpretation of tattooing as a specifically criminal activity is evident from the earliest of telegrams following the outbreak in Tharrawaddy. Not only was tattooing characterized as being indicative of "excitement" and "agitation," but it soon began to be linked directly to rebellion.[78] Tattooing ceremonies were categorized as recruiting exercises for the rebels, redefining the meaning of the practice to conform to counter-insurgency profiles and assumptions. When word was heard of a tattooing gathering, troops were quickly sent to disrupt it, often leading to the burning of the village. As one official claimed, destroying the villages where tattooing took place was essentially "nipping the rebellion in the bud."

The use of tattooing for Rangoon's counter-insurgency purposes was debated among officials seeking to secure the Emergency Powers Ordinance. Burma administrators sought to draft provisions that would make tattooing and the distributing of "charms" illegal and applicable as evidence in support of "offenses under Section 121 and allied sections of the Indian Penal Code."[79] Rangoon officials claimed that they lacked the ability to control the movement of monks and their emissaries who were tattooing in "fresh" districts with the object of promoting rebellion.[80] In other words, possessing tattoos and charms would be used as evidence *for* inciting rebellion. Armed with this reading of what tattooing was in Burmese culture, officials could "legally" arrest

> any person against whom a reasonable suspicion exists that he has promoted or assisted to promote or intends to promote rebellion against the Authority of Government, or that he assisted or intends to assist any rebel, or otherwise has acted or intends to act in a manner prejudicial to the restoration or maintenance of law and order.[81]

As tribunal records will reveal, tattooing, spirit-worship propitiation ceremonies, the use of indigenous medicine, and the wearing of amulets signaled one's involvement in the Rebellion. But they also illustrate how particular traits were marked as elements of enduring Burma's criminal culture.

Marking Rebellion

In the end, the Emergency Powers Ordinance came to embody the intent of the Rebellion Trials and Criminal Law Amendment Ordinances combined. While the latter two were secured through a narrative depicting the Bengali Revolutionary Party involvement in the uprising, the full weight of emergency power was directed against Burmese rebels who were responding to a variety of local concerns and interests. Once these legal powers were established, traces of the Bengali role in the rebellion begin to fade in official accounts as administrators returned their focus onto a local explanation. What matters here is that three narratives were produced simultaneously by colonial scholar–officials in an attempt to explain the rebellion: the *minlaung* model, the Bengali terrorist conspiracy, and the image of the modern, politicized monk in U Oktama. Of these three narratives, two would be conflated to form the picture of Saya San that we accept today. The exclusion of the Bengali connection in practically every account of the Saya San Rebellion and the conflation of the *minlaung*/monk model reflect the manner in which the narrative involving the alleged role of kingship was prioritized in official documentation in order to render the rebellion as traditional, while providing the means of regulating political expression that in fact departed from precolonial forms of protest. As U Oktama would eventually disappear, Saya San would be depicted not only as a quack doctor who saw himself as the restorer of the Burmese monarchy, but he also would be projected as a political operative exploiting the use of GCBA-connected village associations as the infrastructure for the rebellion network. Counter-insurgency legislation both produced and reduced narratives of Burmese resistance while creating the epistemological context for their articulation and authorization in the Special Rebellion Tribunals.

The criminalization of ritual tattooing in relation to rebellion legislation identifies an important moment in the formation of the Saya San narrative. In pursuit of expansive legal and municipal powers, counter-insurgency policy enabled and was enabled by ethnographic constructions of Burmese culture. By identifying, textualizing, and codifying cultural practices that were quite common throughout rural society, colonial officials produced legislation that defined the contours of Burmese social culture through the language and priorities of counter-insurgency policy. Legislation, like official reports, would represent both a stage in the formation of the official narrative of Saya San and an expression of what rebellion meant to colonial officials in a particular context. Rebellion was about migrant communities (Bengalis) and transnational activists (U Oktama) as much as it was about Burmese nostalgia for its vanquished monarchy *(minlaung* model). Counter-insurgency legislation was as much a textual expression of these viewpoints as those found in official reports and other documentation. While previously discussed manuals had already defined the nature of future rebellions, it was counter-insurgency legislation that projected many of these generic traits into the specific events of 1930–31. The Rebellion Trials Ordinance and the BCLAO codified many of these traits by making them a part of the legal discourse on rebellion matters. As objects of debate in correspondence, reports, and legislative proceedings, elements of Burmese culture were imbedded into the administrative context of rebellion, reshaping their meaning and significance to observers. Most importantly, the records that would evolve out of this discourse would establish the interpretive framework in which scholars would engage them.

Notes

1. Government of Burma, L/PJ/6/2020, BRGF, letter no. C42930, December 29, 1930, G/B to G/I, H/D; Government of Burma, L/PJ/6/2020, BRGF, letter no.C429C30, January, 5, 1930, G/B to G/I, H/D; Government of Burma, L/PJ/6/2020, BRGF, Criminal Investigation Department, Ralph Clarence Morris, "Causes of the Tharrawaddy Rebellion," March 26, 1931.

2. Government of Burma, L/PJ/6/2021, BRGF, "Memorandum on Special Powers Already Taken and How Asked for by the Government of Burma in Connection with the Rebellion," May, 4, 1931.

3. The Burma Rebellion Trials Ordinance was introduced for renewal on August 31, 1931, as the Burma Rebellion Trials Bill while the Burma Criminal Amendment Ordinance, itself a reproduction of the Bengali Criminal Amendment Bill, was renewed as a bill and finally as the Burma Criminal Amendment Act also in the fall of 1931.

4. Government of Burma, L/PJ/6/2021, BRGF, docket, W. Johnston, legal adviser, Public and Judicial Department, January 11, 1931.

5. Government of India, L/PJ/6/2021, BRGF, secret telegram, government of India, Home Department, to secretary of state for India, January 13, 1931 (9:30 P.M.).

6. Ibid.

7. Ibid.

8. Ibid.

9. Government of Burma, L/PJ/6/2021, BRGF, secret telegram, Home Department, to Secretary of State (hereafter S/S) for India, January 13, 1931, (10:30 P.M.).

10. Ibid.

11. Ibid.

12. Government of India, L/PJ/6/2021, BRGF, secret telegram, Home Department, to S/S for India, repeating telegram from Burma, January 27, 1931 (5:15 P.M.).

13. Government of India, L/PJ/6/2021, BRGF, secret telegram, Home Department, to S/S for India, February 12, 1931.

14. Government of India, L/PJ/6/2021, BRGF, secret telegram, Home Department, to S/S for India, repeating telegram to Burma, January 27, 1931 (5:00 P.M.).

15. Government of India, L/PJ/6/2021, BRGF, secret telegram, Home Department, to S/S for India, repeating telegram to Burma, January 27, 1931 (5:40 P.M.).

16. Government of India, L/PJ/6/2021, BRGF, secret telegram, Home Department, to S/S for India, repeating telegram from government of Burma.

17. Extract from draft Martial Law Ordinance [sic], government of Burma, L/PJ/6/2021, BRGF, February 12, 1931. All along, civil administrators were resistant to the idea of imposing martial law, at the consternation of army officials called from India to suppress the rebellion. See also *The Burma of AJ: Memoirs of AJS White* (1991) and Government of Burma, L/PJ/6/2021, BRGF, Letter to Stewart, December, 19, 1931, describes Whitehall's desire for Stewart to offer a "categorical denial" of any bickering between Civil and Military officials.

18. Ibid.

19. In comparison to English Common Law, which was the standard adopted within Burma.

20. Dr. Ba Maw in fact, raises this issue in that he could not cross-examine pertinent evidence because it was not included in the appellate record. Further, he argued that the police "deprived the defense of an opportunity to put the evidence to any effective test by cross-examination." To this, the government advocate replied that "the evidence in this case was very much less than might have been put in but in view of the fact that the accused was arrested at the very end of the period for which the Special Tribunal had been constituted and in order to get him in with

the same series of Tribunals, [the] *trial of the accused had to be rushed."* See Government of Burma, L/PJ/6/2021, BRGF, judgment proceedings, appeal no. 1121 of special case no. 5, August 28, 1931.

21. Government of Burma, L/PJ/6/2021, BRGF, minute paper, Public and Judicial Department, February 12, 1931.

22. Ibid.

23. A copy of the proposed Ordinance is found in Government of Burma, L/PJ/6/2021, BRGF.

24. For several examples of the issues surrounding the passage of the BCAA see Burma Legislative Council Proceedings ,vol. XIX, nos.1–2, February 12–14, 1931.

25. Government of Burma, L/PJ/6/2020, BRGF, Press Communiqué, February 10, 1931.

26. Government of India, L/PJ/6/2020, BRGF, letter, no.D.1437/31, Government of India, Home Department, Deputy Secretary to the Government of India to His Majesty's Under S/S for India.

27. One must recall the use of the Moplah example in the letter by Prime Minister Edward Thompson who saw handling Burma in the proper manner as a way of extinguishing the mistakes made in the suppression of that revolt.

28. Government of Burma, L/PJ/6/2021, BRGF, secret telegram, government of India, Home Department, to S/S to India.

29. Government of Burma, L/PJ/6/2021, BRGF, copy of ordinance, no. III of 1931, Burma Rebellion Trials Ordinance, March 12, 1931.

30. Government of India, L/PJ/6/2021, BRGF, telegram, government of India, Home Department, to S/S for India.

31. Government of Burma, L/PJ/6/2021, BRGF, copy of ordinance no. III of 1931, Burma Rebellion Trials Ordinance, March 12, 1931.

32. Government of Burma, L/PJ/6/2021, BRGF, minute paper, draft letter, June 5˙1931.

33. The first trial under the Special Tribunal dealt with the rebellion in Pyapon, and the fifteen defendants found guilty of waging war against the emperor (121 Indian Penal Code) were sentenced for execution. Curiously, it was stated that "there were no Government casualties in Pyapun [*sic*] rebellion, but it was closely connected with 'Tharawadi' [*sic*] rebellion (in which) many Government servants killed, and failure of Pyapun rebels due to lack of opportunity more than lack of intention." See Government of Burma, L/PJ/6/2021, BRGF, secret telegram, government of India, Home Department, to S/S for India, repeating telegram from government of Burma, May 23, 1931.

34. Government of Burma, L/PJ/6/2021, BRGF, untitled memo, sentences of Burma Rebels, (n/d).

35. Ibid.

36. See Government of Burma, L/PJ/6/2021, BRGF for a brief summary of the history of the Bengal Criminal Law Amendment Ordinance, extracts from the Bengal Legislative Council, and copy of the Ordinance.

37. Government of Burma, L/PJ/6/2021, BRGF, confidential minute paper, "Proposal for Promulgation of an Ordinance," January 9, 1931.

38. L/PJ/6/2021, BRGF, Government of Burma, confidential letter, 693W30, December 15, 1930.

39. Secret telegram, G/I, H/D, to S/SI, January 13, 1931.

40. Government of Burma, L/PJ/6/2021, BRGF, secret telegram, government of India, Home Department, S/S for India, January 8, 1931.

41. Government of Burma, L/PJ/6/2021, BRGF, secret telegram, government of India, Home Department, S/S for India, January 8, 1931 (noon).

42. Ibid.

43. Ibid. It is interesting to note that during this time, these same two events were being linked to the Tharrawaddy outbreak that occurred in late December 1930 and January 1931. When, however, the events in Tharrawaddy became associated with Saya San in the accepted narrative, these two events are curiously missing. This is due perhaps, to the puzzling predicament faced by Rangoon authorities who were trying to construct the Saya San myth. All the witness testimony in the trial placed Saya San declaring kingship in December 1930, whence he allegedly initiated the insurrection. Linking the Rangoon violence and the derailed train to Saya San would disrupt the sequence of events and trajectory of the story so neatly woven around Saya San's supposed desire to be king of Burma. The British simply omitted the events of fall 1930 from the narrative.

44. Government of India, L/PJ/6/2021, BRGF, secret telegram, Home Department, to S/S for India, January 8, 1931 (2:30 P.M.).

45. Ibid. Tattooing had already become a significant characteristic of "both" narratives and in this case, was being presented as "evidence" for rebellion-related "excitement."

46. Government of India, L/PJ/6/2021, Secret Telegram, BRGF, Home Department, to S/S for India, January 8, 1931 (3:15 P.M.). U Ottama (Oktama) was a monk who advocated that the monkhood be involved in secular affairs, particularly in the livelihood of peasants. His message was

eventually taken up by the GCBA. See Robert Taylor, *The State in Burma* (Honolulu: University of Honolulu Press, 1987) pp. 182–83.

47. Government of Burma, L/PJ/6/2021, BRGF, confidential minutes, "Proposed Promulgation of an Ordinance to Deal with the Revolutionaries," January 9, 1931.

48. Ibid.

49. Government of Burma, L/PJ/6/2021, BRGF, secret telegram, part II, G/I, H/D, to S/SI, January 11, 1931.

50. Ibid. The Soe Thein GCBA, designated a branch of the original GCBA who split up due to differing views on the Separation issue. It is quite possible that the rebellion and the nature of the government response had to do with the Soe Thein stance of disagreeing with the government's position to separate from the administrative control of India. A brief synopsis of the GCBA and its branches can be found in Taylor, *The State in Burma*, pp. 174–88.

51. Government of Burma, L/PJ/6/2020, BRGF, secret telegram (n/d).

52. Government of Burma, L/PJ/6/2021, BRGF, secret telegram. G/I, H/D, to S/SI, February 2, 1931.

53. Government of Burma, L/ PJ/6/2021, secret telegram, BRFG, G/I, H/D, to S/SI, January, 11, 1931 (1:00 P.M.).

54. Ibid.

55. Ibid. It is quite possible that this was merely a typo, but later statements seem to indicate that the legislation being sought was to be used against the Burmese anyway and that it was not really clear whether the supposed party was involved in the first place.

56. Government of India, L/PJ/6/2021, secret telegram, BRGF, government of India, Home Department, to S/S for India, January, 11, 1931 (2:30 P.M.).

57. Government of Burma, L/PJ/6/2021, BRGF, confidential minute paper, Public and Judicial Department, January 5, 1931.

58. Government of Burma, L/PJ/6/2021, BRGF, W. Johnston, legal adviser, Docket, Public and Judicial Department, January 11, 1931.

59. Ibid.

60. Government of India, L/PJ/6/2021, BRGF, telegram, Home Department, to S/S for India, February 2, 1931.

61. Ibid.

62. Government of Burma, L/PJ/6/2021, BRGF, statement by the governor-general of India, Home Department, January 31, 1931.

63. Government of Burma, L/PJ/6/2021, BRGF, extract from the pro-

ceedings of Council Relating to the Burma Criminal Law Amendment Bill, 1931, at a meeting held on February, 14, 1931.

64. Ibid.

65. Extract, Proceedings from the Burma Legislative Council, 1931.

66. Government of Burma, L/PJ/6/2021, BRGF, Burma Legislative Council Proceedings, February 14, 1931, pp. 139–62.

67. Extracts.

68. Ibid.

69. Government of Burma, L/PJ/6/2021, extract of the Burma Legislative Council Proceedings.

70. Government of India, L/PJ/6/2021, BRGF, secret telegram, Home Department, to S/S for India, January 13, 1931 (10:30 P.M.) and government of India, L/PJ/6/2021, BRGF, secret telegram, January 13, 1931 (9:30 P.M.).

71. Government of Burma, L/PJ/6/2021, BRGF, extract, Burma Legislative Council Proceedings.

72. Government of Burma, L/PJ/6/2021, BRGF, Burma Legislative Council Proceedings, February 14, 1931.

73. Government of Burma, L/PJ/6/2021, BRGF, extract, BLC Proceedings.

74. Government of Burma, L/PJ/6/2021, BRGF, extract, Burma Legislative Council Proceedings.

75. Government of Burma, L/PJ/6/2021, BRGF, Burma Emergency Ordinance, June 1, 1931; Government of Burma, L/PJ/6/2021, BRGF, governor's statement, enclosure no.3, August 1, 1931, BRF.

76. Government of Burma, L/PJ/6/2020, BRGF, telegram, G/I, H/D, to S/SI, repeating telegram from G/B, June 11, 1931; Government of Burma, L/PJ/6/2021, BRGF, telegram part I, G/I, H/D, to S/SI, repeating telegrams from and to G/B, June 9, 1930.

77. Government of Burma, L/PJ/6/2021, BRGF, secret telegram, part III, G/I, H/D, to S/SI, May 23, 1931; Government of Burma, L/PJ/6/2021, BRGF, telegram part II, G/I, H/D, to S/SI, repeating telegram from and to G/B, January 9, 1931.

78. Government of Burma, L/PJ/6/2021, BRGF, minute paper, "Proposal for Promulgation of an Ordinance," January 9, 1931; L/PJ/6/2020, copy of letter, C30, G/B to G/I, H/D. December 29, 1930.

79. Government of Burma, L/PJ/6/2021, BRGF, secret telegram, government of India, Home Secretary, to S/S for India, June 9, 1931.

80. Government of Burma, L/PJ/6/2021, BRGF, telegram, G/I, H/D,

to S/SI, repeating telegram from G/B, June 11, 1931; Government of Burma, L/PJ/6/2021, BRGF, secret telegram, G/I, H/D, to S/SI, June 9, 1931.

81. Government of Burma, L/PJ/6/2021, BRGF, Burma Emergency Ordinance Draft, section 3, June 1, 1931.

Chapter 4

ADJUDICATING REBELLION
The Trial of Saya San

Armed with new legislative and judicial powers, Rangoon officials began to apply their newly secured administrative capabilities toward framing and implementing counter-insurgency policy and strategy. The appointment of a Special Rebellion Tribunal, among several other initiatives, followed closely the blueprint outlined in the Rebellion Trial Ordinance and revealed how administrators would utilize these powers to identify, arrest, and process those suspected of taking part in the rebellion. Through new legal procedures, judicial categories, and trial settings that were specifically reserved for accused rebels, detainees were legally connected to the profiles of Burmese resistance fighters found in turn-of-the century gazetteers and manuals. As discussed in the previous chapter, the most striking of caricatures adopted by administrative officials was the *minlaung* (incipient king) model, a theory that explained peasant uprisings through the image of a pretender-king who would periodically attract followers that believed that he would restore the monarchy and the religion. Judicial officials soon appropriated this idea involving notions of Burmese kingship and linked them to the specific events of 1930–31, codifying the rebellion's connection to the *minlaung* theory through law's authoritative structures. Counter-insurgency jurisprudence would play a crucial role in the construction of the Saya San Rebellion by producing a tighter narrative of events that consolidated divergent instances of political expression into a single, coherent resistance narrative. Law would be instrumental in producing an evidential record that would anchor Saya San's eventual place within the Rebellion Ethnology and Burmese history.

Just as rebellion legislation was conceptualized for and applicable to the entire province of Burma, so too did the series of trials have the effect of rendering the rebellion along those same spatial, cultural, and administrative lines. The specific form and scope of emergency-powers legislation reiterated and operated upon the legal perception that the series of local outbreaks were—as official reports were also insisting—elements of a single, coherently organized, and centrally controlled rebellion. From the start, this framework not only linked various uprisings conceptually, but it enabled colonial judicial officers to accentuate the legal contours of the state by merging and associating particular districts within a geography of rebellion. The province was restructured on the basis of whether or not particular districts were "affected" by the rebellion. The appointment of a special rebellion commissioner, whose purpose was to coordinate counter-insurgency policy between the military and the civil service, oversaw the new administrative landscape that was defined by the threat of rebellion. Finally, directives underlying the all-encompassing reach of the Special Rebellion Tribunal made it possible to present local (and arguably independent) acts of resistance and political expression as chapters within a much larger metanarrative of rebellion, which smoothed over instances that contradicted, diverged, or departed entirely from the dominant narrative. Administrative priorities and counter-insurgency policies (expressed through law) produced the categories, language, and conceptual structures that presented the series of uprisings, disturbances, outbreaks, protests and gatherings as a single, all-encompassing rebellion.

Government lawyers and the Special Tribunal influenced the understanding of the rebellion through their efforts to demonstrate and establish legal coherency among the series of trials between the years 1930 and 1932. The infusion of judicial rhetoric to identify, decode, and translate the meaning of uprisings transformed how knowledge about the rebellion would be retained while initiating the terms through which all subsequent discussions of the movements would take place. Predictably, the creation of an official evidential record, the deliberation of issues in an adversarial context, and the registering of this process through specific legal-documentation projects rendered the rebellion into a particular form that reflected this system of knowledge construction. Trial judgments of suspected rebels (such as the case against Aung Hla in the previous chapter) set the legal precedent for subsequent trials, reinforcing both the authority and continuity of the Tribunal's findings while expanding the application of Carey's *minlaung* framework to explain the criminal nature of village associations. Moreover, by designating the series of outbreaks collectively as "the Burma Rebellion," by appointing a special court to adjudicate transgressions against the State, and by declaring Saya San as the sole "face" behind the various resistance movements, government officials were able to apply counter-insurgency strategies that reconstituted their administrative and legal authority over the cultural space it had delineated and defined.

Legalizing Ethnography

Though numerous scholars have concentrated on interpreting the findings and conclusions provided in official reports and other available documentation, few have examined the legal records connected to the adjudication of the rebellion.[1] Official reports are more comprehensive in scope, but they contain abridged and sanitized conclusions that were derived from the judgments of earlier tribunal cases. As such, the legal records pertaining to the Rebellion Trials present a much closer glimpse of how rebellion in Burma was conceptualized, constructed, and codified within that particular epistemological setting. Not only do these sources reveal how the story of Saya San was created within the context of the trials, but how legal processes and procedures reproduced a singular image of a Burmese rebel that could be applied to suspected criminals in subsequent trials. The notion that Burmese rural communities all shared a singular worldview of resistance was as much a product of judicial rendering as it was a legacy of colonial ethnology.

The structure of the trials under the supervision of the Special Rebellion Tribunal was crucial in creating the appearance of a collective movement bound together by a shared rebellion ideology. Charges were levied against several hundred defendants at one time, who were charged en masse with having conspired to wage war under Saya San even though he was still at large at the time of their respective hearings. While individuals were mentioned in the judicial summaries, many of the accused were tried as a group, suppressing the possibility of detecting difference and individual agency due to the way in which the accused were incorporated into the legal setting. Connections among the various defendants often rested on whether or not one bore a tattoo, if they used amulets, or if they had participated in an act of spirit worship. For the most part, these sessions were used to quickly incarcerate large numbers of suspected rebels by expediting procedures and forgoing stages (such as committal hearings) that were guaranteed in the normal legal system. The abbreviated trials that began in early 1931 and preceded Saya San's (September 1931) functioned as a prelude to the arguments and evidence that would be eventually presented at his own proceedings. In doing so, the records of the Rebellion Tribunal authenticated the ethnographic characteristics articulated in previous situation reports by appropriating them and inserting them into the procedures, language, and records of the judiciary. Examining these sources illuminate the role of law in forging the narrative about Saya San as well as the way in which legal discourses about these very cultural traits would eventually be canonized by the colonial state. Ethnographic knowledge about Burmese culture was appropriated and objectified in the context of trials that would eventually find its way into the archive as historical documents, devoid and drained of their original epistemological contexts.

Whereas the role of law in the rendering of the Rebellion marked an important stage in connecting the events of 1930–31 to particular notions of the Burmese past, the legal affirmation of the Rebellion Ethnology also marked an important stage in securing a commensurate understanding of the rebellion for the future. Judgments, appeals, and evidential records stemming from the special tribunals not only confirmed the origins of the Rebellion, but provided legal precedence and authority for framing future findings and decisions. Just as the trial of Aung Hla provided the context for subsequent trials, so too would the trial of Saya San serve as precedence for trials that were conducted well beyond the official ending of the rebellion in 1932. The textualization of the rebellion through its adjudication provided a specific corpus of materials that would provide Rangoon officials with the types of documents required to produce a final report that would appear legitimate to readers in New Delhi and London. In other words, the trials conducted by the special Rebellion Tribunal functioned not only to link Saya San to the *minlaung* tradition of the past, but it created the textual and legal precedence for producing and preserving knowledge about the Rebellion in the future.

Although the Rebellion Ethnology had begun to emerge well before the events of 1930, attempts to project it to the circumstances surrounding the Tharrawaddy outbreak in general, and with Saya San in particular, commenced in early January 1931. As we have already seen, early reports reveal how quickly Saya San was linked to the conceptualization, planning, and initiating of the rebellion in its early stages. Moreover, Saya San and his followers were almost immediately identified as a version of the *minlaung*-inspired movements of the late 1800s. Representations of Burmese peasants that were once articulated more generally in ethnographic terms by gazetteers and manuals became directly linked to the narrative of circumstances surrounding Saya San through specific, Rebellion-related documentation. In order to keep New Delhi and London updated on these developments, early police communiqués, situation reports, telegrams, and confidential correspondences tended to assert (rather than demonstrate) official positions regarding the origins, character, and facts of the outbreak. Until the implementation of the Rebellion Trials Ordinance and the commencement of the Tribunal hearings, colonial documentation reveal very little as to how colonial authorities reached their conclusions regarding the role of Saya San in the Rebellion. Due to the specific demands of the court setting, legal sources pertaining to the trials provide a fresh view that reveals how colonial lawyers actually borrowed, refashioned, and articulated earlier administrative positions on Burmese resistance to fit the historical narrative to which Saya San's name is now attached.[2]

The Trial Setting

By the time Saya San was eventually apprehended in August 1931, Arthur Eggar and his prosecution team did not have to introduce the details of their case since much of Saya San's profile and his place in the Rebellion had already been made public in numerous official reports and newspapers prior to his trial, a distinct disadvantage confronting the defense team from the beginning.[3] Dr. Ba Maw, lead defense attorney, stated at the appeal that the "appellant was a man of singular misfortune in that he was pursued by his own fame or notoriety, so much so that his name had come to be permanently connected with the rebellion." The concept of a unified Rebellion also allowed the tribunal to view testimonies and material exhibits from previous trials as part of a growing but interrelated evidential record, enabling prosecutors and the tribunal to link the stories of "other" rebels to the narrative involving Saya San. In fact, one trial that covered the events surrounding the capture of the alleged rebel headquarters overlapped considerably with the trial of Saya San, "as the facts relied on by the prosecution in the two cases were practically identical."[4] Evidence establishing tattooing, *nat* propitiation, amulet use, and other elements of the Rebellion Ethnology as integral components of the Saya San narrative was achieved through the combined findings of tribunal hearings over several cases. The cohesive image of the rebellion and its attending legal structures influenced the way in which the rebellion trials were being understood by administratively linking individual instances of resistance into a single narrative. Infusing Saya San into this already-existing model depended on reasserting his preconceived role as a pretender-king and central mastermind behind the Rebellion.

In these and other respects, the trial of Saya San commenced and proceeded under circumstances that would have a direct effect on narrative of the Rebellion. For one, the trial was fast-tracked in order to adhere to a schedule that was determining how long the tribunal could spend to oversee the case. The extraordinary procedures and guidelines provided by the Rebellion Trials Ordinance had nearly expired by the time Saya San was arrested, compelling even the prosecution to admit that the trial "had to be rushed" in order to have it heard under the authority of the Special Tribunal.[5] To compound matters for the defense, allegations against Saya San had already entered the legal record in previous trials of other detainees and were thus already treated as "legal fact."[6] The prosecution's reliance on uncorroborated testimony and the paucity of physical evidence offered in the case gave the defense little room to cross-examine the material record. Dr. Ba Maw, lead defense counsel, suggested that there was a large corpus of evidence that could have been submitted as corroborating evidence, which in turn would have provided the opportunity for cross-examination. Curiously, the government advocate (Arthur Eggar) replied that there was in fact very much "less than might have been put in."[7] Thus, the Special Rebellion Tribunals and the operational setting in which they functioned were crucial to the way in which the narrative about Saya San came to be formed, especially in terms of the alleged coherency of the Rebellion. The legal and administrative structures responsible for the collection, evaluation, and dissemination of knowledge about the rebellion contributed to its unified image.

Given these observations and their ramifications to the types of sources that emerged from the tribunals, the trial of Saya San is crucial to understanding the extent of the colonial government's counter-insurgency effort to reserve and register his role in the Rebellion through the court's documentary machinery. More importantly, the narrative of events, what would crucially be regarded later as the historical facts of the case, would eventually be formulated and sanctioned through the supervision of the Rebellion Tribunal. Though this narrative would eventually pass seamlessly into the hands of scholars (via a definitive blue-book report), the legal rendering of this narrative and its attachment to Saya San was hardly as flawless as one might expect under these circumstances. Assessing these legal records for the first time will reveal not only the way in which the Rebellion Ethnology was eventually connected to Saya San, but more importantly, how the narrative of kingship (to which Saya San is attached) rests uncomfortably on an untenable evidential record.

Legal Sources

The sources for the trial of Saya San are located in judgment summaries collected and preserved within the Burma Rebellion General Files. Three types of documents—the judgment, the appeal, and the judgment order (a review of procedure, evidence, and argument)—provide the closest account of the trial and represent three levels of judicial authorship as the official account grew more complex in content and detail with each stage. In the original judgment document, the case of the prosecution team is described by the presiding tribunal and further elaborated upon in the appeal and judgment order that followed respectively.[8] The latter two documents are more helpful in reconstructing the thinking behind the prosecution's case in that issues of procedure, evidential admissibility, and argument are more closely addressed by the judge conducting the review. A comparison of these documents illustrate that the judges reviewing the arguments of the prosecution often reinforced their allegations by providing supportive references from other cases that served to situate and normalize the legal circumstances surrounding the Saya San trial. In short, the documents reveal that the process of constructing what would become a crucial source in the archival record developed over several stages as a documentation project.

Taken together, a relatively clear genealogy of ideas can be traced among the documents concerning the trials, though interesting deficiencies within these records are also readily apparent. First, the documents are not actual transcripts of the proceedings but summaries written by the tribunal overseeing the original case, the appeal, and the review of the appeal (judgment order).[9] Following the guidelines found in the Rebellion Trial Ordinance, court records stemming from the tribunal were only summarized in order to facilitate the speedy administrative processing of detainees. Not surprisingly, only the prosecution's arguments and tribunal comments are presented,

Defense lawyers

raising serious questions about subsequent documents (and scholarly interpretations) that rely on the content and findings of these legal records. Second, the counter-arguments of the defense team, led by Dr. Ba Maw, are only discernable in instances where they raised a legal issue that warranted the attention of the appellate or review judge. In several instances, it appears that the tribunal, not the prosecution, made counter-arguments on issues of admissibility of evidence, relevance, and interpretation.[10] Reconstructing how the defense team (and especially Saya San) responded to the charges, arguments, and setting of the trial is difficult to ascertain given the nature of the sources.[11] Yet this silencing of the defense's voice (and particularly Saya San's own words in the trial) are in many ways revealing. Although the absence of the defense's case is disappointing, it nonetheless emphasizes the discursive, aesthetic, and persuasive influence of the prosecution's case in the archival record.[12] How was the narrative of Saya San guided by law's interpretive strategies, terminology, rhetoric, and rules that determined who could speak and in what manner?[13] To what extent has our current understanding of Saya San, and the mentalities he is said to represent, relied upon the prosecution's constructions of Burmese ethnology and the events associated with the Rebellion? In what manner has the idea of rebellion shaped our understanding of Burmese kingship in relation to the case of Saya San? In this respect, the presence of the defense's case would only reinforce the point that the arguments underlying the trial of Saya San were framed and mandated in an inherently adversarial context wherein the establishment of innocence or guilt was the predetermined objective of arguments introduced in court. The resulting sources and the narratives they contained were products of this particular legal setting and the procedures prescribing the way in which law made rebellion knowable. Counter-insurgency law was not merely a product of historical forces and circumstances involving the Rebellion, but "an active participant in the process through which history is written and memory constructed."[14]

The outcome of these legal processes (the story) would therefore be affected by how particular categories, issues, and evidence were deemed relevant to the structures, procedures, and terminology (the storytelling) of the legal setting in which this narrative was being constructed. As will be discussed below, the arguments of the prosecution and the Special Rebellion Tribunal shaped and attached the notion of kingship to the narrative about the Saya San Rebellion, keeping in line with the model described by earlier colonial officials. Whereas the prosecution introduced components of the Rebellion Ethnology into the legal record, it was the Tribunal that translated these ideas using the particular vocabulary of counter-insurgency law.[15] The records illustrate that the Tribunal had a formative influence on the final shape of the narrative for it had the authority to decide what could and what could not be admitted into the evidential record. The ramifications of this role to the epistemology of the Saya San narrative cannot be overemphasized: the Tribunal was not only dictating what would be admitted as evidence in the course of the trial, it was in fact determining and transforming what would constitute the historical record.

Ironically, the basis for determining legal admissibility in the trial was also the same criterion for defining its historical relevance, since the available sources would consist only of the evidentiary record that the judges accepted and included in their summaries[16] As a consequence, the legal evidence of the trial and the arguments corresponding to its application serve as the primary evidence and methodology in the history of the Saya San Rebellion.

Whereas the preceding chapter discussed how historical forces shaped counter-insurgency law, this chapter focuses on how law used Burmese ethnohistory to construct rebellion.[17]

Prosecuting Rebellion

The thrust of the prosecution's case alleged that Saya San had organized, influenced (and in some cases), duped peasants into waging war against the British Crown.[18] According to their arguments, Saya San matched the profile specifically detailed in Carey's *minlaung* model in his reference to the symbols and memory of the Burmese monarchy by claiming that he was the new king of Burma. Alleging that his Galon Organization (Galon Wunthanu Athin), a network of village community associations (that adopted the Galon for their symbol), were really political cells linked to the preparation of the Rebellion, government prosecutors charged Saya San with recruiting and intimidating otherwise docile (yet restless) peasants into conducting operations against the colonial administration.[19] Prosecution lawyers argued that Saya San had been planning rebellion two years before the December 1930 uprising by contending that he had "the idea of the Galon Organization ... since 1928, if not earlier."[20] As a result, their task required them to demonstrate that planning for rebellion had indeed occurred in 1928 and through the formation of the Galon Organization, a component of the rebellion narrative that had been missing in earlier trials. In short, the prosecution wanted to establish in the record that the uprising was not merely a "spontaneous" expression of peasant unrest but the result of a well-planned conspiracy.

In the judicial review of Saya San's case, Judge J. M. Baguley summarized the points under which Saya San was convicted of waging war against the king-emperor. It was alleged during the trial that:

(1) At a meeting at Shwenakwin village in the house of Saya Sa [not to be confused with Saya San] he [Saya San] took a leading part in fomenting rebellion
(2) At Magyigone Kyaung he fomented rebellion and organized Galon Societies
(3) He ordered his men to make attacks on Tharrawaddy, Henzada, and Letpada
(4) He ordered the murder of Mr. Fields Clarke, a forest officer who was killed while on tour at We Bungalow
(5) At Alantaung, a hill in the forest, he collected men for the purpose of Rebellion[21]

Dr. Ba Maw, Saya San's lead counsel, focused on each charge and its corresponding evidence separately, while the prosecution viewed the five charges as collectively indicative of his having waged war against the British government. These approaches are important in that they reveal how each side viewed the Rebellion—as a series of separate and unconnected events on the one hand or as a series of interrelated and interdependent events on the other. These perspectives also refer to the politics of the case being argued within the chambers of the local legislature whose divide was deepening due to debate over the Rebellion: Were the uprisings a spontaneous expression of peasants driven by worsening socioeconomic conditions? Or the result of a few fanatics who were motivated by a thirst for power? In either case, the arguments that would be submitted to the Tribunal certainly reflected the politically charged nature of the trial.

The pertinent evidence against Saya San began with a document seized from a household he had allegedly resided in for ten years. The prosecution contended that the note demonstrated that Saya San had been "permanently connected" in "fomenting the Rebellion" well before the outbreak of violence in late 1930. It stated that a new organization by the name of Sandati Galon Organization would be recognized by the General Council of Burmese Associations (one of the largest nationalist organizations) and "utilized according to the wishes of its members."[22] Although the document was dated August 3, 1928, there was nothing within the text to link it to Saya San, nor did it support any allegation that the Galon Organization was a front for rebellion. One had to assume a priori that the prosecution story about the origins and meaning of the document was accurate in order for it to be valid. Curiously, reference to this document appears only in the official blue-book report produced in 1934; it did not seem to appear as evidence submitted in any of the trial records dating back to 1931.

Another document with questionable relevance is a letter dated December 14, 1929, from Saya San to Saya Nyun, presented as evidence of early Rebellion planning. It reads:

> The declaration by the Viceroy that Dominion Home Rule would be granted to India is but a ruse. A political object is achieved only when lives are sacrificed. The Indians in India will like one man, give up their lives next Pyatho (January 1930). Our party has decided not to separate Burma from India, and it is when we follow the lead of India (Lit. When the elder brother dances, the younger brother should dance, and when the elder brother sits, the younger brother should sit too) that we are acting according to the spirit of the decision.[23]

This letter was deemed "to foreshadow" the "violence and bloodshed" that would befall British officials in the coming months. In a rare indication of the defense explanation (and referred to in the record because of the prosecution's rebuttal), Saya San's lawyers claimed that the sacrifices mentioned in the passage was not directed toward British authorities but referred to the ways in which political interests would have to make sacrifices in order to secure consensus, especially in reference to the highly divisive Separation Issue (of Burma from India) that was currently under debate within nationalist and government circles. This explanation was dismissed by the judge conducting the judicial review since Saya San was a known provider of charms and tattooing which rendered the recipients immune to bullets... (the blood) can hardly be regarded as referring to the blood to which his men would have to shed, for according to all the evidence, his men were supposed to be proof against injury, so the shedding of blood contemplated must have been the blood of the opposite party.[24]

In other words, it was the intervention of Judge Baguley that connected "the blood and violence" within the letter. It had to be directed toward the British since the Burmese used tattoos that were believed to make themselves invulnerable. Therefore, the letter was considered direct evidence of Saya San's intention to rebel in the coming months. However, an examination of the document's text shows no reference at all to "blood and violence" in the first place. The counter-argument (pertaining to tattooing) was actually in reference to the judge's own commentary on the letter, not from the original text itself. Moreover, the government continued to refer to the positions articulated in the Rebellion Ethnology by presuming that tattooing was indicative of rebellion, though this relationship had not been established beyond assertions made in earlier reports. Judicial intervention on the relevance of the evidence rested on, and was directed toward, assumptions and arguments that stemmed from its own comments and prejudices, not from the document under examination.

In fact there was actually very little reliable material evidence to show that Saya San had the idea for rebellion in 1928 and that the formation of the Galon Athins were connected to the uprisings. The 1928 note and the 1929 letter relied on the prosecution's unproved characterizations of their meaning and content. Both documents hinged on a narrative that was symbiotically and tautologically dependent on them as sources. Not only are the circumstances surrounding their admittance peculiar, but their reliability as sources for the historical is questionable as well.

The evidence of the case was based primarily on prosecution witnesses, many of whom were asked to describe the events leading up to the outbreak of the Rebellion. San Pe told the Tribunal that Saya San had lived with his family for ten years and had given him a membership card that stated:

> Enlistment ticket No. 1587—Maung Sein Aye, aged 25 years, has been recognized as a member of (A) Company, on his taking oath that he will abide by the rule of the Galon Organization [Dated] The 9th Lazan of Pyatho (27th December 1930) [signed] Thupannaka Galuna Raja.[25]

Naturally, when witnesses were brought forward to testify about meetings involving these village units, the legal assumption would be that they were involved in preparation for the Rebellion. For example, witness Po Aung deposed that both he and Saya San had been members of U Soe Thein's branch of the General Council of Burmese Associations (GCBA), and that in December 1930 he received a letter from Saya San instructing him to meet at his house in the village of Shwenakwin, whereupon Saya San addressed those at the meeting and said "People are now getting into trouble with the capitation tax. We must collect men and loot guns and rise in rebellion."[26] Po Aung's testimony was corroborated by another witness, Ba Aye, who heard the same alleged speech. In all, two witnesses testified that Saya San had ordered membership cards for the accused Rebellion Organization and two witnesses stated that Saya San had openly discussed rebelling against the British.

From what can be gleaned from the judicial summaries, the defense conceded that meetings had indeed taken place but denied that rebellion was the subject of these gatherings. The Tribunal was faced with deciding whose testimony was more credible, Saya San's or the prosecution's witnesses. In their ruling on Ba Aye's testimony, the tribunal concluded that

> He is a very resolute person. Probably he is a scoundrel. But he was, in our view, in the innermost counsels of the persons who fomented the rebellion. The first time he gave evidence before us was last April, and he has given evidence in all the rebellion cases before us. We believed him then and so did the Court of Appeal. We have accepted his evidence in all these cases.[27]

In reference to Po Aung, they observed:

> Po Aung is a very different character. He is a timid person, and we think he was brought to this rebellion because he was a friend of Saya San in Kamamo. He was, in our view, thoroughly afraid of Saya San and his organization. His evidence however is clear and straightforward.[28]

The Tribunal's criteria for accepting the testimony of the prosecution witnesses exemplifies the type of reasoning that went into the creation of the legal record. Ba Aye's testimony was accepted on the grounds that the Tribunal determined "in their view" that he was in the "innermost counsels of the rebellion," a conclusion that had not been established by the prosecution or evident in the witness's statement. More curiously, Ba Aye had apparently appeared before the court before, as a prosecution witness against other defendants, as he had agreed to the terms of amnesty offered by the government. His frequent appearances as a prosecution witness and the acceptance of his testimonies in past cases seemed enough to establish his credibility. Similarly, Po Aung's testimony was accepted on the unsubstantiated inference (on the part of the Tribunal) that he was Saya San's "friend" who was thoroughly "frightened" of the alleged leader. In both instances, the witness testimony was accepted on decisions reached by the Tribunal that were independent of any specific argument presented by the prosecution. Thus, the fact that Saya San planned and organized the Rebellion through the formation of the Galon Village Organizations as early as 1928 is based in part on two witnesses whose credibility was established not by the prosecution, but by the judges of the Special Tribunal. Whether or not Po Aung and Ba Aye were credible witnesses or actually present in the first place are actually minor points. More crucial to the ethnology of the Rebellion narrative is recognizing the way in which this element of the Saya San story became entrenched within the historical record through the legal processes of the Special Rebellion Tribunals.

Tattooing as Terrorism

Another witness, Tun U, testified that in the late summer of 1930, Saya San had ordered the printing of five thousand similar cards resembling the example given by San Pe. These cards played a significant role in the case against Saya San since they refer for the first time, to a "royal" title, *Thupannaka Galuna Raja* or King of the Galons. The Galon or Garuda was a mythical bird in Southeast Asia that was often pitted against the Naga (snake), similar to the association between the fox and the hound. Members of the organization were alleged to have tattooed the image of the Galon defeating the Naga, a symbol that mirrored Burmese intentions to defeat the British. In the prosecution's eyes, the Galon–Naga motif symbolized the very idea of rebellion and the inherent cultural traits that underlined its very conception. The membership card, according to the prosecution, illustrated not only Saya San's rank as leader and founder of the Galon Village Associations, but it signaled his self-identification as *king* of the Galons and his intention to use Burmese kingship as an ideological platform from which to launch his revolt.[29]

In their effort to attach Saya San to the formative stages of the rebellion, the prosecution had to demonstrate that the Galon Associations were the political wing of the Rebellion. Drawing upon a produced knowledge of Burmese rituals, mythology, and medicinal practices, the government lawyers melded together an argument that not only came to criminalize aspects of Burmese culture, but one that refined the Rebellion Ethnology where it would endure into contemporary scholarship as the discourse through which these features would be discussed. They chose specifically to focus on the symbol of the Galon–Naga and the act of tattooing. Although the practice of tattooing in Burma had a wide and varied tradition (such as a means of identifying with one's service group), the British attempted to argue that the act of tattooing and specifically the tattooing of the Galon's defeat of the Naga was an initiation ritual that Saya San undertook as part of his recruitment into the rebel associations.[30] The prosecution attempted to argue that the choice of the symbol for the Galon Organization and their tattoos was completely intentional, for the symbol of the Galon defeating the Naga triggered the "hereditary lawlessness and contempt of authority" in the "ignorant, gullible and superstitious" villagers who associated themselves with the Galon and the Naga with the British.[31] Thus, the legal connection between the Galon Association and the Rebellion rested upon an anthropological interpretation of tattooing as a practice and the Galon as a symbol of revolt.

This interpretation actually relied on evidence presented in an earlier rebellion trial (Special Rebellion Case No. 1 of 1931) in which a prosecution witness, Po Yon, stated the following:

> I asked Po Htin why he had the "gallon" mark tattooed on his arm. He said that those people bearing these tattoo-marks would fight the Government when the Government servants came to demand capitation-taxes and land revenue. "Galon" is the symbol of victory over the "Naga." The "Naga" represents foreigners, such as the English, the French, the Italiens [sic], and the Russians. It is said that if a man has a "gallon" tattoo mark on him he becomes invulnerable, and the shot fired at him become[s] coloured flour.[32]

The defense countered that the Galon tattoo was a prophylactic against snakebite, which drew criticism from the British High Justice Cunliffe, until U Ba U, a Burmese member of the Tribunal, supposedly intervened and said:

> Judge, if you think that a man who has a tattoo mark on him should be presumed a rebel, I think I had better get down from the bench and take my seat along those accused in the dock. See my tattoo marks....Judge, you may think we are childish in our belief, but we all believe, especially the villagers, that these tattoo marks render us immune to snake bite.[33]

Even though the prosecution's explanation for the meaning of the Galon symbol depended on hearsay testimony and despite the fact that the tattoo apparently had an equally ambiguous epistemology, their interpretation was deemed sufficient enough to prove that the Galon Village Associations were the political and administrative wing of the Rebellion. Thus, testimony and evidence referring to meetings of the

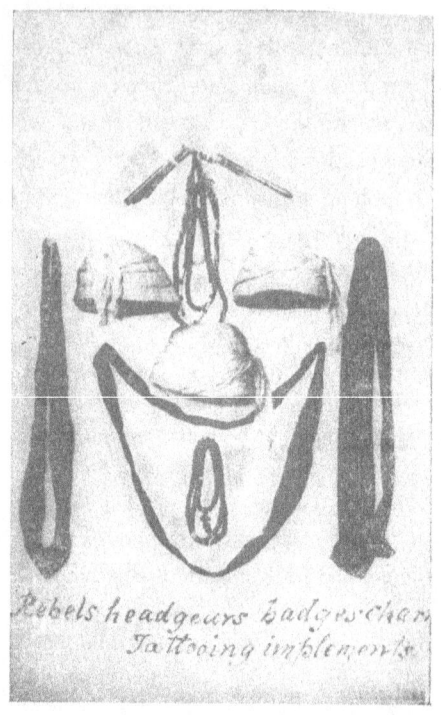

Badges of rebellion displayed in "mocking" fashion

village organizations automatically were categorized as representing rebel activity.[34]

In fact, tattooing was considered evidence of the Rebellion's coherency and organization. Outbreaks in different districts were linked to the Galon Association and Saya San because "the symbol adopted by the Htandaw Rebels was that of the galon, in the same form as the marks found in Tharrawaddy."[35] Yet, when the prosecution came upon conflicting evidence that contradicted their Galon paradigm (if one accepts that interpreting the meaning of a tattoo is reliable evidence in the first place) they rationalized their evidence to fit the theory. In one instance, the Special Tribunal found it

> a curious thing however that we have not found a single "galon" tattoo mark on any one of the accused....It seems, therefore, to us quite likely that the "galon" mark had been now definitely aban-

doned. The actual tattoo marks of which we have been supplied with the list are of a varied and puzzling character. The evidence with regard to their signification is conflicting. *It is difficult to find an outstanding common factor among them*; but it may be noticed that the "necklace design" is found on a very large number of the people accused. We are of the opinion that this necklace design was part of a symbol adopted by the rebels indicating sympathy with the enrolment [sic] in the rebels' forces.[36]

Not only was the Tribunal intentionally looking for coherency through tattooing, but they adjusted the argument and chose an arbitrary tattoo (the necklace) to fit the preconceived theory that the Rebellion was a coherent movement. Although this adaptation of the necklace design actually dislodged Po Yon's testimony linking the Galon tattoo to the village associations, out of this methodological dilemma sprang the idea that tattooing was "a well known concomitant of rebellion in Burma."[37] In presenting Burmese peasants as having tattooed the Galon–Naga symbol on their bodies as an act of resistance, judicial officers were in fact inscribing upon the social body of the Burmese peasantry the very meaning of rebellion.

Establishing Kingship

The Tribunal's special procedural flexibility, evident in the deliberation of the prosecution's opening arguments, became fully obvious as the case turned to reconstructing the events associated with the outbreak of the rebellion in 1930. Whereas the early direction of the trial had dealt with pre-1930 planning, the thrust of the case dwelt on establishing the traditional character of Saya San and demonstrating his aspirations to rebuild and claim the defunct Burmese monarchy.

The prosecution hoped to show that between the months of October and December 1930, Saya San began holding coronation ceremonies in order to consecrate his identity as the new king of Burma and to recruit and inspire peasant soldiers. The entire character of the prosecution's case, and indeed the history that stemmed from it, hinges upon the arguments and evidence that were presented to demonstrate Saya San's kingship. Interestingly enough, the whole case rested on the testimony of a single witness and the admissibility of one curious document.

Maung Chone, a prosecution witness, claimed to have been a part of Saya San's retinue which convened on October 28, 1930, at the Pagoda in Taungnyogale Village. He recounted that,

> All of us who went with Saya San sat down in a row including Saya San except Tun Lin and Yan Lin. They stood up and held a white flag each with the figure of a "gallon" and "naga" painted thereon. Then Saya Daing read something. After he had read it "May there be victory, may there be victory."[38]

Besides there being only one witness in the record to testify on this alleged event, the Tribunal and the Appellate Court deemed the event "somewhat in the nature of a coronation."[39] This is especially troubling, for nothing in the description suggests that the event even resembled a traditional coronation ceremony.[40] Yet, both judicial summaries and the appellate documents indicate that it was the Tribunal, not even the prosecution, who reached this conclusion. Although the issue at that point in the trial was whether or not the event took place, noticing how it was classified is important because it illustrates the way in which the Tribunal presumed what the nature of the ceremony was and the role Saya San was to play within it. And all from a single witness, whose ambiguous testimony was deemed admissible on the determination of the Tribunal that "this man is an extremely stupid man and too foolish to be able to have made up the story which he tells."[41]

The prosecution attempted to support Maung Chone's testimony with what they claimed was Saya San's diary, the final piece in the puzzle that would tie their case together. Although the records do not indicate whether or not the document presented was ever shown to be a diary in the Western sense of the term (for keeping a diary is not a characteristic of Burmese culture), Saya San is reported to have denied that the "diary" was his. Consequently, the issue of identifying the name of the item apparently was not raised, and the Tribunal turned to determining whether or not the diary was the authentic diary of Saya San.

The prosecution introduced an expert witness to establish the author of the diary by calling in Mr. Ghosal, Principal of the Insein Detective School. Mr Ghosal was asked to compare the writing of the diary with a written statement known to be Saya San's. In his comparison, Mr. Ghosal testified that the diary was surely Saya San's for "whenever the writer of this diary makes a letter containing a circle he draws it in a peculiar manner, and he finds the same characteristic in the letters of the appellant."[42] Yet, neither the defense, nor historians for that matter, even questioned the expertise of Mr. Ghosal, even though his credentials as a handwriting expert rested only on his personal assurances and despite the fact that he could neither read nor speak a word of Burmese, which has its own techniques and procedures for writing characters.[43] Mr Ghosal's deficiency in Burmese was downplayed by the prosecution, which stated that an expert could identify characteristics of a written language even though "the expert is ignorant of that language."[44] The Tribunal agreed that his testimony on the handwriting was admissible "provided the expert understands sufficient [sic] of the script to know what the writer of any document was trying to reproduce on paper."[45] Yet this argument, which was introduced by the Tribunal (who was supposed to be hearing positions, not introducing them), assumed a priori that the alleged writer was known when the issue was whether Mr. Ghosal was a reliable expert witness, not whether he could determine what was being written. Nevertheless, Mr. Ghosal's expertise was accepted and his testimony was admitted into the record that the diary was Saya San's.

Perhaps to belay any concerns about Mr. Ghosal's inability to read Burmese, the diary was also examined

> by members of the Tribunal, two of whom were well acquainted with Burmese...the diary was accepted by the Tribunal as the genuine diary (of Saya San) both on the general appearance in handwriting and by internal evidence which it contains.[46]

Maung Ba, the presiding appellate Judge, concurred with his colleagues and commented in his review,

> I have compared the writing in the diary, Ex. J, with the writings in those exhibits (B, B1, D, D1, and F). I also consider that there is a striking similarity between those writings. I therefore hold that the entries in the diary are in Saya San's handwriting. I also agree with the Special Tribunal that this diary showed inherent possibility of its truthfulness.[47]

Consequently, on the partial basis of Mr. Ghosal's, the Tribunal's, and one Appellate Judge's self-declared expertise in handwriting, the diary was deemed to be Saya San's and entered into the record. The other factor contributing to the diary's admissibility and declaration of "authenticity" was the opinion of the Tribunal that found that

> The very fact that this document is an exact confirmation of certain evidence relating to certain ceremonies spoke[n] of by the prosecution, showed the inherent possibility of its truthfulness. The diary can be regarded as the type of mind (Saya San) possessed and the type of action and method (Saya San) advocated.[48]

The Tribunal's statement regarding the authenticity of the diary is extraordinary, for it reveals a peculiar circularity, not to mention complicit attempt to write the prosecution's arguments. The Tribunal opined that since the internal details (within a not-yet-authenticated diary) made reference to events whose own verification depended on whether the diary's authenticity could be established, then the document should be considered genuine. In short, the admissibility of the diary into the evidentiary record was accepted on the grounds that it contained information that seemed to corroborate the prosecution's story. Incredibly, upon this ruling rests the weight of the prosecution's case and the entire narrative of the Saya San Rebellion. The original diary has yet to be located.[49]

Authenticating the Narrative

The trial of Saya San reveals that the narrative of the rebellion was created within the procedural and methodological boundaries of counter-insurgency law. Exploring how the narrative was constructed within this particular legal setting leads one to consider how evidence

Special Rebellion Tribunal

was presented and qualified to support the history of the Saya San Rebellion. Although reinterpreting the historically problematized narrative might merit equal attention, such a task would lead one away from studying the manner in which the narrative was created, how sources were made, the role of ethnology in their legal discourse, and what the trial reveals about colonial law and knowledge production. In addition, examining the prosecution's case discloses how a particular view of Burmese history (constant rebellions, periodic appearances of pretenders to the throne), and the *minlaung* idea, played a singular role in the legal construction of Saya San's criminality.[50] Saya San was considered part of a longer, chaotic, narrative of Burmese history that was attempting to reassert itself in the face of modernization. The implication of the government's case was that the Burmese (at least those taking part in the Rebellion), were not capable of participating in the political reforms or mechanisms for participation being introduced in India, urban Rangoon, and in other colonial cities. Yet, Burmese peasants were in fact employing the very modes of

Adjudicating Rebellion   129

political organization that the British were claiming (through the tone and character of the Rebellion narrative) were not being embraced by rural populations.[51] The network and utilization of *wunthanu athin*s (nationalist village associations) clearly indicate that the political landscape of Burma in the 1930s was of a varied nature and more complicated than the prosecution and the findings of the Special Tribunal permitted. These examples of political mobilization, contextualized within the rebellion discourse, were seen as precursors to the growth of a "genuine" nationalist movement, something local officials were desperate to subdue.[52] The Rebellion narrative was a smoothing over of these contradictions within Burmese politics, for it created a clear distinction between the civil administration and the Galon village networks by linking the latter with traditional Burma, although it was actually modeled on the colonial infrastructure.

This incongruence with British norms, this inability to engage in the workings of the colonial state by using the recognized language, institutions, and procedures of the authorities are exemplified in the arguments and evidence produced in Saya San's trial. Material and testimonial evidence was used to establish not only the traditional character of the Rebellion but also the very nature of Burmese political expression. To Rangoon officials, the message was clear: the Burmese peasantry could not articulate protest or dissatisfaction in a language other than through rebellion. Predictably, the prosecution fashioned a case that presented Saya San as leading a rebellion of superstitious peasants, duped into believing that he could protect them with invulnerability tattoos and spells as only a king of Burma and "quack doctor" might do. In a sense, the very idea of political leadership in Burma was relegated to being understood only within the traditions, imagery, and boundaries of Burmese kingship. The translation of the Rebellion and the identifying of its causes demonstrated that Saya San and other rural leaders were informed and constrained by their restrictive history and culture. The criminalization of Burmese tattooing exemplifies the manner in which a common practice was appropriated and reconstituted as a singular element in the rebel profile. Tattooing was taken out of its cultural context and bound to a particular temporal, special, and legal reality that was informed by ideas of rebellion and revolt. Specifically, the Galon, a symbol that had a long and varied tradition in Southeast Asia, was soon confined through the legal process to represent the very concept of rebellion in Burma. In sum, it seems that Burmese culture was on trial as much as Saya San. For the entire case rested on evidence and arguments that implied that the very seeds for rebellion, the very root of the unrest, and the periodic terrorism that characterized the early 1930s could be located within the traditions, values, and history of the Burmese.

From this vantage point, the trial of Saya San might even be seen as a site for the production of knowledge, as Burmese culture was codified, materialized, and standardized in the archive of the court.[53] The special procedures, allowances, and flexibility afforded to the prosecution by the Tribunal point to a legal system that enabled knowledge about the rebellion to be carefully accumulated, sanitized, and controlled. Following Nordholt's findings in Dutch Indonesia, the language of law and the methodology of litigation managed the various facets of Burmese culture that were brought under court examination, which smoothed over their meanings to correspond to the accepted version of events.[54] Special Rebellion Tribunal judges determined what would be admitted into the evidential record, effectively deciding what would and especially what would not become the basis for subsequent reports that would eventually end up as "historical" documents in the archives. The narrative about the Saya San Rebellion could not have been shaped in any other way than as it arrived, considering the theater and script in which it was constructed. In essence, the trial was as much an expression of counter-insurgency policy as it was a site for producing counter-insurgency knowledge. The very process of creating the narrative demonstrated the capabilities and continued relevance of the Rangoon administration in Burma to New Delhi superiors (who openly questioned counter-insurgency policies), as well as to those overseeing events from London. The administration's ability to translate, dictate, and narrate the story of Saya San to the Home Office was a measure of its legitimacy within the Empire as much as it was a statement about legitimacy in Burma.

As sociolegal scholarship has shown, principles of *stare decisis* and the interpretation of the present is often governed by the law's relationship with the past, especially if cases are deemed by judges to be similar in context.[55] This was precisely the basis of interpretation adopted by administrators and judges who were charged with adjudicating the Rebellion in that the "facts" of the case were deemed relevant to the notion of Burmese resistance since they appeared to have precedence in the form of similar uprisings that occurred in the past. Yet these "facts" that were linked to the accepted character of Burmese kingship were recognized and made as such only through the prescriptive rhetoric of the prosecution's charges and the validating authority of the Tribunal. Furthermore, examples drawn from the past that were used as a basis for showing precedence had only emerged from an image of Burmese culture that was itself constituted within the context of pacification. Associating Saya San as a pretender-king was part and parcel of an enduring colonial ethnology that cast Burmese peasants as historically immobile while it also reflected a particular legal context that drew upon this interpretive strategy to serve specific counter-insurgency purposes. These connections reflect an interpretive community in the writing and documenting of Burmese rebellion as district officers, police, lawyers, and judges wrote, read, and delineated Burma in a familiar administrative and judicial "language"; aware that future readers would most likely share the same concerns, experiences, and requirements of the authors.

Counter-insurgency law not only formulated and regulated the terms through which Burmese rebellion was defined by the administrative community, but it also served to delineate and demarcate the boundaries of the Burmese community in relation to British colonialism. Peasants who took part in the rebellion were deemed as unable to comprehend or take part in the technologies of development and progress that were being initiated by the colonial state. Thus, during the trial of Saya San, government lawyers presented a particular reading of the Burmese past as they made their case about the Burmese present. The law's involvement in the writing of this history was one of dictation, dispute management, and preservation; it selected and shaped key elements from the more general positions articulated in early ethnographic documents while reconstituting them to fit the narrative being associated with Saya San. Not only was dispute management figuratively represented in reestablishing normalcy in the countryside, it was also illustrative in the trial, and in the attempt to portray textually, a particular way of speaking and thinking about the Rebellion.[56] As a result, another layer of documentation emerged, obfuscating earlier versions and validating others for future archival sources that would eventually be relied upon by subsequent historians of the Rebellion. Colonial knowledge was produced through several stages, involving different writers and readers; but in this case, it was consistently appropriating the interpretive strategies of past authors. In doing so, colonial law condensed the more generalized assertions predicted in Carey's Rebellion Ethnology into the more narrow narrative associated with Saya San, which would become its own template upon which further interpretations of Southeast Asian rebellions would rest. This transformation of colonial ethnographic knowledge was produced in the series of trials and appeal hearings of Saya San, that reared records which would be used in the formation of the seminal blue-book report, *The Origins and Causes of the Burma Rebellion (1930–1932)*.

Notes

1. Michael Adas (1979), Oliver B. Pollack, Patricia Herbert (1982), and Kenji Ino (1987), represent the few scholars who have made reference to the trials that were conducted between the years 1931 and 1933.

2. Documents clearly demonstrate that until his capture, Rangoon officials knew "nothing definite" about the man called Saya San, who apparently had several names. See Government of Burma, L/PJ/6/2022, Burma Rebellion General Files (BRGF), Judgment, August 28, 1931, and L/PJ/6/2022, BRGF, copy of letter no.4265C31, August 12; Government of Bengal to the Government of India for Saya San's numerous aliases.

3. Government of Burma, L/PJ/6/2022, BRGF, criminal appeal no. 1121 of 1931, September 29, 1931, Nga San Sa (a) *Saya San v. King Emperor*, Special Tribunal Case no. 5, August 28, 1931 (hereafter Criminal Appeal no. 1121).

4. Government of Burma, L/PJ/6/2022, BRGF, Special Tribunal Case

no. 4, Alantaung Case, *King-Emperor v. Saya San and Others,* August, 28, 1931.

5. Government of Burma, L/PJ/6/2022, BRGF, Criminal Appeal no. 1121.

6. Government of Burma, L/PJ/6/2022, BRGF, Special Rebellion Trial Judgments nos. 1–4.

7. Government of Burma, L/PJ/6/2022, Criminal Appeal no. 1121.

8. The tribunal consisted of J. R. Cunliffe (president), A. J. Darwood (member), and Ba U (member). L/PJ/6/2022, BRGF, judgment, August 28, 1931. The appellate judge was Maung Ba and the judgment order was reviewed by J. M. Baguley, both processed on September 29, 1931.

9. These proceedings (if still in existence) have never been consulted by scholars though they are referred to in the official blue-book report *Origins and Causes of the Burma Rebellion, 1930–1932.*

10. Government of Burma, See L/PJ/6/2022, BRGF, judgment, August 28, 1931; L/PJ/6/2022, BRGF, appeal, September 29, 1931; and L/PJ/6/2022, BRGF, judgment order, September 29, 1931.

11. The documents refer to a written statement that Saya San presented in court, which was unfortunately excluded from the final record but apparently disclosed that the organization of villagers into his so-called Garuda Associations (Galon Wunthanu Athin) were for peaceful, nonviolent, demonstrations against tax collection, not for rebellion as the prosecution alleged. See L/PJ/6/2022, BRGF, judgment, August, 28, 1931.

12. Austin Sarat and Thomas R. Kearns, "Editorial Introduction," in Sarat and Kearns (eds.), *The Rhetoric of Law* (Ann Arbor: University of Michigan Press, 1996), pp. 2–3.

13. Sarat and Kearns, p. 5.

14. Austin Sarat and Thomas R. Kearns, "Writing History and Registering Memory in Legal Decisions and Legal Practices: An Introduction," in Sarat and Kearns (eds.), *History, Memory, and the Law* (Ann Arbor: University of Michigan Press, 1999), p. 2.

15. Vicente L. Rafael, *Contracting Colonialism: Translation and Christian Conversion in Tagalog Society Under Early Spanish Rule* (Durham: Duke University Press, 2003 [3rd edition]); Johannes Fabian, *Language and Colonial Power* (Berkeley: University of California Press, 1986); Austin Sarat and Thomas R. Kearns, *The Rhetoric of Law* (Ann Arbor: University of Michigan Press, 1996).

16. The decisions of the Tribunal not only set a precedence for "future audiences," (Sarat and Kearns, 1999) but for future historians as well,

since the available sources would consist only of the evidentiary record that the judges accepted and included in their summaries.

17. Austin Sarat and Thomas R. Kearns, "Writing History and Registering Memory in Legal Decisions and Legal Practices: An Introduction," in Austin Sarat and Thomas R. Kearns (eds.) *History, Memory, and the Law* (Ann Arbor: University of Michigan Press, 1999), pp. 1–24.

18. Government of Burma, L/PJ/6/2022, BRGF, Judgment, August 28, 1931. Saya San was formally charged with rebellion and abetment of rebellion under Section 121 of the Indian Penal Code.

19. The *athin* or association movement spread from the cities into the countryside, signaling a growing trend of political integration using new forms of organization and communication. The *wunthanu athin* movement was one of several formed to provide villagers with the means to articulate their concerns while linking them up with urban religious and political groups. See Patricia Herbert, "The Hsaya San Rebellion (1930–1932) Reappraised," working papers no. 27, Monash University, Center for Southeast Asian Studies, 1982.

20. As cited in Government of Burma, L/PJ/6/2020, BRGF, Ralph Clarence Morris, "Origins and Causes of the Burma Rebellion, 1930–1932," March 2, 1934. However in Government of Burma, L/PJ/6/2022, BRGF, Judgment Order, September 29, 1931, the earliest evidence of conspiracy is a letter dated November, 6.1929.

21. Government of Burma, L/PJ/6/2022, BRGF, Criminal Appeal no.1121 of 1931, Judgment Order, September 9, 1931.

22. Government of Burma, L/PJ/6/2020 BRGF, "Report of the Enquiry Committee (GCBA)," September 3, 1928, as found in "Origins and Causes of the Burma Rebellion, 1930–1932," March 1931, p. 7.

23. Government of Burma, L/PJ/6/2022, BRGF, J. M. Baguley, Judgment Order, September 29, 1931.

24. Government of Burma, L/PJ/6/2022, BRGF, Criminal Appeal no. 1121 of 1931, Judgment Order, October, 11, 1931.

25. Government of Burma, L/PJ/6/2022, BRGF, Judgment Summary, Special Tribunal Case no. 5, *King Emperor v. Saya San*, August, 28, 1931, [dated] September, 29, 1931.

26. Government of Burma, L/PJ/6/2022, BRGF, Judgment Order, Criminal Appeal no. 1121 of 1931, Special Tribunal Case no. 5, October, 11, 1931.

27. Government of Burma, L/PJ/6/2022, BRGF.

28. Ibid.

29. Yet if one looks at the original document, the text also includes the

term *Thammada,* which can mean "president." It is interesting that the official report, after having referred to this piece of evidence, excludes the term in its text. See also Patricia Herbert's comments regarding Saya San's use of this term in her inspirational study, "The Hsaya San Rebellion (1930–1932): Reappraised" (Centre of Southeast Asian Studies, working papers no. 27; Melbourne: Monash University, 1982).

30. Crown service members, soldiers, religious bondsmen, craftsmen, and even those monks who failed their exams, were said to receive a special tattoo during the Konbaung period. See Michael Aung-Thwin, *Pagan: Origins of Modern Burma* (Honolulu: University of Hawaii Press, 1985), p.90, and Than Tun's translation of the *Royal Orders of Burma,* vol. 5.

31. There are some references to the Galon (Garuda)–Naga symbol in Southeast Asian Buddhist literature, especially in reference to the legend of the Buddhist Saint Upago (Upagupta). See John Strong, *The Legend of Upagupta: Sanskrit Buddhism in Northern India and Southeast Asia* (Princeton: Princeton University Press, 1992), pp. 183, 187–89, 191, 204.

32. Government of Burma, L/PJ/6/2020, BRGF, *Origins and Causes of the Burma Rebellion (1930–1932),* p. 3.

33. Ba U, *My Burma: The Autobiography of a President* (New York: Taplinger Publishing, 1958), pp. 110–11.

34. This is despite the fact that the formation of village organizations *(wunthanu athins)* were a legal and highly effective way that urban- and rural-nationalist groups were able to communicate with each other. Through the colonial government's counter-insurgency program, many such village associations were censured and shut down.

35. Government of Burma, L/PJ/6/2020, BRGF, *Origins and Causes of the Burma Rebellion (1930–1932),* p. 3.

36. Italics are my emphasis. Government of Burma, L/PJ/6/2022, BRGF, Judgment Order, Criminal Appeal no. 1121 of 1931, Special Tribunal Case no. 5, October, 11, 1931.

37. Government of Burma, L/PJ/6/2020, BRGF, frames 22–44, *Origins and Causes of the Burma Rebellion (1930–1932),* March 1931, p.3.

38. Government of Burma, L/PJ/6/2022, BRF, frames 670–71, J. M. Baguley, Judgment Order, September, 29, 1931.

39. Ibid.

40. Maurice Collis's description of the coronation ceremony in his Trials in Burma (1938) should not be considered seriously as a primary source for that event (as some scholars have done) since the author reveals that he examined "a court judgment" as a basis for his description.

41. Government of Burma, L/PJ/6/2022, BRGF, October, 11, 1931.
42. Government of Burma, L/PJ/6/2022, BRGF, frame 681. Judgment Order, Appeal no. 1121 of 1931, October 11, 1931.
43. Consider, for those familiar with the writing of Burmese, how the proper method of *walone* is supposed to be written. See John Okell's introduction to the Script, volume 3 (Dekalb: Center for Southeast Asian Studies Publications, Northern Illinois University).
44. Government of Burma L/PJ/6/2022, BRGF, Judgment Order, Appeal no. 1121, October, 11, 1931.
45. Ibid.
46. Government of Burma, L/PJ/6/2022, BRGF, Judgment Order, Criminal Appeal no. 1121 of 1931, Special Tribunal Case, no. 5, October, 11, 1931.
47. Government of Burma, L/PJ/6/2022, BRF, Frame 659, Appeal no. 1121 of 1931, Special Case no. 5, September 29, 1931.
48. Government of Burma, L/PJ/2022, BRGF, judgment summary.
49. Scholars, including the author, have only had access to Burmese-language copies of the diary (found in journals and newspapers) or translated versions found in British documents. Extracts of the diary were released by the colonial police and Criminal Investigation Department to local newspapers.
50. Henk Schulte Nordholt in Peter Pels and Oscar Salemink (eds.), *Colonial Subjects: Essays on the Practical History of Anthropology* (Ann Arbor: University of Michigan Press, 1999) suggests that much of traditional Bali was invented by colonial administrators eager "to find" Old Java in Southern Bali and projected many characteristics, such as imagined Hindu–Javanese legal principles, into Balinese society.
51. Patricia Herbert shows that the *wunthanu athins*, the nationalist village associations that were being used as an alternate conduit to the political network established by the British, were a qualitative break from the *minlaung*-inspired uprisings in the late nineteenth and early twentieth centuries, in that the imagery tactics and messages they employed were not derived from pre-annexation traditions.
52. Government of Burma, L/PJ/6/2021, secret telegram, G/I, H/D, to S/SI, repeating telegram from G/B, May 16, 1931.
53. Courts have been considered as archives in that their records serve "as the materialization of memory" (Sarat and Kearn, 1999).
54. Law was used in Dutch Colonial Indonesia to interpret and construct culture as well. The "adat law approach" used juridical concepts to record and redefine local customs and institutions. Henk Schulte

Nordholt (in Pales and Salemink, 1999) suggests that the legalist approach, which stressed formal rules and institutions, directed the focus of research as well as informed interpretations of change and continuity.

55. Austin Sarat and Thomas K. Kearns (eds.), "Writing History and Registering Memory in Legal Decisions and Legal Practices: An Introduction," in *History, Memory and the Law* (Ann Arbor: University of Michigan Press, 1999).

56. Austin Sarat and Thomas R. Kearns, editorial introduction, in Sarat and Kearns (eds.) *The Rhetoric of Law*, (Ann Arbor: University of Michigan Press, 1996), p. 9.

Chapter 5

CODIFYING REBELLION
Origins of a Resistance Narrative

The sentencing and execution of Saya San in November 1931 did not mark the end of the Rebellion for the colonial administration as new outbreaks continued to emerge in districts throughout Upper Burma and the Shan States. As a result, legislative powers were extended and subsequent Special Tribunals would oversee the trials of hundreds of suspected rebels, building upon the findings made by the original tribunal and the Rebellion Ethnology upon which it (and the narratives it produced) were based. These trials, conducted between the years 1932 and 1933 not only connected the stories of resistance to those that were produced at the onset of the outbreaks, but they consolidated the strategies, rules, and paradigms employed by earlier counter-insurgency officials into a roughly hewn, but recognizable discourse. They recorded the activities of other rebels while emphasizing the criminalized nature of Burmese culture that had been deemed readable through the prism of rebellion. Narratives that were potentially disparate, contradicting, or contextually at odds with Saya San's were fused with elements from his story through the prescriptive authority of the courts. What had been originally conceived of as a "local" disturbance in 1930 was by 1932 being designated "the Burma Rebellion," reflecting the manner in which counter-insurgency policies and tactics delineated the epistemological field of "Burma." Administratively, this shift in how the rebellion was being viewed was expressed more comprehensively through reports that merged district accounts

Saya San exiting Tharrawaddy Jail

into single documents that charted the Rebellion over specific periods of time. Distinctive patterns among the various outbreaks were delineated by projecting the *minlaung* profile and other characteristics of the Rebellion Ethnology into districts such as Thayetmyo, where a rebel leader was even designated as another "Saya San."[1] Tattooing, rituals of allegiance, and the distribution of charms and amulets were identified as key elements signaling not only the unified nature of the Rebellion, but the common cultural worldview that was seemingly shared among rural communities.

By 1933, the Rebellion was being classified as having reverted to "dacoity," suggesting that the main impulses for organized resistance had dissipated and that the responses to the outbreaks had been largely successful. If in its earliest inception the goal of the rebellion was aimed at overthrowing the government, it was now deemed less organized and unwilling to engage security forces directly.[2] Now only random acts of banditry, theft, and other acts of civil disobedience characterized the situation—perhaps the reflection of a growing military presence on the one hand or a lack of a cohesive strategy on the part of rural cultivators on the other. At the same time, declaring the end of the Rebellion also enabled the Burma government to announce to both local and external audiences that its counter-insurgency measures were largely successful and that the province was once again under administrative control. Satisfying enquiries from colonial offices in London and New Delhi were a priority as affairs of the Empire regularly drew attention from policy makers in Parliament, who were concerned over the manner in which business in the colonies would be perceived by the domestic electorate. In fact, it was from a series of questions stemming from Parliament over the continued detention of sentenced rebels and debate over the economic or political origins of the Rebellion that contributed to the production and release of one of the most frequently cited sources in the historical record.[3]

The Origins and Causes of the Burma Rebellion (1930–1932)

The official blue-book report *The Origins and Causes of the Burma Rebellion (1930–32)* was published to establish the Crown's counter-insurgency expenditure, the causal factors of the Rebellion, and the manner in which detainees were managed throughout the course of the outbreaks. The report was hardly easy reading: one official described it as "an ill-digested mass of extracts from the judgments in the various trials" whereas another thought that it was such a "dull and uninspiring production" that it was not worth even "placing copies in the Library of the House."[4] Yet, the document served as the final statement by Rangoon officials on what they saw as the foundations of the Rebellion, as certain critics within and without Burma attributed the unrest in rural areas to a failure in economic policies, a potentially damaging indictment of the colonial administration.[5] The report represented the view that the Rebellion was political in nature, the result of urban-nationalist activities in rural areas combined with the misguided aspirations of delusional peasant activists. The forty-four-page report was divided into thirty-nine sections, organized according to the structure, order, and findings of the Special Rebellion Tribunal's sessions. Moving away from district-oriented narratives that characterized earlier reports, the blue-book was conceptually a product of counter-insurgency law, deemphasizing the varied and often tenuous links among the outbreaks into a single, explainable account of the Rebellion. Passages and sections from judicial summaries of the trials were directly inserted as the text of the report, highlighting the continuities between the narrative content of the trials and the content of subsequent official documentation. At one level, the report functioned to codify the positions established in the courts about the nature of the Rebellion, reproducing the ethnographic categories, interpretive strategies, and legal findings through the authority invested in its blue-book status. Examples of modern, socially acceptable, and legal forms of political mobilization were cast within a traditionalist garb, suggesting that these tools of reform were not only irreconcilable with the worldviews of rural cultivators, but that these organizations were actually being employed for treasonous ends. In this way, the document was very much immersed within the politics arising between and within the metropole and the colony; it was directed toward superiors in the Indian administration as well as towards those in Parliament who continued to raise questions about the affairs of the Burma government and its management of the Rebellion.

From another level, the report reified the view that the Rebellion was a unified, cohesive movement by fusing judicial findings into a single narrative, reinforcing the connectedness of the Rebellion through the textual structure and chronological sequencing of the report. Although outbreaks occurred in various districts, at different times (and often through different means), the narrative structure and content of the report presented the picture of a single Rebellion by reasserting the uniformity of its ethnographic character. The report was considered to be authoritative, grounded in evidence, and anchored to the legitimacy associated with the legal process. As one official described it, "the account has been confined to facts found by the Courts and consists of direct quotations from judicial records."[6]

As a result, Bertram Carey's *minlaung* model of Burmese kingship and resistance became officially sanctioned as the overarching cause of the Rebellion, successfully projecting a vision of Burmese resistance that emerged during the pacification years of the 1880s and 1890s into the historical context of the 1930s. By doing so, the report implied that little had changed in Burma in regard to political expression; rural Burmese were unable to participate in the forms of modern governance that had been introduced by colonial authorities. Farmers and other village communities were presented as only being capable of participating in violent resistance movements, dacoity, and other forms of disobedience, ignoring the opportunities of reform that were available to and being adopted by urban-based elites. In addition, the report split the political landscape of British Burma into two separate fields by presenting the Rebellion as a lingering example of culturally determined, impenetrable peasant traditionalism that prevented rural communities (and the majority of the population) from maturing politically like their urban counterparts. More importantly, this assessment contributed to the debate over whether Burma should be separated from India, where nationalist parties were expecting wide-ranging reforms and political liberalization. With the majority of the rural population being cast as incapable of comprehending political reform, the case for separating Burma from India would appear stronger. Thus, the report allowed the Rebellion to be presented and regarded by the government as a continuing manifestation of deeply rooted Burmese cultural constraints inhibiting the development and acceptance of modern political forms. It was the very nature of the Burmese psyche and nostalgia for the monarchy that rendered peasants unable to comprehend and to participate in the colonial system.

Yet, immersed within this ethnographic statement about the political stagnation of rural Burmese, lay a far more critical contention—that the growth, spread, and influence of village associations, the very example of urban political models said to be lacking in the countryside was, in fact, nothing more than a front for the organization of the Rebellion and its traditionalist visions. *The Origins and Causes of the Burma Rebellion (1930–1932)* (OCBR) was more than a statement explaining the series of uprisings within the context of Burmese kingship; it was a clear attempt to represent examples of novel rural political organization as elements anchored within the Rebellion Ethnology. The growth of the *wuthanus athins* throughout rural Burma were characterized and explained within the context of the *minlaung* model, regarded as a strategic network of terrorist cells intent on restoring the monarchy and overthrowing the government rather than as an example of mass mobilization. In short, the report misrepresented the ability of rural political leaders to adopt and apply new forms of political organization to fit the needs of the countryside. Instead, local associations were cast as terrorist sleeper cells, consisting of gullible Burmese peasants awaiting the return of their king.

The Politics of Rebellion

The report wasted little time in establishing the tone and direction of its brief. It stated categorically that it sought to correct the mistaken opinion that the Rebellion was caused primarily by economic factors, such as the fall in paddy prices that might have had a direct effect on the lives of rural cultivators.[7] Although "economic stress" may have "aggravated" the situation, the report argues that the Rebellion was "almost entirely political in origin" and it was from this point of view that the writer of the report hoped to present the narrative of events.[8] In outlining the general causes of the Rebellion, the opening section referred to one of the earliest documents produced by the colonial government, *Causes of the Tharrawaddy Rebellion* (March 1931), extending what originally had been an assessment of that particular district to the entire province.[9] This report stated that the main causes of the Tharrawaddy Rebellion were:

(1) a deep-laid conspiracy against the government organized by Saya San with the aid of *wunthanu athin* leaders and members; both *pongyis* and laymen, and secretly countenanced by the GCBA (Soe Thein), and GCSS leaders
(2) the GCBA-volunteer movement under the guise of which the *galon athins* were formed by Saya San
(3) the hereditary disposition of the Tharrawaddy people to violence, lawlessness, and contempt of authority
(4) the rooted antipathy to pay taxes, which has been a marked feature of Tharrawaddy District for some years past

(5) the continual fostering of the spirit of lawlessness and sedition by leaders of the GCBA and GCSS like U Oktama, the stormy petrel of Burmese politics, and

(6) the ignorance, gullibility, and superstition of a people, which make them easy prey of plausible impostors like Saya San with his *galons*, tattooing, medicines, and charms to render them invulnerable

Drawing from this early report established an important sense of intertextuality among the many colonial documents that were issued by the government while providing a sense of historical continuity with the events that were associated primarily with Saya San. By referring to earlier published reports and communiqués, *OCBR* established its precedence (both in a legal and historical context) while tautologically affirming those very documents and positions it relied on. In other words, making reference to events in Tharrawaddy made the claim that the findings established in March 1931 were essentially applicable to the assessment being made in 1934, and that despite the growth and variances that emerged since the first outbreak of violence, this report could confidently establish its salient features, define its contours, and translate its exotic meanings. Referencing the earlier report established its authority as a text and provided an important sense of coherency and continuity. Linking the two reports also implied that there existed an identifiable "origin" to the entire Rebellion; that it was in Tharrawaddy and through Saya San's involvement in the *wunthanu athin* movement that the uprising was first conceptualized, germinated, and hatched. If *Causes of the Tharrawaddy Rebellion* could be viewed as the first chapter of the official story, then *The Origins and Causes of the Burma Rebellion (1930–1932)* could serve as its conclusion.

Three of the six points also made reference to political organizations that had begun to play an important role in the politics of the province since the 1920s. The General Council of Burmese Associations and the GCSS (representing the interests of an increasingly politicized religious sector) had emerged as major players in state affairs and were regarded as part of a growing nationalist movement. Within these two organizations, English-educated, Burmese civil servants and so-called politicized monks aligned themselves to various individuals, parties, and interests—many of them directly and indirectly linked to the concerns and influences of these two organizations. Some branches were committed to reform through existing channels but others, like those following the outspoken Soe Thein, were more radical in the government view and would not be unlikely to stir trouble in rural areas. Making reference to these groups in the report placed these urban-nationalist groups directly under the scrutiny of counter-insurgency officials and within the parameters of the Rebellion narrative. Thus, the Rebellion was being regarded as a product of these nationalist groups, enabling the government to criminalize their activities, curb their influence in rural areas, and check the movement of their leaders.

Yet, the other three points referred to "causes" that were considered an inherent part of Burmese cultural sensibilities, elements that were part of the Rebellion Ethnology. As a result, the report made two claims: on the one hand, the rebellion was a product of urban nationalists; but on the other it was historically inevitable due to the hereditary disposition of Burmese villagers to be swayed by magic, superstition, and the charisma of manipulative leaders. In essence, rural communities were being made to be apolitical—incapable of articulating political reform through accepted channels and forms. Furthermore, it was urban nationalists who played on these well-known mentalities of village cultivators, pointing to the strictly political nature of the Rebellion. Although the report would actually attempt to conflate the two explanations through its discussion of the *wunthanu athins*, the legacy of this binary framework would directly influence the manner in which scholars would engage the history of the rebellion.

Wunthanu Athins

Since the 1920s, reformists identified the importance of bridging the gap between village communities and their urban counterparts, resulting in a wide variety of organizations designed to articulate rural concerns. The implementation of the dyarchy legislative council in 1923 created the demand for political parties, platforms, and a means to connect with the public.[10] Some of the key organizations, clearly drew inspiration from external sources such as the Young Men's Buddhist Association (YMBA) and its eventual successor, the General Council of Burmese Associations. The majority of members of the YMBA were part of a growing number of intellectual elites that were among the first to be educated in tertiary institutions like Judson College. For these young graduates, the question of reform was often conceptualized along and through those limited avenues allowed by the colonial administration. Exposed to ideas of nationalism, Communism, and other ideologies conceptualizing social change, political issues were articulated through what were identified as "Buddhist terms" in an attempt to construct a loose notion of affinity linking all Burmese.

Unlike the earlier generation of elites who sought to work within the system, a new generation of reformers emerged in the political scene between early 1920 and 1936 that sought to reject the colonial state and its administrative order. These political parties were more successful in penetrating the countryside and securing at least nominal ties with a wide range of village leaders and activists. While politics at the top were often divisive, the particular differences over ideology, patronage, and the role of the political monks did not always filter into the countryside. The challenge for many of these reform-minded activists was determining how to articulate their programs to a populace that had a limited exposure to the formal vocabularies and ideas associated with the colonial administration. Reform and its goals could be expressed through symbols and media that were culturally recognizable.[11]

With the formation of secular political organizations like the GCBA and the monk-led GCSS, the political landscape was becoming more sophisticated and complicated as new forms of political organization became increasingly available to reform-minded elites. Significantly, monks became more politically active and interested in issues once dominated only by elites within the civil service and the growing number of university-trained students. Monks such as U Oktama and U Wisara were able to employ Buddhism as a language through which secular issues could be engaged, while providing a means of articulating the problems and challenges of reform to rural communities not familiar with the terms and concepts used by the colonial administration. In order to create more effective means of communicating with rural populations, the GCSS trained and appointed groups of political monks to act as advisers in village-based, nationalist organizations, *wunthanu athin*. The success of these organizations politicized the countryside very effectively, though in many cases did not succeed in unifying it. Yet, it was through these associations that anticolonial sentiment, nationalism, and the decline of Buddhism became a recognizable platform for villagers. The movement of monks within the countryside attracted the attention of colonial administrators, especially those that were clearly connected to nationalist activities. Thus, it was perhaps unsurprising that counter-insurgency policies were aimed to curb the influence and spread of the *wunthanu athins* by tracking and limiting the movement of "political *pongyis*." The manner in which this was accomplished deserves a closer look. For the report connected these village associations with rebellion and cast urban activists in the countryside as "wandering" medicine men, quacks, and opportunists. In fact, although Saya San was recognized as formerly a member of the GCBA and member of an investigative committee into village concerns, his agenda (which included protecting villagers from abuse, the communal use of forestry products, and the Separation Issue), was reduced to a mad obsession to resurrect the monarchy. In short, the Rebellion Ethnology provided the means to control how the political landscape in rural Burma was perceived.

Coherence

The use of judicial records to anchor the report under the legal authority of the Tribunal allowed its compilers to emphasize the traditional character of the rebellion and the peasant worldview it was said to represent. At the same time, the quotations from the proceedings that were selected for the report highlighted the alleged connection between the spread of the *wunthanu athins* and the Rebellion. Familiar sections of Saya San's story were presented not only to remind readers of his *minlaung* profile, but to show how this narrative of kingship could both translate and incriminate the activities of the *athins*. These village associations were not only a front for rebellion activities, but they were considered to be superficial structures that masked more enduring, traditionalist tendencies on the part of Saya San and his followers. Key features of the Rebellion Ethnology that made Burmese kingship, royal proclamation, spirit performances, *gaing* rituals, and tattooing the essential terms of rural resistance were presented in the report as also being inherently connected to the recruitment, organization, and spread of these village groups. Furthermore, the presence of this emerging network throughout the countryside was made to be a coherent arm of urban-nationalist organizations, suggesting that the rebellion was not only unified, but that it was directly tied to more radical wings of the GCBA. In effect, the report sought to establish that the *wunthanu athins* were no less than terrorist cells that played on peasant nostalgia for the monarchy and perverted acceptable forms of mobilization techniques for political ends.

In summarizing the first four trials that preceded Saya San's under the Special Rebellion Tribunal, the report made several references to the manner in which "the rebels made use of the wunthanus athins in making their preparations to fight against the Government."[12] In the trial of Aung Hla (Dedaye Case, trial no.1), the appellate judgment asserted that the sixty-year-old village elder had portrayed himself as a king to the villagers, but beneath this guise he was also the president of a local circle of *athins*, part of the thirty local associations in the area that were connected to "the Central" *athin* in Rangoon."[13] In the second case tried by the Special Tribunal, the central figure Saya Sa was identified as "the President of Shwenakwin Wunthanu Athin" who had held meetings to discuss the question of taxes, the collection of arms, and retaliatory measures for those in the village who did not join the local chapter of the village association. Saya Sa's role as a key figure in the Rebellion leadership was connected to one U Han Tha, whose place in the Rebellion and in the *wunthanu* network was established in the third trial. Throughout the early pages of the report, passages linking the *wunthanu* activities to the ethnography of the Rebellion, made reference to the distribution of amulets and charms or to the taking of oath-water that bound members of these cells to each other and the resistance movement.[14] But perhaps most significant to this rendering was how tattooing and specifically the Galon symbol was used to associate the *minlaung* component of the Rebellion Ethnology to the function and character of the *wunthanus athins*. The attempt to connect Burmese kingship as the central component explaining the identity of these village associations would have the effect of directing the manner in which the Saya San Rebellion would be interpreted in the decades to come.

While tattooing was established quite early in the rebellion as a significant feature of the Rebellion profile, the discourses connecting tattooing activities and particular symbols with the *wuthanu athins* did not come to full form until the publishing of *The Origins and Causes of the Burma Rebellion (1930–1932)*. Tattooing did several things in building the case against the village associations. On the one hand, it linked a popular form of ritual adornment and healing to the political aspirations of urban nationalists. As discussed, bearing a tattoo was imagined to not only signal one's possible involvement in the Rebellion (in its power to confer invulnerability), but it was thought to also mark one's allegiance and rank in particular village associations.[15] Of particular significance was the Galon tattoo, which was a symbol of considerable attention in the trial of Saya San. Not only was this symbol claimed to acknowledge Saya San's royal persona as "the Galon King," but it was the name adopted by the very *wunthanu athins* that were operating in the districts most affected by the Rebellion. If government advocates were correct in interpreting the tattoo's implied meaning (that the Burmese would defeat the British just as the Galon will defeat the Naga), then the symbol chosen for Saya San's *wunthanu athins* revealed an underlying mission. Several documents and judicial exhibits were highlighted from the trials that recounted the establishment of a GCBA-endorsed organization called the Sandati Galon Organization and evidence claiming that Saya San was calling himself "*Thupannaka Galuna Raja*" or "King of the Galons."[16] Although there was apparently some debate as to what the term *Thupannaka* actually meant, the Tribunal established its definition and judged that Saya San was responsible for the founding of the Galon Athins, that he imagined himself king, and that the symbol was deliberately chosen for the village associations—for the meaning of the Galon and its representation as a tattoo disclosed the very intentions of the Burmese to overthrow the government.[17] By presenting carefully chosen extracts from the trials, the report functioned to smooth over discrepancies in the legal record and provide a consolidated view of how urban-based forms of political organization were informed by culturally stagnant images of monarchy and its enduring place in Burmese society.

Beyond linking the idea of Burmese kingship to the spread of village associations and the eventual outbreak of rebellion, the use of tattooing as a category in this counter-insurgency discourse also functioned to present an image of a single, coherent Rebellion. The report reconfirmed that tattooing activities signaled attempts to recruit and conscript villagers into the uprising, whether they believed in the efficacy of the symbols or not. Common symbols such as the Galon, letters of the Burmese script, animals, and *nats* were interpreted to denote the interconnectedness among various rebel groups.[18] Wandering ex-monks, a standard component in Saya San's profile, were said to be crucial agents in the preparation for rebellion. Unlike their more orthodox and "authentic" brethren in the monasteries, these characters donned the robes in order to appeal to village sensibilities, and were manipulating this reverence for Buddhist monks in order to recruit potential rebels. The alleged movement of Saya San during the Rebellion was a key factor in establishing his singular influence in subsequent outbreaks; for his elusiveness in the early months of 1931 were attributed to his ability to disguise himself as a monk in order to conduct meetings with other potential rebels.[19] For example, in describing the spread of outbreaks in the Shan States, the account stated that an *athin* was formed by a Burman *pongyi* who distributed needles, swore in recruits using *thitsaye* (oath-water), and promised formal tattooing to follow. This *pongyi* was also reported to be practicing alchemy, and pretending to have powers that rendered him invulnerable to harm.[20] Another account in the Southern Shan States reported that a *pongyi* claiming to have supernatural powers and medicine to cure all types of diseases was not only inserting needles in the people, but that he had established a camp named Aungchanthamyo, planned to host a "victory festival," and that he ascended a throne and proclaimed himself "king."[21] It did not matter whether these monks were identified as Saya San or his lieutenants, for the point of these reports was to establish that a clear pattern existed when it came to recruiting, and that a system of symbols denoting resistance could be identified as signaling an impending revolt.

Following the section discussing Saya San, the *OCBR* turned to passages drawn from other trials of detained rebels, connecting their narratives to his by reinforcing the idea that the formation of *athins* was intrinsically connected to the type of tattooing, needle distribution, and the use of oath-water that he established as central to the recruitment process. In doing so, the report codified these practices as categories denoting Burmese rebellion, removing them from the myriad cultural contexts and fixing them within the particular narrative associated with Saya San. Yet the spread of the rebellion could not be attributed to the movement of Saya San alone, as many of these characteristics were not just being applied to him, but to the whole of rural Burmese village society.[22]

From this point of view, the report itself could be seen as a textualized rendering of the Rebellion, structured chronologically to cover the movement from its inception to its spreading to other districts, represented in the different numerical sections structuring the document. The concern in the report with coherency and ordering is demonstrated in its attempt to structure the narrative in as linear a fashion as possible, beginning with the inherent nature of Burmese to rebel as the original source of the problem, citing the findings of Carey's guidebook as precedence. Cultural and historical factors support this origin, refining and entrenching the Rebellion Ethnology as the underlying source of the events called "the Burma Rebellion." As such, Saya San is presented as a product of Burmese culture and a fulfillment of the expectation that the monarchy would one day return. Other rebel leaders not only followed his lead, but were bound to use the same vocabulary of resistance, despite the available organizational strategies found in the *wunthanu* framework. Each instance of rebellion, represented by a section number and a corresponding passage from judicial summaries, was nonetheless bound to structure and character of the original outbreak in Tharrawaddy, fusing them into a single narrative. To the compilers of the document, the Rebellion was not just a series of spontaneous uprisings occurring throughout the province, but a series of interconnected outbreaks that were linked by a culture of resistance and political-organization structure that could be harnessed, contained, and translated for the paper. The *OCBR*'s reliance on judicial findings and the judgment summaries of the Special Tribunal attest to the authority and legitimacy placed on counter-insurgency law, which contributed to the process of translating and ordering of Burmese resistance culture into an easily accessible form.

Incoherence

In presenting a consolidated view of the Rebellion that fused district to district, merged one rebel group to another, and conflated nostalgia for the monarchy with the ability to articulate political reform, the report also effaced striking instances of variance, tension, and competition among various rural activists. Even as government officials actively promoted Saya San as the instigator of Rebellion, other accused leaders were also reported to have donned the image of king, evoking the symbols of the throne, and promising followers a restoration of the precolonial order.[23] In a trial preceding Saya San's, Aung Hla, a sixty-year old president of a local *wunthanu athin* in the Dedaye Township, was said to have declared himself "King" and his sons "Crown Princes." Officials even stated that he and his family were "protagonists in the rebellion" and that "there can be no doubt that he (Aung Hla) was regarded as the head of the movement."[24] By the time Saya San's trial commenced and the records of his trials were made available for reports such as the *OCBR*, accused rebels such as Aung Hla slipped out of official view, permitting Saya San to dominate both the official narrative and the manner in which the Rebellion was understood. Thus, while Saya San was said to have imagined himself king (an image allegedly shared by many peasants in rural Burma), other rebel leaders were also regarding themselves as Burmese royalty, potentially hinting at the variety of interests and agendas that were emerging in the countryside by the early 1930s.

Evidence of such variances appear frequently and can be discerned from a document allegedly written by "a well-known rebel chief," Myat Aung, in regard to cooperation between two rebel units led by Saya Sa and Han Tha (two lieutenants of Saya San). The report highlights a passage from the Tribunal's judgment, which contextualizes the letter as indicative of the nature of "the working amalgamation" between the two forces and the close alliance that had been forged between the two leaders. On closer examination however, it is possible to see that differences among village activists were sometimes strained and disorganized, hardly the centralized network that was being projected by the report.

> U Han Tha and Saya Sa,—I write to tell you that if the Bos are at variance with one another and work in [a] disconcerted manner as they are now doing, I cannot imagine how the country can be conquered. In order to ensure easy and immediate victory, Saya Ka and I have now combined. Other Bos and we should combine, and after consultation capture Tharrawaddy town. Only by capturing Tharrawaddy will mother-country Burma be conquered at an early date. [25]

The report went on to quote the Special Tribunal as saying that "such a document leaves little doubt of the aims of local leaders" since Myat Aung was "President of the Taikkyi circle of *wunthanu athins.*" Documents and testimony related to *wunthanu* affairs were automatically connected to rebellion activity while evidence suggesting collaboration between village groups were similarly criminalized. At the same time, one might also read the same document as demonstrating the decentralized nature of the countryside, as Myat Aung comments on the manner in which local village leaders work individually within their personal networks due perhaps to differing agendas and pressures. In a similar case, a letter was retrieved and presented to the tribunal as evidence of the coordination between Galon groups, but it also reveals the incoherent nature of such rural activity and the predominance of patron–client-based loyalties, concerns, and worldviews in village politics.

> This is my command to the Taungbyat Bo and others for your obedience. To recover the country there could be success only when united effort is made. I therefore order you to come. Is it because you mind family affairs more than the country's interests that you have failed to come? Is it because you are contemplating to recover the country relying upon your own abilities? Now, on receipt of this command from me, your Saya, you must hasten to me. If you fail therein I will not recognise you. Note this is my command. I will leave your organization and your weapons well alone. [Signed] Saya Gyi[26]

Beyond revealing the more complex nature of village resistance movements during this period, the passage also hints at the differing notions concerning community, political affinity, and geopolitical identity. While "Saya Gyi" (who the report contends is Saya San), admonishes his junior to think of the "country" rather than "family affairs," this account also suggests that village leaders may have experienced attempts to unify rural and urban political interests quite differently, with local concerns and priorities outweighing the rhetoric and vision of nationalist leaders.

In fact, competition within nationalist organizations, such as the various factions within the GCBA, continued within the countryside as local leaders and charismatic individuals competed for prestige and influence among villagers with urban-trained recruiters. One proclamation, alleged to show that Saya San was working outside the parameters of the Soe Thein branch of the GCBA, also illustrates the various sources of authority that were being used by reformers to attract followers into their personal networks. Urban-based associations were wary of

Quacks, including those in the guise of hermits and monks, [who] pose themselves as possessing medicines and amulets which have the power of making persons under their spell invulnerable and proof against sticks and dahs, demand fees from the unwary for their trouble. These quacks are not recognized nor encouraged by U Soe Thein GCBA controlled by the Thetpan Sayadaw, and therefore should be shunned. Notice is given that the famous Sayadaw U Oktama and the GCSS disapprove of the conduct of certain district associations, that are issuing tickets not recognized by Soe Thein GCBA.

The picture one gets is that attempts to mobilize villagers into a single, organized, and coherent association was far from what was happening on the ground. Members of urban-nationalists organizations were not only competing among themselves, but also with local headmen, traditional healers, and marginalized monks who had not been successfully integrated into these larger reform structures. Differing political vocabularies, symbols, and explanations emerged from local communities in order to make sense of the economic changes they were experiencing while external voices attempted to present new ways of articulating reform. As these processes of political integration were presented under the rubric of "rebellion," local intentions, methods, and characteristics were effaced through the Rebellion Ethnology that guided the manner in which this knowledge was recorded. Attempts to rally villages into a larger political network were automatically categorized as preparation for armed resistance, rendering these differences and conflicting loyalties as indicators of a coherent movement that sought to urge the countryside into open rebellion.

Read from this perspective, the use of tattooing as an indicator of rebel activity could show the possibility of incoherency in the Rebellion even though the report was attempting to demonstrate quite the opposite. In one passage of the same trial, the report remarks that a peculiarity in the case emerged on the issue of tattooing symbols, for the tattoos borne by the accused were of an inconsistent nature, despite the fact that the two groups of rebels had allegedly combined forces. The judges were provided with a list of tattoos that were of a "varied and puzzling character" in that it was "difficult to find an outstanding common factor among them." The report quotes the statement of the Special Tribunal, which says that it was "curious" that not a single Galon tattoo mark could be found on any one of the tattoos, but since Saya San's palace had been located and destroyed, it could be inferred that the Galon tattoo had been discredited in favor of the "necklace design."[27] Beyond the fact that the report was relying on the Tribunal's understanding of tattooing practices was the attempt in the report to reify the coherency of the Rebellion through the perceived uniformity of tattooing symbols. The adoption of the tattooing element as a central component of the report's narrative not only reveals the connections between the trials and the official report, but it illustrates how forms of Burmese culture were being objectified and authorized to denote the coherency of the Rebellion despite lingering hints of its incoherency.

Conclusion

Indeed, *The Origins and Causes of the Burma Rebellion (1930–1932)* functions as a repository of "facts," held together by a single narrative sequence that was fine-tuned by judicial officers and sanctioned by the colonial government. The report fixed particular arguments, perspectives, and paradigms that would significantly shape the way in which the Rebellion would be engaged by scholarship. These conventions guided the manner in which the narrative would be considered by identifying its main protagonists, defining the story's parameters, and by configuring the rebellion so as to appear neatly coherent, recognizable, and manageable. The focus on "origins" would compel future commentators to understand the alleged causes of the movement whereas others would unintentionally be attracted to interpreting the colorful characteristics of the Rebellion. One Burmese writer even went so far as to use the title "The Real Origins and Causes of the Burma Rebellion" in an effort to respond directly to the contentions of the report.[28] More significantly, the discussion of the rebellion in dichotomous terms (superstition v. rationality, political v. economic, traditional v. modern, Burmese kingship v. British administrative authority) would also prescribe the manner through which future interpretations would be presented and considered. The legal structures that dictated how the narrative was shaped eventually dissolved, leaving readers with a predetermined set of debates and questions surrounding the Rebellion. Most importantly, the image of a single rebellion, organized by a single protagonist and carried out by an undifferentiated peasant community, would endure in studies to come. The report functioned to codify and authorize an older, more rigid view of rural Burma that was hewn out of much earlier assessments of village communities during the pacification period of the 1880s and 1890s. Treated from this point of view, the politicization of the countryside in the 1920s and 1930s was rendered to be inert, static, and detached from more urban settings. As protest grew more violent and expressive, the mechanisms and institutions underlying this growing network were criminalized, simplified, and drained of their more complex character. Scholars would treat the report as a "primary" source—a pillar upon which the facts, narrative sequences, and the place of Saya San could rest.

Notes

1. Government of Burma, L/PJ/6/2020, BRGF, confidential report, "The Rebellion in Burma, April 1931–March 1932," police department, no. 429630, September 14, 1932.
2. Government of Burma, L/PJ/6/2020 BRGF, *The Origins and Causes of the Burma Rebellion (1930–1932)*, Rangoon, 1934, p. 2.
3. Government of Burma, L/PJ/6/2020, BRGF, minute paper, file 1126, March, 20, 1934; L/PJ/6/2020, G/B, BRGF, letter, R. A. Butler to George Hall, Esq. (House of Commons), May 29, 1934.
4. Government of Burma, L/PJ/6/2020, BRGF, minute paper, file 1126.
5. Ibid.
6. Government of Burma, L/PJ/6/2020.
7. Government of Burma, L/PJ/6/2020 BRGF, *The Origins and Causes of the Burma Rebellion (1930–1932)*, Rangoon, 1934, p.1.
8. Ibid.
9. Government of Burma, L/PJ/6/2020, BRGF, Ralph Clarence Morris, *Causes of the Tharrawaddy Rebellion*, March 1931. Patricia Herbert,

"The Hsaya San Rebellion: Reappraised" (Melbourne: Monash University Centre of Southeast Asian Studies Working Papers, 1982).

10. Robert H. Taylor, *The State in Burma* (Honolulu: University of Hawaii Press, 1987), pp. 174–98.

11. Ibid.

12. Government of Burma, L/PJ/6/2020, BRGF, *The Origins and Causes of the Burma Rebellion (1930-1932)*, Rangoon, 1934, p. 4.

13. Ibid.

14. Ibid., p. 6.

15. Ibid.

16. Ibid., pp. 7–8.

17. Ibid., p. 10. Saya San allegedly stated that the literal meaning of *Thupannaka Galuna Raja* was "Great Galon Bird of the Letpan Tree."

18. Ibid., p. 6.

19. Ibid., p. 2.

20. Ibid., p. 12.

21. Ibid., p. 13.

22. Ibid., p. 22.

23. Ibid., p. 3.

24. Ibid., p. 4.

25. Ibid., p. 5.

26. Ibid., p. 15.

27. Ibid., p. 6.

28. U Chit Maung, "The Real Origins of the Burma Rebellion 1930–1932," in Ma Ma Lei, *A Man Like Him* (Ithaca: Cornell Southeast Asia Publications, 2008; orig. 1948).

Chapter 6

INTERPRETING REBELLION
Binary Structures and Colonial Remains

The publishing of *The Origins and Causes of the Burma Rebellion (1930–1932)* and its eventual distribution to relevant government libraries and offices marked for all intents and purposes the administrative end of the Rebellion.[1] To Rangoon officials, the process of compiling the report satisfied requests from Parliament to account for the Rebellion financially, justified the implementation of counter-insurgency policies, and provided the opportunity to demonstrate the ability to understand (and therefore control) the communities and cultures within Burmese society. The report also provided closure and coherency by bringing together the findings of several official documents into a single text—unifying the various events, individuals, and geographical contexts into a containable and manageable narrative. In a deft move, the series of disparate and uncoordinated uprisings that were regarded by colonial administrators as a threat to the very existence of British Burma were recast as a single rebellion, reinforcing the province's conceptual, territorial, and historical boundaries. Just as maps visually created new cultural, psychological, and historical spaces through which new forms of identity were marked, so too did reports such as *The Origins and Causes of the Burma Rebellion (1930–1932)* delineate a particular epistemological terrain upon which legitimacy and authority of the colonial administration in Burma were articulated.[2]

Yet the act of publishing the report also pointed to an important stage within the historiography of the Rebellion as its inclusion into what would be categorized as the Burma Rebellion General File authorized the contents as "history" and marked its status as a "source" in the archive. In an administrative context, the document operated as the final assessment of the Rebellion, a text that signaled closure for officials in London and in New Delhi. If considered within the context of post-Rebellion scholarship however, the report was the foundational source upon which subsequent interpretations were made. *The Origins and Causes of the Burma Rebellion (1930–1932)* was thus a history at the interstices, to borrow from Thonchai Winichakul— only in this context it did not demarcate a space between encounters, between national identity and history, or between cultural processes, but between the epistemological contexts of the colonial administrator and the scholar.[3] As will be discussed in the following sections, the report acted to affirm the Rebellion Ethnology, representing its final manifestation within the context of the Burma Rebellion General File while also functioning as the founding source for a generation of scholars studying Saya San.

Scholar Officials

The earliest Western references to the Saya San Rebellion outside official records were the published memoirs of administrators that were stationed in Burma during the early 1930s. These authors describe the Rebellion as it had affected them, which more often than not had little to do with the sequence of events associated with Saya San. However, writers such as Gwynn (1934), C. V. Warren (1937), Maurice Collis (1938), and A. J. White (reprinted 1991), skillfully inserted their own experiences into the well-known official narrative giving the reader a blend of personal and secondhand knowledge. Although these writers were not attempting to write a formal history of the Rebellion, they might be associated with the construction of Saya San in that they adopted both the narrative and the interpretative posture of the final blue-book report, which articulated official administrative findings on the events in question.[4] By emphasizing the use of amulet-wearing, oath-taking, tattooing, and the rituals surrounding the supposed coronation ceremony of Saya San, these observers reinforced the ethnographic character of the Rebellion, an understanding of events that reflected British images of Burmese cultural history. As postcolonial scholars have observed in a wide variety of historical contexts, indigenous populations were often rendered in official documentation as being forever informed by timeless cultural restrictions that left them incapable of understanding European modes of political expression and unable to articulate dissent in a manner other than revolt. Thus, the character of rebellion in British Burma (expressed through its exotic nature) was at a fundamental level conceived along dichotomous lines—modern/traditional, rational/irrational, static/progressive, secular/religious, and Europe/Asia. Professional historians who consulted these published volumes not only continued to interpret the Rebellion within this binary framing, but they would erroneously cite these works as primary sources for those circumstances concerning Saya San—even though not a single one of these writers had any direct connection to the events being described.[5] In addition, while subsequent research would scrutinize the works of Gwynn, Warren, Collis, and White for the "facts" that they contained, many would only identify problems in interpretation, racial bias, or analytical perspective as their fundamental shortcoming. For many scholars, the structure of revolt remained visible within these accounts, even though they were linked to documents in the official record. As secondary sources, these works constitute the transition stage between the official documents of colonial offices and the earliest versions of scholarship on the Rebellion.

Colonial Historians

G. E. Harvey (1946) and D. G. E. Hall (1950), two of British Burma's earliest twentieth-century British historians, offered many of the same characterizations that Warren and Collis had made, and therefore did not alter the image of Saya San that had been constructed thus far. Harvey seems to have been influenced by the report (or at least by the positions contained within it), stating that there was a "tradition of brigandage in Tharrawaddy" where "there had always been such rebellions, led by monk–magicians, from time immemorial, under the kings."[6] Both historians seemed to have been influenced by official documents since both restricted their assessments of the Rebellion within contours of the arguments posited by the official blue-book report. Not only did they continue to focus on "the origins" and "causes" of the uprising, but the report's categories through which these themes were examined were adopted as well as its binary structures. For instance, although Hall disagreed with the finding of the report (that posited political factors rather than economic ones as "the cause" of the Rebellion) he suggests that the Rebellion was "anti-foreign" and due "largely to economic discontent," adhering to the dichotomous framing of the report. On the other hand, Harvey agreed somewhat with the report's finding, contending that

> It was not economic [in origin], for it originated in a comfortably-off area where the taxes were if anything lighter than elsewhere, it broke out two months before the slump arrived, and it had been plotted for two years.[7]

This particular argument, which seems to have originated in an early source that was later adopted in the *The Origins and Causes of the Burma Rebellion(1930–1932)*, demonstrates the extent to which official statements might have informed Harvey's reading of the Rebellion.[8] In fact, Harvey rejected any political causes for the Rebellion, reasoning that since the Burmese were already well-represented in the legislature, the ultimate cause "was superstition pure and simple, superstition of so crude a type that no reader in England can even imagine it."[9] Harvey chose to punctuate what Collis, Warren, and White had actually only implied—that the cause of the Rebellion was one and the same with the characterization of the Rebellion.[10] Being one of the first Western historians of Burma, many subsequent scholars consulting Harvey's work would be committed to making superstition a criterion by which the Rebellion was interpreted or determined to consider "superstition" in a more culturally sensitive manner.

The earliest works by scholar–officials set the tone for subsequent scholars by focusing on the themes and patterns provided by the official report. For Warren, Collis, Harvey, Hall, and White, the Rebellion was considered as being predominantly superstitious and political in nature rather than economic and rational in origin. Scholars who consulted these works often considered their own interpretations within the conceptual framing introduced by these authors. Interestingly enough, while Saya San was explicitly mentioned as having organized and instigated the Rebellion, scholarship up to that point had only spoken of the event in general terms as "the Tharrawaddy Rebellion," "Burma Rebellion," or "Burma Revolt." It was not until almost twenty years afterward that the focus of the Rebellion would center on Saya San, setting his current place in the history of Burma.

Post-independence Scholars

John Cady's *A History of Modern Burma* (1958) continues to be a seminal work for the period under review. Utilizing many British government documents from various departments, correspondences, parliamentary papers, and police reports, Cady reintroduced the historical narrative of the revolt as "the Saya San Rebellion" and he is the first Western historian to call it as such. Although more carefully documented than his predecessors, Cady's narrative of the Rebellion remained substantively similar to earlier accounts since he relied almost exclusively on British documents that measured the uprising by its inherently traditional Burmese characteristics and sensibilities. He writes:

> The rebellion led by Saya San...differed qualitatively from other contemporary forms of nationalist protest [and] from the spontaneous anti-alien riots mainly because it was a deliberately planned affair based on traditional Burmese political and religious patterns.[11]

Cady's view does not dismiss these features as "superstitious," but he does juxtapose the Rebellion participants with the nationalist Western-educated Burmese that were operating within the British system. His structuring of the Rebellion introduced three new binary pairings in which the Saya San Rebellion was differentiated from other types of political expression occurring in Burma during the 1930s: Burmese–Western, rural–urban, and kingship–nationalism. In fact, Cady argues that these dichotomies were precisely the reason the Rebellion failed politically: the leadership did not reconcile the political differences between the peasantry and urban-educated elites in Burma, and they ignored the political alternatives suggested by leaders in London and India.[12] In other words, Cady's take on the Rebellion suggests that Saya San and his followers were incapable of cooperating with the growth of new urban nationalists and were unresponsive to colonial arbitration because their worldview was inextricably informed by Burmese ideas of political legitimacy and protest. While entirely more sophisticated than earlier works and outwardly more sensitive to his predecessors' overstatements, Cady continued to evaluate the Saya San Rebellion as a traditional protest movement within a modern colonial world, continuing its dichotomous rendering. Furthermore, earlier colonial views were sustained in Cady's assessment that Burmese rural communities were constrained by particular cultural barriers that limited the range and form of political activism. Yet his work serves as an important stage in the historiography of the Rebellion since it attempts for the first time to recognize that localized forms of political expression (albeit in traditional terms) were apparently at work alongside the growing number of Western-inspired nationalist associations in the countryside. He ultimately rejected any association between the forms, but he nonetheless provided several other dichotomous pairings for future historians to consider.

Other postindependence Burmese historians, in response to earlier impressions that the presumed characteristics of the Rebellion were a cause for the uprising, presented Saya San as an early nationalist hero and the Rebellion as an expression of nationalist concerns. Usually, these interpretations stress economic factors as a cause for popular dissatisfaction rather than the supposed "superstitious" nature of the Burmese, perhaps to compensate for earlier overstatements by British scholar–officials. Whereas they admitted that the character of the Rebellion had been articulated through a distinctively Burmese

Interpreting Rebellion   165

cultural vocabulary, these scholars pointed to exploitation of the Burmese farmer and worsening economic conditions as a cause of these grievances.[13] For many, the Rebellion was not an aimless happenstance that occurred from time to time, but a legitimate movement based on economic grievances. Thus, this nationalist interpretation, a persuasion exemplified by historians such as Htin Aung, Maung Maung, U Chit Maung, and the commission that produced the work *Taungthu Lethama AyeDawpon*,[14] attempted to legitimize the Rebellion by infusing ideas of popular revolt into the discourse about it. Burmese scholars were more concerned with creating a national history and downplaying the indigenous characteristics of the Rebellion in favor of terms and ideas thought to be more rational and justifiable to the professional historians. What had once been rejected as a disorganized rabble of medicine men and gullible peasants had been transformed by these observers into a demonstration of early nationalist sentiment.[15] Focusing on economic causes soon became the perspective adopted by Burmese historians eager to correct the views of British historians and to legitimize the efforts of their countrymen in the 1930s within a nationalist context. Needless to say, these historians had merely chosen to accentuate economic causes rather than political ones, a choice which only reinforced one pair of the dichotomous categories introduced in the official 1934 report.

This economic perspective, a view espoused by Western-educated Burmese, has also been studied closely by scholars in the West who were less concerned with establishing legitimacy in the Rebellion as they were with quantifying and clarifying the causal factors of the rebellion that had been buried, to some extent, in the statistics of official reports. Written a generation later and no doubt infused with the intellectual currents that informed both peasant studies and Southeast Asian studies, Michael Adas's *The Burma Delta* (1974) and James C. Scott's *The Moral Economy of the Peasant: Rebellion and Subsistence in Southeast Asia* (1976) provided in-depth analyses into the economic conditions underlying the uprisings in the 1930s . For these scholars (like their earlier Burmese colleagues), the traditional vocabulary of the Rebellion was less a factor in the cause of the insurgency than the unforgiving demands of the rational state's economy.[16] Heavy and consistent taxation, high-interest loans, absentee-landlordism, the erosion of traditional forms of economic safety valves, interracial labor tensions, and dipping prices in the value of paddy all contributed to the worsening social conditions of 1930 Lower Burma.[17] Despite avoiding the nationalist slant that early studies into the economic conditions of Lower Burma had displayed, these scholars still maintained the original sequence of events and, more importantly, positioned their studies within the familiar dichotomous structure that continued to inform scholarship on the Saya San Rebellion.

Located alongside nationalist discourse, but on a different path from what was being produced in Burma, was a growing number of Western scholars interested in studying "Burmese nationalism." Linked inextricably to anticolonialism, scholars began to trace the development of nationalism through several innovative and creative approaches. Most recognized quite early the significance and role of the Buddhist *sangha* in Burmese politics and thus framed their studies of these religious-political elements under the rubric of nationalism. Buddhist undertones and other traditional characteristics became a part of, not separated from, the nationalist movement in Burma.[18] Donald E. Smith (1965), adopting a Burmese–Western framework (while implying a traditional–modern one), typified the Saya San Rebellion as:

> an authentic expression of traditional Burmese nationalism... [owing] nothing to western political ideologies or institutions and receiv[ing] neither inspiration nor political techniques from the Indian nationalist movement.[19]

Ten years later, E. Michael Mendelson presented Saya San as "a nationalist ex-monk," a political *pongyi* who disregarded his vows of detachment from worldly affairs to lead a native movement.[20] These scholars seem to have accepted Saya San's central role (in recognition of Cady's work) but identified Buddhism as having played a more significant role in articulating revolt than previously detected. To these scholars, superstition or traditional beliefs were no longer adequate for describing the Rebellion's vocabulary or motivations. Economics was certainly a contributing factor in the Rebellion, but it was Buddhism that provided the blueprint for explicating these early nationalist sentiments. Ironically, scholarship had shifted their attention back to studying the Rebellion's features as opposed to its causes, perhaps because legitimacy was not an issue of concern for these outside observers. Yet, by emphasizing Burmese nationalism and placing the Saya San Rebellion within this framework, scholars began a program of legitimation by interpreting indigenous symbols and Buddhist motifs as expressions of nationalism. Whereas historians within independent Burma had chosen to deemphasize the traditional character of the rebellion in hopes of appealing to the sensibilities of Western political movements, external historians embraced those discarded symbols and validated them by infusing them with nationalist qualities.[21] Burmese (and by implication "traditional") nationalism was as legitimate as Western (or "modern") nationalism. The effort to give agency to Southeast Asian culture unintentionally rekindled the approaches of earlier scholars by focusing on the exotic characteristics of the Rebellion, maintaining the official narrative, and preserving the underlying variables upon which the Rebellion had always been evaluated.

One particular consequence of examining the Rebellion within a general Burmese nationalist interpretation, and specifically within a religious–nationalist strain, was that rebellions in Burma since 1885 were beginning to be seen as typically restorative in nature in that Burmese sought to reinstate precolonial institutions as opposed to replacing them with Western institutions.[22] Reinstalling the monarchy and *sangha* as the two institutional pillars of the Burmese state was contrasted by scholars with the secular colonial institutions of the British that some members of the Burmese elite were seeking to implement.[23] Although religion was given more relevance to political expression than earlier scholars had afforded, it was still seen as being linked primarily to the precolonial order and nostalgia for the monarchy. As a result, scholars renewed their typifying of the Saya San Rebellion as being "a traditional movement" expressive of the growing resistance to the modernizing and unfamiliar world of the West. Thus, the perceived goals became for some the defining factor in understanding the Saya San Rebellion.

Autonomous History

As Southeast Asian studies in the United States saw a new emphasis in the 1960s and 1970s on "internal," "local," and "marginal" perspectives, the Saya San Rebellion was thrust under the scrutiny of scholars keenly aware that the type of methodology John Smail urged, and the writing of autonomous history he envisioned, could be applied to anticolonial uprisings.[24] This relatively new approach, which stressed an indigenous viewpoint based on Southeast Asian themes and foci (as opposed to external, European colonial ones) produced fresh explanations for the Rebellion despite the continuity of the traditional–modern dichotomous structure. Under this new framework, Buddhism, indigenous spirit beliefs, and peasant values were demonstrated as having played a much larger role than ever before, a testament to the depth and sophistication of these so-called traditional movements. The most important distinction for this community of interpretations is that categories such as "Buddhism," "millenarianism," or "kingship" are not validated by Western ingredients (such as nationalism) or placed within a framework of linear, progressive history; they are considered important and relevant as viable rubrics of study in themselves. Whereas earlier scholars such as Donald Smith and E. Michael Mendelson might have looked at Burmese Buddhism as a reflection of (Western) nationalism and then examined Burmese popular movements within that pseudo-synthesis, this next generation of scholars would choose to acknowledge Buddhism as a subject of analyses without a qualifying variable. The Saya San Rebellion as an event was placed within these "autonomous categories" as opposed to being examined within the history of the British in Burma, as earlier studies had done.[25] The concern by scholars to demonstrate the movement's motivations represented simultaneously a desire to legitimate indigenous responses to colonialism by illustrating their complexity; and an apparent reaction to earlier scholarship that had implied that a traditional movement was inherently that of a simple and unsophisticated culture. The difference between this new scholarship and the earlier focus on Burmese nationalism was that indigenous-conceptual systems began to be regarded in their own terms, as opposed to being validated under the rubric of nationalism, anticolonial rebellions, peasant grievances, or colonial economics. Thus, the intellectual climate of the 1960s–1970s, which sought to give agency and importance to Southeast Asian culture, broadened the range of interpreting the Saya San Rebellion while at the same time providing a similar anti-British political texture that earlier nationalist historians had constructed.[26]

E. Sarkisyanz's *Buddhist Backgrounds of the Burmese Revolution* (1965) examines "the Saya San revolt" as an expression of Buddhist millenarian ideas that were in themselves part of a much longer history of Burmese–Buddhist politics. Perhaps in the closest manner to what Smail envisioned (although it appears that Smail had no influence on his work), Sarkisyanz studied the eventual development and implementation of socialist ideas in Burma as the most recent phase in the culture's long tradition of Buddhist kingship, religion, and politics. In this way, his work marks a transition from those who studied the Rebellion within the context of nationalism to those who were beginning to study these cultural ideas within an indigenous and "autonomous" framing. Scholars who had attempted to link Buddhism with nationalism could only sustain such a theme within the limited chronological space and array of twentieth-century institutions, whereas Emanuel Sarkisyanz's approach provided a much broader perspective that encompassed most of Burma's premodern and modern cultural institutions. A complex mixing of millenarian beliefs in a *Setkya-min* (*cakkavartin*) who would prepare the world for the prophesied Golden Age under the Future Buddha (*Metteya*) and an eschatological revitalization of both the Buddhist doctrine and the *Sangha* were cited as making the cultural conditions under the British and Saya San's Rebellion relevant to Burmese ideas of protest.[27] Sarkisyanz's work in 1965 was a path-breaking study concentrating on how ideas of Buddhist millenarianism, kingship, and traditional symbolism served as the ideological framework for the Rebellion. By focusing on *mentalités*, the Saya rebellion was examined within *la longue durée* of Burmese Buddhism, which addressed for the first time the ideas that might have given meaning to the Rebellion. From this point of view, the Rebellion was conceptualized in religious terms rather than as a singular response that grew out of British colonialism. Thus, the beliefs in a future Buddha, a future monarchy, a resurgent religion, were all features of a complex ideological system that in many ways defined Burmese identity. Sarkisyanz's study for the first time used the events of the Saya San Rebellion to discern a much more enduring and entrenched conceptual belief system that the British had written off as being "superstition." Whereas earlier historians had devalued the uprising as an attempt to reinstate traditional institutions, Sarkyisyanz gave depth and meaning to these ideas, thereby broadening our understanding of Burmese culture and its connection to conceptions of resistance. The hegemony of Western categories or periodization no longer defined how the Rebellion narrative might be interpreted, which allowed for a different explanation as to what the Rebellion meant to the Burmese. Not only could the Rebellion be examined for its traits of Buddhism, but the event itself becomes projected beyond the confines of "rebellion" into an expression of Burmese Buddhism. Interestingly, Sarkisyanz's linking of the Rebellion to Buddhist ideology (in an effort to counteract British characterizations), unintentionally supported British contentions that the Rebellion's characteristics were a primary factor for the uprising. Clarification of what these ideas constituted did not fundamentally alter the way in which these ideas were associated with the Rebellion.

A decade later, Michael Adas returned to the subject of the Saya San Rebellion in *Prophets of Rebellion* (1979), which continues much of what Sarkisyanz had examined but carries it further by emphasizing the need of "a prophetic leader" to take on the role of a messianic figure in these "revitalization movements."[28] Adas noticed that ideas of millenarianism and eschatology also provided a vocabulary of protest in other societies, where a colonial presence had disrupted the indigenous order. By extending this model to Indonesia, Africa, and New Zealand, Adas demonstrated that the millenarian-informed revolts were not necessarily particular to Burma but exemplified in several other colonial situations. Adas's motif further entrenched the *singular* role of Saya San in the uprising and the traditional Burmese beliefs he was said to represent. Where Sarkisyanz had attempted to rescue these ideas from the confines of the rebellion paradigm, Adas' work reconnected the discussion of Saya San to the colonial context and the narratives it produced.

Adas was most interested in those revitalization movements in which a prophet figure led and inspired indigenous peoples against European colonial states. Specifically, he sought to examine the relationship between prophet leaders and protest through an examination of the causal factors for revolt. In similarity to Sarkisyanz, millenarian traditions are identified as concepts that provide the blueprint for articulating peasant "discontent and frustration," as well as contribute to the character and legitimacy of the prophet–leader and his methods of organization. Yet, Adas did recognize that there was a certain level of cultural "ambivalence" in that many of these movements did demonstrate certain levels of toleration for foreign ideology and organizational patterns. In this, Adas shifts the pendulum slightly from Sarkysianz's approach and the nationalist studies that preceded *Prophets of Rebellion*. His interpretation engages the role of Western influences whereas Sarkysianz does not, and retains the autonomy of indigenous categories where Smith and Mendelson do not. This interpretative accommodation was one of the first to recognize the ambiguities of colonial culture (in Burma) and the difficulty of utilizing ideal categories of pure "nativism" on the one hand or pure "assimilation" on the other. This approach also extended to Adas's comments regarding the variable causes of the Rebellion. It was the political displacement of elites, it was economic dislocation, and it was the accelerated institutional changes that created the type of cultural trauma that compelled both peasant and elite groups to take up violent measures of protest. Thus, *Prophets of Rebellion* was both a departure from and a derivative of earlier scholarship. Although the essence of the Saya San narrative was maintained and in some cases elaborated through his pan-colonial typology involving the prophet–leader, Adas raises several provocative issues that question not only our understanding of rebellion and revolt, but also the role in which such millenarian ideas were translated among different social groups.

Although scholarship had extended the understanding of the Saya San Rebellion, it did not alter the dichotomous structure characterizing earlier works. Scholars appreciated and focused on indigenous symbols and conceptions informing the Rebellion, but in doing so prolonged the categorization that the Rebellion was steeped in traditional Burmese culture. These studies, instead of dismissing indigenous expressions of revolt as "superstition" embraced them as part of a much wider Southeast Asian matrix of beliefs. To specialists in ethnography, religion, and ritual studies, the Saya San Rebellion provides a case example of how a traditional society responded to the encroachment of and confrontation with the Western colonial state. Rebellion was a lens through which to study particular vicissitudes of Burmese culture.

Due in part to emphasis on the traditional characteristics of the Rebellion, scholars also began examining the communities they thought most often embraced these traditional conceptions—peasants. Perhaps best viewed within the traditional–modern dichotomy, the influence of peasant studies provided scholars with approaches that could more closely differentiate the way in which village communities articulated their dissatisfaction with the colonial powers, as opposed to the ways in which Western-educated urban elites exercised their grievances. The peasant–intelligentsia dichotomy also allowed scholars to acknowledge the differing systems of political ideology that a Burmese–British framing did not imply. Not all Burmese accepted Saya San's ideas of kingship, and not all Burmese incorporated Western forms of political organization and political expression.[29] Focusing on the peasant's role in the Saya San Rebellion also permitted scholars to examine the uprising in the context of Socialism, a framework adopted by historians in Burma. However, focusing on the peasant and the corpus of ideas associated with him implicitly affirmed the observations made in *The Origins and Causes of the Burma Rebellion (1930–1932)*, that peasants were at the heart of the Rebellion and that urban concerns were in no way associated with the revolt. Again, the binary framing of earlier interpretations directed the way in which subsequent scholarship would posit their interpretations. The machinery of the official report was still at work.

Perhaps in response to the arbitrary divisions between the world of the peasant and the urbanite, Patricia Herbert's work (1982)[30] was a welcome contribution to the field and challenged much of what had been written about Saya San, especially the "traditional" characterization that had been attached to the movement. Guided by her extensive research into Burmese newspaper accounts and oral interviews, Herbert's study challenges the traditional typology of the Rebellion by suggesting that the sources did not clearly support this image. Through a careful study of documents alleged to be Saya San's, Herbert noticed that much of the language used was not in the typical honorific style that a potential "Burmese king" might use. Furthermore, the creation of the village associations deemed to be the front for the Rebellion network was interpreted as being much more akin to "modern" forms of political organization than "traditional" ones. In short, Herbert argues that the Saya San Rebellion was a movement conceptualized perhaps on some level in traditional terms, but equally influenced through the organizational and administrative techniques adopted by Western-educated intelligentsia.

While Herbert is the first to raise issue with the royal characterization of Saya San and implicitly the traditional formula of the Rebellion, her study left that issue alone in favor of demonstrating the Rebellion's more modern features, exemplified by the *wunthanu athin* movement.[31] By illustrating how the *wunthanu athin* movement was a relatively new channel through which villages could communicate with national-level organizations (like the General Council of Burmese Associations), Herbert effectively argues that it was through this political environment and not necessarily traditional Burmese motifs that Saya San founded his movement.[32]

Currently, scholarship has not strayed too far from the course that had been laid out by twentieth-century scholars.[33] Although Herbert's interpretation argues that the Rebellion was actually organized along modern (and by implication, Western) lines of political protest, it nonetheless retained the traditional/modern framing. Stressing the use of twentieth-century modes of organization, this interpretation recognized the role of Western-educated elites in the early stages of nationalist movements, and viewed the Saya San Rebellion as an attempt to unite the peasantry with urban leaders. In this way, the work rekindled the efforts of earlier historians who had contextualized the Saya San Rebellion within a discussion of nationalism, but it adeptly avoids the normative examples of nationalist coloring that usually problematizes such interpretations by focusing on organizational strategies. Whereas it did not uniformly dismiss the scholarship that championed "autonomous history," it nonetheless deemphasized the "traditional" character of the Rebellion in favor of a more "modern" one. Even though the pendulum has simply swung to the other side, Herbert is the first to detect problems in the historical narrative, and her contribution cannot be understated.[34]

Interpretive Strategies

In assessing the existing scholarship on the Saya San Rebellion, a few characteristics deserve repeated attention. Clearly, interpreting the events, rather than clarifying how and whether they occurred, has preoccupied the attention of scholars.[35] From the earliest works to the most current contributions, scholars have concentrated on determining the causes of the Rebellion or scrutinized the Rebellion's characteristics in an effort to define and understand them. Interpretations have varied, but only within the parameters and terms presented in official documentation. Changes in theoretical orientation account for alternative readings of the Rebellion's characteristics, to interpret the Rebellion from a variety of viewpoints; but no fundamental departure from the dichotomous framework has yet to be offered. Scholars have unconsciously maintained this framing in their approach and method, often only altering slightly the binary positions that previous scholars had taken.

The ramifications of this interpretative pattern not only conditioned the way in which the Saya San Rebellion has been examined as a whole, but determined how characteristics within the Rebellion narrative would be included in scholars' analyses and how they would be situated within that discourse. For example, on the grounds that the Rebellion was caused by inherent superstition, Harvey dismisses the Rebellion as having little relevance to the history of British Burma, therefore affording very little to the event in his history of Burma. Subsequent scholars in Burma and the West reacted to this polemical stance by emphasizing the economically motivated origins of the Rebellion as an alternative explanation to Harvey's.[36] In hoping to make the Rebellion relevant to Burmese history, these scholars unknowingly employed the dichotomous structure found in official reports that framed the origins of the Rebellion in terms of economic strain or political aspirations. Reducing the emphasis of and attention to those Burmese *mentalités* that had been categorized by Harvey as "superstition" may have temporarily served the purposes of nationalist historians; but it left subsequent scholars somewhat unsatisfied with the way in which indigenous cultures were presented in colonial histories.[37] As suggested earlier, historians began examining the conceptions behind the emblems of the Rebellion and posited a more clarified reading of its ideological superstructure, although the emphasis on a traditional reading of the Rebellion had not been fundamentally altered. Although valuable in its own right, this strand of historiography excluded other forms of ideological influence—Western, Indian, Chinese—and excluded considering the role of those groups that embraced such ideas. Thus, in their attempt to encapsulate the Rebellion within a definitive interpretation (which is itself part of the problem), scholars found themselves emphasizing one characteristic over another, one group over another, one ideology over another, which in the end only reinforced the dichotomous thinking about the Rebellion. Employing this formula required subsequent historians to qualify and locate their contribution within earlier works, which only reinforced this interpretative cycle. One of our most recent contributions was clearly a reaction to almost fifty years of scholarship that had placed Saya San alongside other traditional-based anticolonial movements.[38]

The most important result of this dichotomous structuring of the Rebellion by scholars is clearly the candid assumption that the Rebellion narrative was historically accurate. The facts and evidential foundations supporting Saya San's role in the Rebellion—the basis for all the Rebellion's historiography—has received little attention. Had scholars examined the narrative for historical accuracy, not just interpretative viability, they might have noticed some of the following discrepancies. Many of the sources cited for the narrative were actually not primary in nature and really did not support the story they were purported to establish. Many of the government reports, which comprise the bulk of sources regarding the rebellion, were not primary documents, but summaries of earlier sources left unexamined. In practically every aspect of the Rebellion that involved Saya San, the sources cited did not directly verify the event that they were supposed to support. In many cases, other scholars' references to a particular source were employed without scrutiny or sometimes one of the Rebellion's participants, who actually might not have been present in Burma at the time, were utilized to support an event as having occurred. These narrative conventions (or ways of evaluating the Saya San story) link scholars and observers into a community of interpretation that stretches across disciplinary, spatial, and chronological lines. One example may illustrate this affinity.

Robert H. Taylor's rendition of the Rebellion narrative (1987) credits Albert Moscotti's monograph *British Policy and the Nationalist Movement in Burma (1974)*[39] and Maung Maung's *From Sangha to Laity* (1980)[40] as secondary sources for his version, encouraging readers to consult the latter for the fullest account.[41] Maung Maung in turn cited three sources for his version of the narrative: a 1965 Union of Burma publication entitled *Taungthu Lethama Ayedawpon* (An account of the peasant crisis) and two colonial reports—*The Rebellion in Burma, April 1931–March 1932* and *The Origins and Causes of the Burma Rebellion (1934)*. An examination of the *Taungthu Lethama Ayedawpon* reveals that its version of the narrative was drawn primarily from *The Origins and Causes of the Burma Rebellion (1934)* and other British documents. Although Maung Maung describes this volume as "a sober, factual presentation of the events," the basis for this assessment stems from his comparison with newspaper reports from the period—not from a close examination of the volume's sources.[42] Taylor's survey of the Saya San narrative relies on Moscotti and Maung Maung, who in turn had adopted the findings found in the official blue-book report (*The Origins and Causes of the Burma Rebellion [1930–1932]*). The acceptance of the report as a primary source and the citing of other scholars as references contributed in part to contestable facts in the narrative remaining undetected.[43]

Beyond relying on the findings of earlier scholars has been the curious use of secondary sources as primary sources for specific events in the Saya San narrative. In particular, the works by Collis and Warren have been treated as if everything they wrote was personally observed or experienced while in Burma. Collis describes events that were occurring in British Burma as he remembered and as they were reported in official circles. In fact, he left before Saya San was captured and before much of the story about Saya San had been established in his trial. Yet, his descriptions of Saya San's coronation ceremony and other traditional aspects of the Rebellion have been used as if he were an eyewitness.[44] Collis's *Trials in Burma* does indeed contain reflections from experiences in Burma, but the sections dealing with the Saya San narrative are clearly not of "a primary nature." Saya San's supposed proclamation of kingship under the title *"Thupannaka Galuna Raja,"* was based on Judge U Ba U's description from the Saya San trial, which was a detail heard secondhand, and not witnessed as the citation implies.[45] In a similar fashion, Warren's *Burmese Interlude* has been utilized as if the work were entirely a recording of events that the forestry officer experienced.[46] Although it appears that Warren did take part in quelling a few skirmishes, his description of Saya San's personal file, the planning of the Rebellion, the traditional character of the rebels, and other specific details of the uprising were not part of his personal experiences. At the time of the initial uprisings in Tharrawaddy and according to documents contemporaneous to the events, detailed information about Saya San was not known by senior officials in Burma and yet Warren's book casts the impression that this information was known by him at the outset of the uprising. The section dealing with the narrative of the rebellion was actually constructed after Warren's experiences, although scholars have used him as if he were a credible observer contemporary to the events. What is only partially a memoir of events has been erroneously cited as a primary source, and further disguises any indication that the sources closest to the narrative remain undetected.

Due to the use of Collis and Warren as primary sources, details purporting to be the words or thoughts of rebels were also treated as being primary in nature by later scholars even though they were of questionable origin. In John Cady's *A History of Modern Burma* (1958), the author attempts to establish the political-religious character of the Rebellion by providing a transcript of a rebel oath allegedly taken by all Galon members:

> We are banded together to drive out all unbelievers...till we are free of the rule of the English...I will obey all superiors of the Galon society...so that our religion may be saved from the unbeliever.... Grant that I may help destroy all...unbelievers. Protect and help our religion, O ye greater and lesser Nats....Grant us liberty to the Galon King dominion over this land.[47]

Cady cites Moscotti whose own transcript of "the oath" was based on Warren, a citation acknowledged by Cady. Yet, scholars have not examined the problematic circumstances surrounding this supposed oath, demonstrating the extent to which Warren has been summarily accepted as a primary source.[48] Warren claims that he found the oath and translated the document himself, but the original was given to one "McGregor," perhaps a senior official or military officer. The original has never been examined but the translation has become a primary source. These discrepancies in the scholarship surrounding the Rebellion are examples of one assumption being placed on top of another. Not only have scholars assumed that earlier scholars had thoroughly gone through the sources, but some observers were mistakenly thought to be eyewitnesses to all the events that they discussed in their published recollections. There was also an assumption that the traditional aspects of the Rebellion were historical fact. Despite indications suggesting that the association of Saya San with a *Setkyamin* was perhaps only a "rumor," despite noting that the origins of the rebel oath were less than certain, and despite the use of government sources (which were produced after the fact) to establish the historicity of an event, the traditional coloring of the Rebellion and the role of Saya San within that story remained intact.[49] The problem in the cases was that scholars were citing sources that were thought to verify the actions of Saya San. Even government sources published during the years of the Rebellion were themselves based on earlier sources.[50] The primary sources in the history of the Saya San Rebellion were not actually earliest known sources to the events described, and were therefore not tested or scrutinized for reliability. This oversight actually compounded the "traditional" texture of the Rebellion narrative since the corpus of documents most commonly cited all professed this characterization.

The character and focus of subsequent interpretations had as much to do with the sources upon which their studies were based. Just as *The Origins and Causes of the Burma Rebellion (1930–1932)* attempts to define rebellion in Burma, so too do scholars address the causes, circumstances, and features of the revolt that made it "unique" to Burma. The residual effect of defining Burmese rebellion through what was interpreted as "Burmese culture" was that later scholars, seeking to study particular forms of Burmese culture, began studying these elements within the context of Rebellion, thus reinforcing both the perception of these cultural features and the narrative and situation to which they were attached. Tattooing, millenarianism, invulnerability rites, *nat* ceremonies, and mystical charisma became part of a Rebellion ethnology, cultural features associated most poignantly with the Saya San Rebellion.[51] Frequent rebellion, according to the confidential 1934 report, was even declared a natural occurrence in Burmese culture.[52]

Thus, the concept of rebellion in Burma came to be defined through cultural characteristics selected by British officials. This project continued with scholars who, in pursuing to understand these particular aspects of Burmese culture, ended up associating them strictly through rebellion—further submerging the actual origins of the historical narrative and reaffirming the findings made by British officials in their reports. Scholarship is therefore epistemologically connected to the counter-insurgency program initiated by British officials since it validated the official version of events espoused by government reports and adopted the way in which Burmese cultural features were typified as representing rebellion.

The Remains of the Rebellion Narrative

In all, the last sixty years of scholarship on the Saya San Rebellion have remained remarkably similar. Admittedly, recent contributions have tended to be more creative, interpretative, autonomous (in some cases), and thorough in terms of historical method; and yet they can still be found deficient in three ways. First, the narrative of the Saya San Rebellion has remained intact, even though there appears to have been problems with the most frequently cited source for that narrative.[53] Second, no historian has closely examined the trial records of Saya San in order to substantiate the findings contained in the *The Origins and Causes of the Burma Rebellion (1930–1932)*. Third, in terms of methodology, scholars had done essentially what prosecution lawyers did in trying to build a case against Saya San at his trial. Just as Rangoon officials made claim after claim, utilizing various forms of evidence to fit their preconceived theory, so too did scholars shape their interpretations to fit the narrative, often giving as much credence to the testimony of their colleagues as the prosecution treated the testimony of its own witnesses.[54] This concern with interpretation and similarity in method with colonial officials seems to have contributed to the presumption that the narrative that had served as the basis for "the history" of the revolt was accurate.

The consequence of this presumption seems to be that scholars did not see the need to reexamine the sources but to concentrate on interpreting the uprising. Consequently, Ralph Clarence Morris's *The Origins and Causes of the Burma Rebellion (1930–1932)* was allowed to function as the most important primary source of the Rebellion.

Few ventured beyond the report to examine the judicial sources or the earlier district-oriented documents that provided the basis for the report's text.[55] By leaving the report unchallenged, the sequence of events, the facts of the narrative, and the interpretation of that narrative created the particular discourse through which the Rebellion would be studied.[56] As a result, the past seventy years of scholarship have only been discussed within the parameters and categories originally presented in the Morris report. The various approaches of the Rebellion—superstitious v. rational, political v. economic, Burmese nationalism v. Western nationalism, complex v. simple, peasant v. intelligentsia, traditional v. modern, rural v. urban—have all provided useful frameworks for analysis but inextricably excluded discussion of synthesis, complication, or a mixing of patterns.[57] By focusing on millennial conceptions informing the Rebellion, one excludes the role of the General Council of Burmese Associations, Tats, *Wunthanu Athin*, *Dobama Asyione*, the Youth Improvement Movement, and other forms of political organization and influence that were spreading into the countryside in the 1930s.[58] Arguing for a strictly modern organizational pattern would not only exclude the possibility of religious ideas being used to articulate protest, but it would assume that the two could not be working simultaneously or by different groups in different areas and in different ways.

Scholarship functioned on the assumption that the rebellion was a unified movement that could be categorized as a monolithic entity. Such a framework left little room for the Rebellion to take on different characteristics in different parts of the country, despite reports indicating that such disparities and multiple actors certainly existed. As such, the coherency of the rebellion continues to serve as a major trope in Burma scholarship, suggesting that Burmese peasants and rural communities envisioned change and political reform from a single point of view, impervious to the variety of influences and priorities that might have affected them by an equally multifaceted colonial administration and middle-class elite. Whereas interpretations meant to provide agency and importance to indigenous mentalities may have championed Burmese sensibilities, they have nonetheless overlooked the differences among rural and urban activists, the various ways in which Buddhism is imagined, and the opportunities that contemporary forms of organization offered to grassroot reformers. Through the Saya San Rebellion, resistance became a category through which particular aspects of Burmese culture were discussed, influencing the manner in which one perspective of Myanmar's political potential in the 1930s has been understood.

Notes

1. Government of Burma. L/PJ/6/2020, BRGF, *The Origins and Causes of the Burma Rebellion (1930–1932)*, Rangoon, 1934.
2. Matthew H. Edney, *Mapping an Empire: The Geographical Construction of British India, 1765–1843* (Chicago: University of Chicago Press, 1990).
3. Thongchai Winichakul, "Writing at the Interstices: Southeast Asian Historians and Postnational Histories in Southeast Asia," in Abu Talib Ahmad and Tan Liok Ee (eds.), *New Terrains in Southeast Asian History* (Athens: Ohio University Press, 2003).
4. Maurice Collis, *Trials in Burma* (London: Faber, 1938); C.V. Warren, *Burmese Interlude* (Plymouth: Skeffington and Son, 1937). These works were written well after the Rebellion had ended and Saya San had been executed. In fact, Collis's description of Saya San's coronation ceremony, a frequently cited passage, was not witnessed by the writer as the book (and its use by scholars) tends to imply. On p. 217, Collis even reveals that he examined "a court judgment" as a basis for his description. Warren's description of the Rebellion narrative is clearly a reiteration of the official version and not a personal account of his experiences.
5. Ibid.
6. Godfrey Eric Harvey, *British Rule in Burma 1824–1942* (London: Faber and Faber, 1946), pp. 73–74; Daniel George Edward Hall, *Burma* (London: Hutchinson House, 1950).
7. Ibid., p. 73.
8. Harvey appears to have adopted the views stated in *OCBR*, p. 43., L/PJ/6/2020, Burma Rebellion Files, frame 44. He may have been reiterating a common view that "preparations must have commenced six weeks or two months before the economic distress felt to any serious extent." L/PJ/62020, Government of Burma, Burma Rebellion General File, letter no. C30, government of Burma to government of India Home Department, p. 7, December 29, 1930.

9. Harvey, *British Rule in Burma 1824–1942*, p. 73.

10. Michael Adas has made a similar distinction between locating the causes and characteristics of the Rebellion, arguing that while messianic and millenarian content certainly informed the Rebellion to an extent, this is entirely different from factors of causation. Michael Adas, *The Burma Delta: Economic Development and Social Change on an Asian Rice Frontier, 1852–1941* (Madison: University of Wisconsin Press, 1974), p. 201.

11. Cady, *A History of Modern Burma* (Ithaca: Cornell University Press, 1958), pp. 309–10

12. Ibid., p. 319.

13. Many cited the observations of U Saw, the representative from Tharrawaddy, who wrote to a British Member of Parliament about the Rebellion in Burma. His pamphlet caused such commotion in Britain that Burma officials confiscated U Saw's printing business and halted production of the document. See *The Burma Situation: A Letter to W. Wedgwood Benn M.P.*, July 1931, L/PJ/6/2020, BRF, frames 304–24.

14. See U Htin Aung, *A History of Burma, by Maung Htin Aung* (New York: Columbia University Press,1967); U Maung Maung, *From Sangha to Laity: Nationalist Movements of Burma, 1920–1940* (New Delhi: Manohar,1980); U Chit Maung's essay, "The Real Origins and Causes of the Burma Rebellion," in Ma Ma Lei's *Gyane Gyaw Thu Lolu*, Rangoon (1968), and *Taungthu Lethama Ayedawpon*, Rangoon: Burma Historical Commission (1965). For a more recent example of this trend, see U Khin Maung Nyunt's essays, "Supannaka Galuna Raja" and "The Peasant Revolution in Perspective" in *Selected Writings of Dr. Khin Maung Nyunt* (Yangon: Myanmar Historical Commission, 2004).

15. It is also evident that this nationalist perspective of the Saya San Rebellion interpreted the movement to be a well-organized and planned undertaking if it were to be accepted as part of growing nationalist sentiment. This view was also one that was espoused by official British circles, who wanted to assert that the Rebellion was not spontaneous *(The Origins and Causes of the Burma Rebellion [1930–1932])*. The main body of the Burmese nationalist interpretation did not really differ in substance from British documents (for it adopted the facts of the narrative and the role of Saya San); but it did apply a greater sense of legitimacy than earlier British commentators were apt to give.

16. I treat James C. Scott's *The Moral Economy of the Peasant* perhaps too generally as an investigation into "the traditional economy" of the Burmese (and Vietnamese) peasant, therefore invoking a traditional v. modern dichotomy.

17. See Adas, *The Burma Delta*, pp. 185–208; Cady, *A History of Modern Burma*, pp. 277–80; Robert Henry Taylor, *The State in Burma* (London: C. Hurst, 1987), pp. 123–47.

18. Religion in this sense becomes relevant to political studies since it is considered a form of nationalism. Although scholars at this stage attempted to recognize different forms of political expression in Burma, they were nonetheless validating indigenous ideology by employing Western categories (such as nationalism) to translate local vocabularies. A response to this trend places "religion" as a category in itself, as will be discussed in the later examples by Sarkisyanz (1965) and Adas (*The Burma Delta*).

19. Donald Eugene Smith, *Religion and Politics in Burma* (Princeton: Princeton University Press, 1965), p. 107.

20. E. Michael Mendelson, *Sangha and State in Burma: A Study of Monastic Sectarianism and Leadership* (Cornell University Press, 1975), pp. 206–9. See also Robert Solomon's article "Saya San and the Burmese Rebellion," *Modern Asian Studies*, 3, 3 (1969): 209–23.

21. Ironically, the prosecution team that presented the case against Saya San characterized these symbols as representative of Burmese rebellion.

22. This view was explicit in *The Origins and Causes of the Burma Rebellion (1930–1932)*. Saya San's attempt to crown himself king was interpreted as part of the *minlaung* pattern, a British-created formula that had pretender-kings (*minlaung* actually means *incipient-king, prince,* or *king-to-be*) periodically claiming (illegitimately) to be king. See *The Origins and Causes of Burmese Rebellion (1930–1932)*, p. 1, L/PJ/6/2020, Burma Rebellion Files, frame 22; and B. S. Carey, *Hints for the Guidance of Civil Officers in the Event of Outbreak of Disturbances in Burma*, confidential, reprint copy 1931, L/PJ/6/2020, Burma Rebellion files, pp. 578–85.

23. Harry Benda, "Peasant Movements in Southeast Asia" (New Haven: Yale University, Southeast Asian Studies Reprint no. 15, 1966).

24. John Smail, "On the Possibility of an Autonomous History of Modern Southeast Asia," in *Autonomous Histories Particular Truths; Essays in Honor of John Smail*, ed. Laurie Sears (University of Wisconsin Center for Southeast Asian Studies, monograph 11, 1993).

25. Admittedly (according to his own criteria), Smail would have argued that focusing on the Saya San Rebellion as an event would still be adhering to colonial history as it is depicted as an occurrence within the contours of the British in Burma. A more autonomous reading of the Rebellion would be to consider the events, as Sarkisyanz does, through

the prism of a locally defined category that transcends the boundaries of British involvement in Burma.

26. Victor Lieberman, *Strange Parallels: Southeast Asia in Global Context* (Cambridge: Cambridge University Press, 2003), pp. 9–15.

27. Sarkisyanz, *Buddhist Backgrounds of the Burmese Evolution*, pp. 161–65

28. Adas adopts Anthony Wallace's term *revitalization movements*, which the latter "describes as a deliberate, organized, conscious effort by members of a society to construct a more satisfying culture." See Adas, *Prophets of Rebellion*, pp. xvi–xvii.

29. See Harry Benda, "Peasant Anti-colonial Movements in Southeast Asia" (1966). Benda encourages a dichotomous framework of traditional–nationalist in order to differentiate among the variety of uprisings in Southeast Asia.

30. Patricia Herbert, *The Hsaya San Rebellion (1930–1932) Reappraised* (London: Department of Oriental Manuscripts and Printed Books, British Library; Clayton, Victoria: Australia: Centre of Southeast Asian Studies, Monash University, 1982).

31. Herbert investigates the sources linked to the traditional reading of the rebellion and questions the accuracy of that characterization. Her research led her to some of the very sources that this study examines. Herbert mentions that the facts surrounding the Hsaya San Rebellion, "the biggest anti-colonial uprising in Burmese history, are quite well known and only need outlining." See Herbert, *The Hsaya San Rebellion (1930–1932) Reappraised*, p. 1.

32. Herbert then suggests that the *wunthanu*'s failure to successfully satisfy peasant grievances resulted in the peasants' uprising, presumably in rejection of options such as noncooperation and other tactics favored by Western-educated leaders. This would imply a return to the traditional ideas that her study questions if "the Rebellion" is seen as a monolithic, coherent, movement that was inextricably connected. See Herbert, *The Hsaya San Rebellion (1930–1932) Reappraised*, p. 12.

33. Robert Taylor in *The State in Burma* adopts Herbert's take on the Rebellion. See pp. 198–99 for a restatement of Herbert's analysis.

34. Anne Foster, "Alienation and Cooperation: European, Southeast Asian, and American Perceptions of Anti-colonial Rebellion, 1919–1937" (Ph.D. diss., Cornell University, New York, 1995). Anne Foster's dissertation examines how Western colonial powers (England, Netherlands, and the United States) reacted to anticolonial rebellions in terms of their

foreign policy. Her work accepts the accuracy of the narrative. Parmimal Ghosh's *Brave Men of the Hills: Resistance and Rebellion in Burma* (London: Hurst & Co., 2000) examines anti-British uprisings in Burma from 1824 to 1932 and attempts to extend Patricia Herbert's arguments within a larger chronological framework, but also leaves the structure of the Rebellion narrative uncontested.

35. Every scholar has treated the events within the historical narrative as being factual. Included within these events as a fact, not as an interpretation, is that the Rebellion was led and organized by Saya San.

36. Harvey's position was in many ways an amplified form of the sentiment found in *The Origins and Causes of the Burma Rebellion (1930–1932)*. The "superstitious" segment of the report was actually a component of the report's overall argument to demonstrate the political motivations of the Rebellion exemplified by Saya San's attempt to crown himself king. The multiple descriptions within the report of Hindu–Buddhist symbols of kingship, amulet-wearing, tattooing, and other "badges" of the Rebellion were meant to support the notion that the Rebellion had to do with the gullibility and superstitions of Burmese peasants whose political pretensions longed for such a king. *The Origins and Causes of the Burma Rebellion (1930–1932)*, pp. 1–3, 6–7, L/PJ/6/2020, Burma Rebellion Files, frames 22, 24, 26

37. Although beyond the scope of this study, I would agree with other scholars that a dichotomous structuring of Southeast Asian culture is a feature typical of colonial scholarship, and was partly the perspective that Van Leur and Smail hoped to counteract by their strategies.

38. Herbert's first statements demonstrate her "reaction" to the overemphasis of earlier scholarship toward a traditional characterization of the Rebellion. Herbert, *The Hsaya San Rebellion 1930–1932 Reappraised*, p. 3.

39. Albert Moscotti, *British Policy and the Nationalist Movement in Burma, 1917–1937* (Honolulu: University of Hawaii Press, 1974).

40. Maung Maung, *From Sangha to Laity*.

41. See Taylor, *The State of Burma*, p.198 in footnotes 132–33.

42. Maung Maung, p. 257 in endnote 2–3. Interestingly, Maung Maung judges the sequence of events accurately because he confirms it with newspaper accounts, which he implies are inherently factual. An examination of press releases and legislation controlling the press reveals that almost every newspaper covering the Rebellion was censored and sanctioned by the local government. Newspapers that were permitted to

comment on the rebellion merely reiterated information from government press releases. It seems that these newspapers, although *Burmese*, should be considered in the same historiographical context as official government documents. See press communiqué. February 10, 1931, and the following extract from the *Times*, February 11, 1931, L/PJ/6/2020 BRGF.

43. In all fairness, it was not the task of Moscotti, Taylor, or Maung Maung to check the veracity of the narrative in their works. Each was more focused on discussing the role of Saya San within Burmese nationalism. As discussed earlier, the need to establish Saya San's place within the latter discourse was probably a contributing factor to the acceptance of the historical narrative.

44. Sarkisyanz cautiously uses Collis to introduce the idea that Saya San was "rumoured" to be a *Setkya-min*, an ideal universal conqueror. He also uses U Ba U's autobiography, which describes the events surrounding the capture of Saya San's supposed jungle palace. Both references are actually secondary recollections, not actual citations establishing the inference of Saya San's kingship as fact. See Sarkisyanz, *Buddhist Backgrounds of the Burmese Revolution*, pp. 161–62, footnotes.

45. Judge Ba U was in fact part of the tribunal that determined what would be accepted as legal facts in the trial of Saya San, an issue discussed in a later chapter. However, citing him to verify Saya San's supposed declaration of kingship should be approached with caution. See Sarkisyanz p.162, footnotes 1–2 for this use.

46. C. V. Warren, *Burmese Interlude* (Plymouth: Skeffinton and Son, 1937). Warren is described by Sarkisyanz as an eyewitness to one of the battles against rebels. His descriptions are used side by side with official legal and government reports as if he were privy to the information those documents contained as well. See Sarkisyanz, *Buddhist Background of the Burmese Revolution,* p. 162, footnotes 1–7.

47. As paraphrased in Cady, *A History of Modern Burma*, pp. 311–12.

48. Sarkisyanz does mention his reservations about the oath, mentioning, "There seems to be no other published record of this Rebel Oath except the translation made from the Burmese original by Warren . . ." who happened to be involved in the British military actions against Saya San's peasant revolt. See Sarkisyanz *Buddhist Background of the Burmese Revolution,* footnote 3, p. 162. The difficulty here is that Warren's experiences in counter-insurgency measures are assumed to be against "Saya San's revolt," when at the time it was not really known who was behind the Rebellion. See subsequent chapters for alternative narratives proposed by the British.

49. See Cady, *A History of Modern Burma*, p. 311, footnote 72. See also Maitrii Aung-Thwin, "Genealogy of a Rebellion Narrative: Law, Ethnology, and Culture in Colonial Burma," *Journal of Southeast Asian Studies*, 34, 3 (2003): 393–419.

50. *The Origins and Causes of the Burma Rebellion (1930–1932)*, p. 1, L/PJ/6/2020, Burma Rebellion Files, frame 23, states, "The Local Government then referred to the fact that the Burman was by nature restless and excitable, that the Burmese peasantry were incredibly ignorant and superstitious and that belief in the efficacy of charms and tattooing as conferring invulnerability was still widespread: *quoted with approval the prophetic observations made in 1914 by Mr. B. S. Carey that rebellions would recur from time to time.* . . . ." The series of confidential reports issued in 1931 all make reference to Carey's handbook on jungle warfare in Burma, which establishes the traditional *minlaung* motif and the idea that rebellions will occur in Burma periodically.

51. See Maitrii Aung-Thwin, "Genealogy of a Rebellion Narrative."

52. Ibid.

53. Although discussed in greater detail in chapter 3, the most significant problem with the use of *The Origins and Causes of the Burma Rebellion (1930–1932)* is that the document was used by scholars as a primary source to verify the accuracy of the Rebellion narrative when the document was actually a later synthesis of earlier findings in previously published documents. It should not have been considered a primary source.

54. This is not to say that scholarship has had the same intentions as those colonial officials who constructed the narrative through their documentation projects or in debates of the Burma Legislative Council. It is interesting, however, that the methods of scholars who have sought to reconstruct the history of the Rebellion have resembled the methods of the colonial official who constructed the sources behind this history.

55. To their credit, Michael Adas and Patricia Herbert did examine some of the judicial sources referred to in the report. They did not, however, probe or question the context from which these judicial decisions were reached. Herbert also noticed the copying of Morris's *Rebellion in Tharrawaddy* text but did not raise any issues concerning the superimposing of that district perspective onto the entire country. This may in itself account for Saya San's preferential role as the Rebellion leader—his supposed actions in Tharrawaddy were artificially extended by a rushed report to the rest of Burma. It is no wonder that officials were to comment that after the uprising in Tharrawaddy (late December 1930), infor-

mation regarding Saya San was unknown until he was caught in early August 1931.

56. Briefly, the Rebellion would always be considered through a discussion involving its "unique" Burmese characteristics and reasons for the uprising. Saya San would always be discussed as the peasant leader seeking to restore indigenous institutions.

57. Although Herbert, Taylor, Ghosh (and to some extent Adas), recognize the role of the urban intelligentsia and other forms of Western political mobilization that may have influenced the character of the Rebellion as a whole, little attention has been paid to understand the blending of the influences, especially from a more district-oriented perspective. Overarching generalizations on the nature of the uprising, which seek to make sense of the Rebellion as a whole, actually presume that it was a coherent movement in the first place. This trend to smooth over the contradictions of the Rebellion's character, as opposed to recognizing them as such, might account for the longevity of the acceptance of the official narrative.

58. Actually, British officials responsible for constructing the case against Saya San attempted to link the *wunthanu* movement with the traditionalist ideas that they stated informed the Rebellion. See *The Origins and Causes of the Burma Rebellion (1930–1932)*. Their arguments were less than adequate. Scholars who began and ended their scrutiny into the sources with the Morris report would not have been able to recognize these problems.

Chapter 7

SANCTIFYING REBELLION
Colonial Discourses and Southeast Asian Resistance

The lingering presence of the official narrative and its prescriptive structures within scholarship highlights the intimate relationship between colonial documentation projects and postcolonial research. Scholars broadened the manner in which we thought about the Saya San Rebellion by reinterpreting past assessments, shifting our theoretical priorities, and in doing so provided new viewpoints from which "the historical narrative" was engaged. Alongside these worthwhile ventures, particular narrative features remained embedded within this scholarship and the sequence of events and caricatures that have come to be associated with Saya San continued to make a substantial mark on how we conceptualized the shape of modern Burmese history and Southeast Asian culture in general. In particular, Southeast Asian mentalities began to be explored from the point of view of religious resistance, drawing from similar trends and interests in European peasant history.[1] The characteristics that were once treated as ethnologies of superstition and limited to the context of colonial Burma were now being regarded as important emblems of a pan-Southeast Asian cultural matrix. Within this epistemological context, "rebellion" became a prescriptive category through which religious worldviews of Southeast Asians (and Burmese in particular) were located and understood. The melding of religion (and especially millennial Buddhism) with revolt ushered in a fresh perspective through which Southeast Asia could be delineated as a field of analysis, while it also entrenched the Rebellion Ethnology and its colonial heritage more firmly within the scholarship of the Saya San Rebellion.

This epistemological heritage stretched beyond the dichotomous structures found in the Rebellion's official rendering, as scholars returned to the original Rebellion Ethnology in hopes of reading against the grain of colonial documents in order to distill the essence of a (single) Southeast Asian worldview. Just as ethnographers, officials, and lawyers attempted to produce a coherent understanding of the outbreaks in Burma, so too would scholars seek a similar coherency in the study of regional anticolonial rebellions, albeit with an emphasis on Southeast Asian agency and distinctiveness. Reacting to colonial accounts of rebellion that reduced descriptions of symbols, agendas, and ritual to "superstition," as well as to post-Independence historians who were eager to celebrate these movements as early expressions of secular nationalist sentiment, area-studies commentators attempted to infuse religion "back" into the Rebellion Ethnology, suspecting that previous commentators had intentionally excluded or mistakenly omitted religion from the official record. Armed with a new theoretical framework developed by John Smail and a reinvigorated focus on peasants (borrowed from European studies), Southeast Asian specialists began to look at the Saya San Rebellion within the longer context of religion in order to view the events within a fresh sociocultural context. Smail's seminal article called for the writing and conceptualization of "an autonomous history" of modern Southeast Asia that placed emphasis on utilizing internal criteria—categories, periods, narratives, and contexts—for the writing of the region's history. For nearly thirty years, scholars had struggled with the problem of "modernity" and its association with colonialism, which had dominated the way in which events, categories, and processes had been studied and considered by regional specialists.[2] Rebellions were often written as "interruptions" in the progressive narratives of the colonial state, whereas the categories of analysis reflected the political-economic priorities of colonial officials, a perspective that nationalist historians (in Smail's view) failed to address adequately.[3] If Southeast Asians were revolting against the colonial state and its policies, it was suggested that in doing so they were articulating these concerns through "autonomous" cultural expressions that were independent of the meanings prescribed to them by colonial officials. Rebellions, by their very nature, were potential subjects revealing the essence of what it was to be "Southeast Asian." Smail's intervention urged scholars to consider events such as the Saya San Rebellion from a point of view outside the framework and narratives of British colonial history and administrative categories. The delineation of Southeast Asian mentalities through religion and revolt answered this call and influenced the way in which Saya San would be regarded.

Although religion (and particularly Buddhism) had long been established as a set of complex belief-systems that enabled administrators to know indigenous communities in India and in Burma,[4] these ideas were often associated by colonizer and colonized alike with Southeast Asia's traditional past, the antithesis to the trajectories of modernity offered in the colonial project. Area-studies-trained scholars retuned their gaze upon symbols and forms of resistance culture (as described in colonial documents) in order to demonstrate the relevancy of these mentalities in decoding and delineating the Southeast Asian worldview. Referents to outcast monks and unorthodox rituals during times of civil disturbances were no longer dismissed as beyond the fold of religion (as colonial documents attempted to establish) but fully within the prescriptions and expectations of everyday Southeast Asian beliefs and practice. Works by E. Michael Mendleson Melford Spiro, and Manning Nash, paved new ground in the study of Burmese Buddhism by asking new questions that focused on local forms and understandings of what were considered more orthodox doctrines. As a result of these new directives, and in conjunction with the emergence of studies that began to show that European peasants were capable of expressing resistance and identity through millenarian expectations, scholars would begin to suggest that Southeast Asians exhibited similar eschatological experiences, taking the study of revolt and resistance in new directions.[5] "Folk" Buddhism, forest monks, medicine men, and other "marginal" figures began to draw more scholarly attention as alternative sources of authority and legitimacy than that asserted by the colonial state. Existing beliefs in a coming Buddha *(Metteya/Maitreya)*, and a golden age that would restore the purity of the religion, suggested to scholars that Southeast Asian peasants could conceptualize changes in their world (like colonial rule) in a richly nuanced and surprisingly global language. Even as millenarianism was found to be relevant in several historical settings, it was deemed particularly useful within the context of exploring Southeast Asian anticolonial rebellions and peasant movements.[6] Interest in millenarian movements and cargo cults soon began to be applied to the Southeast Asian sociocultural landscape, providing a category of analysis that would enable scholars to read peasant behavior through this trans-cultural vocabulary, refocusing our gaze upon the region's particular mentalities while raising the importance of peasant views within the field. These studies explored resistance uprisings through the prism of millenarianism in an attempt to illustrate the ways in which communities of Southeast Asians responded and conceptualized their encounters with European–American colonialism.

As a result of these intersecting epistemological trends, the Saya San Rebellion became one of the region's quintessential examples of a millenarian-inspired revolt, the subject of this chapter.[7] Folk Buddhism and in particular Burmese millenarianism provided a likely explanation as to why peasants apparently followed Saya San blindly to their deaths, how more references to kingship could explain motivations for resistance, and more importantly, how the changes under colonial rule might have been interpreted by rural communities through a religious vocabulary. Regarded in this manner, rebels were motivated not by simplistic notions of resurrecting the monarchy (as colonial reports had insisted in the *minlaung* model), but in the hope that their actions would somehow usher in the golden age of *Maitreya* Buddha (the fifth Buddha of our world cycle) whose appearance was believed to signal the renewal of the religion, the world, society, and their individual spiritual potential. To peasants, the loss of the monarchy, the decay of Buddhist institutions, economic hardship, and the erosion of personal village social networks were seen as the conditions of decline that were prophesized to precede the rise of a new king (a *cakkavartin* or universal conqueror) that would either pave the way for or become the future Buddha.[8] Scholars such as Mendleson, Sarkisyanz, and later Adas, a student of Smail, would eventually reconsider the uprising as one chapter within the much longer context of Burmese Buddhism, highlighting the way in which religious concepts provided a vocabulary for conceptualizing the changes and traumas of the British colonial state.[9] This casting of a Buddhist future by scholars was significant in that it infused a sophisticated and complex conceptual doctrine into the worldview of the Burmese peasant, which had otherwise been characterized as only "superstition, plain and simple."[10] For many in Southeast Asian studies, this exciting approach highlighted the power and potential of local knowledge, and provided Southeast Asians with the agency that had been previously denied to them by colonial and nationalist historiographical traditions.

Reinterpreting the events associated with Saya San through the glaze of millenarianism was meant to intervene in the original casting of the Rebellion Ethnology by stressing a novel, indigenously derived, religious framework, partly the result of the field's newfound directive toward writing "autonomous history" and intellectual trends emerging from European case studies.[11] Features of the Rebellion Ethnology were no longer simply regarded as elements of a static, irrational, and simplistic cultural system but indicative of a dynamic, rational, and complex vocabulary capable of articulating resistance and revolt through distinctly Southeast Asian terms and meanings. By exploring the relationship between resistance and religion, area-studies scholars sought to more clearly define how Southeast Asians conceptualized their world and the significant challenges put forth by colonial systems. Delineating Southeast Asia (and Burma) through this new initiative allowed scholars to reconsider the narratives of revolt within a completely new framework, enabling evidential records to produce novel meanings for the field on the one hand, while reifying these records and their sanctity as sources on the other. From this perspective, the Rebellion narrative continued to be affected by particular epistemological contexts, in that scholars used the narrative to delineate a more complex, more sympathetic, but ultimately equally exotic notion of Southeast Asian resistance culture. Seen from this perspective, the Rebellion Ethnology and its attending narratives were envisioned as revealing a different type of Southeast Asia than previously presented.

While earlier colonial officials had used the events to confine Burmese to modes of behavior anchored in the past, the millenarian view provided new categories that defined peasants and their ability to articulate and experience change in reference to the future. Although a tradition of area-studies specialists hoped that reading rebellion in this manner would highlight a more authentic notion of a Southeast Asian worldview, such attempts (in the case of Saya San) also reified the legacy of the colonial archive and its prescriptive qualities. Intended to depart from earlier assessments of the Rebellion, this new interpretation actually confirmed the place of the Rebellion Ethnology by anchoring its novel suggestions in the findings produced by counter-insurgency documentation projects.

This chapter explores how the category of Burmese Buddhist millenarianism (as it relates to resistance movements) is connected to colonial modes of knowing and intellectual trends in Southeast Asian research.[12] I historicize the millenarian reading of the Saya San Rebellion for what it reveals about its evidential origins in colonial law and legislation, its production and preservation in the archive, and for its lasting imprint on the direction and character of Southeast Asia as a field of study.[13]

Losing Religion

Despite this important shift in perspective, the millenarian interpretation did not depart dramatically from the evidential record or the paradigms that stemmed from colonial sources. Kingship was still central to this new framework, as it had been established and maintained in the Burma Rebellion General Files.[14] As discussed by Patricia Herbert, the "royal" interpretation that cast Saya San as a product of Burmese traditional notions of kingship and nostalgia for precolonial social institutions was founded on the authority of the *minlaung* model.[15] Based on the precedent established by political officers such as Bertram Carey, British administrative scholars focused on the supposed political aspirations of the Rebellion by treating (their own) references to kingship outside the sociocultural worldview of Buddhism. Whereas references to Buddhist symbolism were no doubt included in official reports, these elements were regarded as nothing more than attempts to obscure the actual motivations for insurgency, rendering the importance of religion as peripheral, even manipulative in its application. Saya San was thus a pretender-king, whereas his followers and emulators were often "ex-*pongyi,*" charlatans, or "quack doctors" beyond the sanctioned boundaries of what Burmese culture was defined to be. "Wandering" *pongyis* were presented as being outside the fold, not only beyond the control of the colonial administration, but beyond the sanction of religious codes as well, as medicinal practices and other leadership positions in village communities were deemed as deviations of scripturally defined duties. Causes of the Rebellion were recognized and articulated in predominantly secular terms, distilling religion from the *minlaung* model and other features of the Rebellion Ethnology. Saya San was not only illegitimate as determined by the laws and authority constituting the colonial state, he was deemed illegitimate to what was constituted (in the eyes of the British) as the Burmese cultural worldview. Post-Independence scholars (especially commentators within Burma) contributed to this distilling of religion by distancing themselves from both the negative characterization of "traditional" elements and the symbols themselves, choosing instead to focus on the collective consciousness of peasant communities that the Rebellion was seen to represent in order to offset the question of legitimacy raised by the British. Though "nationalist" historians still recognized the connection between Burmese kingship and the Rebellion, they downplayed its emphasis (in reaction to British depictions) by arguing that peasants had few other models or options to rely upon. In doing so, the category of religion was more or less left in the margins of the Rebellion archive, as early commentators focused on the politics of representation and their implications on the colonial and postcolonial state.

With the emergence of area-studies programs, scholars began to notice that these depictions of the Rebellion and its participants obscured the possible religious dimensions of the Rebellion, draining its ideological context while fixing the memory of the Konbaung monarchy and its collapse as the sole reference for revolt. Critics would suggest that British (and Burmese) accounts had overlooked religious connotations in the symbols and rhetoric in the evidential record, distorting not only the ideological grounds for participating in the Rebellion, but the conceptual framework for making sense of the overwhelming changes occurring in Burma. Religion needed to be infused "back" into the Rebellion Ethnology in order to understand the hidden narratives contained in (and beyond) official documentation. The eventual interest in millenarian Buddhism and its connection to the rebellion was part of this effort to find the religious worldview that had been only hinted at in the official discourse. As indigenous-language-trained scholars began to point out the intimate relationship between religion and the state, kingship returned to the conversation within a new, religious context. Saya San may have regarded himself as a king—but in the eyes of his followers, in the symbols of his coronation, and in the words of interested scholars—he was much more.

Recovering Religion

The insertion of religion into the conversation about the Saya San Rebellion was not solely the result of scholars interested in anticolonial-resistance movements, though in its latter permutations this seemed to be the case. Nor was thinking about religion and revolt a product of scholarship within Burma, as scholars there were more preoccupied with how the Rebellion might be integrated into a national history of the country. Saya San was presented as a leader of a peasant's "revolution," separated from the urban-nationalist movement but important nonetheless as the Rebellion signaled a shared anticolonial sentiment.[16] It is significant to note that not a single scholar within Burma explored the Rebellion from such a perspective—Was it merely forgotten or were there other explanations? For the most part, it was North American and European-based scholars of Burma (and specifically anthropologists) that were responsible for bringing religion more squarely to the attention of scholars. Scholars such as Manning Nash, Spiro, and Mendelson were interested (among many topics) in the sociology of belief systems of Burma, and in their seminal works provided the intellectual and empirical contexts for considering the cultural framework within which the Saya San Rebellion took place. For these doyens of the field, the Burmese conceptual landscape was a sophisticated and complex array of beliefs, exhibiting the ability of communities to adapt, appropriate, and reshape external influences throughout history. Although formal institutions, ideologies, and social networks of Burmese Buddhism were certainly key areas of research, so too did "less formal manifestations of Burmese religion" such as the cult of *nats,* the magical powers of *Sayas* (teacher/master), and the *weikza* demand our attention. Understanding the broad spectrum of Burmese belief systems provided the tools to delineate what it was to be Burmese, and in doing so "folk Buddhism" became a crucial category that would eventually contribute to the conflation of religion and kingship with the Saya San Rebellion.

Millennial Possibilities: Saya San as a Weikza

In a series of seminal articles, Mendelson proposed that the study of *weikza* (spiritual teachers endowed with special powers) and the associations formed around them, should be considered as a third tier of religious belief in Burma, along with Buddhism and *nat* worship.[17] These charismatic individuals form religious communities *(gaing)* that were beyond the regulation and recognition of the Buddhist *Sangha,* creating systems of ritual and personal relations that melded spirit worship, astronomy, and Buddhist teachings. He suggested that the study of *weikza* was important, not only in that they provided spiritual guidance "between" Buddhas (between the time and teachings of Gotoma Buddha and the coming of the Future *Maitreya* Buddha), but that they provided an alternative system of ritual and belief that operated between and among the fields of Buddhism and spirit worship.[18] *Weikza* were believed to have achieved special knowledge and expertise in the fields of "astronomy, alchemy, cabbalistic signs, mantras, and medicine." Masters were known to be able to fly, travel underground, assume a variety of shapes, become invisible, and live for great periods of time.[19] *Weikza* were also important because they were believed to be waiting for the arrival of *Maitreya* Buddha, who was destined to appear at the end of this world cycle and without whom they could not achieve Nirvana. According to Mendelson's interviews, one particular *weikza* (Bo Min Aung) was actually considered to be (or become) the *Setkya-min* (universal emperor) who would not only prepare the way for *Maitreya* but become the future Buddha of our *kalpa*. Small religious associations *(gaing)* formed around such a teacher and his disciples, creating a community beyond the village and outside the purview of more established Buddhist institutions.[20] Followers of a particular *weikza* were drawn to the possibility of addressing concerns at the moment, as opposed to waiting for the possibility of spiritual bliss in the sacred future. Public ceremonies involving flags, thrones, victory leaves, and *nat* worship were part of the social experience, whereas the sale and distribution of holy water, medicine, and beads exemplified their commercial relations. Interestingly, not only did Mendelson's observations find reference in the types of descriptions attributed to Saya San's supposed coronation ceremony (found in the official blue-book report of the Rebellion), he (Mendelson) identified elements within the Saya San Rebellion as the "locus classicus of *gaing* studies," basing his assessment somewhat tautologically on that very report.[21] Thus, the figure of the *weikza* and the beliefs surrounding his relationship to the future Buddha constituted what might be considered "millennial Buddhism," a localization of external ideas into something quite distinctly Burmese. Yet in his interest in *weikza* and as a substratum of Burmese beliefs, Mendelson set the groundwork for connecting Saya San to the *gaing* experience and indirectly to beliefs associated with the future *Maitreya* Buddha. This initial connection was provocative. If the networks, ceremonies, and ideologies of the Rebellion were indeed indicative of *gaing* organizational patterns and millennial beliefs tendencies, it was possible that Saya San and others like him could be understood within a completely different paradigm, outside the rubric of the Rebellion Ethnology. But the authority and influence of the archival sources (especially *The Origins and Causes of the Burma Rebellion [1930–1932]*) would prove to be too great to overcome. Despite Mendelson's important suggestions, Saya San's possible millennial connections to *weikza* communities would be interpreted only through the lens of the Rebellion, rendering its features, symbols, and rituals as part of the Rebellion Ethnology, rather than as an expression of autonomous community formation. Even Mendelson was unable to break away entirely from the prescriptive power of the report, suggesting that participants of the Rebellion seemed more intent on focusing on the idea of an imminent king, rather than *Maitreya* as a key figure. But others inspired by Mendelson's work would not be as hasty to dismiss the future Buddha or millenarianism from the narrative. The growing tide of interest in millennial movements and cargo cults in other fields had already given a new perspective on peasant studies, resistance, and religion in society.[22] Even though *weikza* and *gaing* identity were only loosely connected to notions of the fifth Buddha, it was this particular element of Buddhism that was identified, isolated, and infused into the discussion of Saya San. As a result, millenarianism would bring an added dimension to the Rebellion Ethnology, despite having very little evidence in the colonial sources or indigenous accounts saying anything about *Maitreya* Buddha.[23] Scholars would begin to consider (but also conflate) the place of *gaing* religious communities in the 1950s and 1960s with mainstream "peasant" behaviour of the 1930s, establishing millennial Buddhism and religion squarely within conversations of rural life and Burmese peasant revolts.

Preparing for the Millennium:
Saya San as Cakkavartin

Sarkisyanz's *Buddhist Backgrounds of the Burmese Revolution* (1965) was a seminal contribution to Burma Studies as it sought to situate Burmese history within the context of its Buddhist ideology, and it was the first to seriously establish Mendelson's millenarian ideas as framework for understanding the rebellions of the 1930s. The relevant chapter on Saya San was one event within this long history that explored how existing notions of Buddhist kingship, order, decline, and renewal could provide a vocabulary for expressing resistance to the British colonial state. Sarkisyanz's foundational work relied on the same sequence of events and characteristics of the narrative that were introduced in the *OCBR*, but it developed the *minlaung* model much further than ever before. While the official version had relegated the causes of the Rebellion as an expression of political motivations on the part of Saya San and blind nostalgia on the part of the peasants, Sarkisyanz contextualized the economic crisis enveloping the agricultural sectors of the economy in Buddhist terms—arguing that the conditions were interpreted by rural communities as the end of the world before which an ideal ruler and Future Buddha would appear to set things right.

Saya San was rumoured to be the *Setkya-min (cakkavartin)* the universal conqueror who would prepare the way for *Maitreya* Buddha (or in some cases become *Maitreya*).[24] According to several Theravada Buddhist traditions, the purity and sanctity of Gotoma Buddha's teachings would decline after five-thousand years, which would correspond to a collapse of its institutions, oppression of the poor, violence, and the absence of socially responsible, righteous political leaders.[25] In the midst of this chaos, a leader would arise to prepare the way for the future Buddha, whose teachings would renew the religion and golden era that was associated with it. Following the basic structure and causal focus of the *minlaung* interpretation articulated in the report, Sarkisyanz reiterated that Saya San built his palace on a sacred mountain, reenacted the traditional coronation ceremony, and issued royal proclamations—only this time it was done within the context of Buddhist millenarian beliefs that had been significantly missing in both colonial and nationalist accounts. Peasants regarded Saya San not merely as a claimant to the throne, he was *the* king that would prepare the way for (or become, in some traditions) *Maitreya* Buddha. A Buddhist future, not the restoration of the past, was at stake here.

Sarkisyanz's exciting intervention asked us to consider that militant folk Buddhism, along with economic grievances, was a considerable factor explaining the motivation and mobilization of villagers against the colonial state. Dissatisfied with previous explanations surrounding "the origins and causes" of the Rebellion, Sarkisyanz continues the discussion by suggesting that the Saya San Rebellion was a "nativistic" response, an attempt to disengage with the rapid and impersonal socioeconomic forces that were sweeping through village society in favor of a worldview that was culturally and psychologically more familiar and comforting to the large majority of rural communities.[26] The restoration of familiar symbols, patronage relationships, and communal values were articulated through "Buddhist" notions of change that were associated with the advent of an ideal ruler that would usher in a golden age. To be sure, economic hardship was a causal factor, but it was through Buddhist notions of decline and restoration that would provide cultivators with the vocabulary for understanding the social changes brought forth by the British colonial administration. Sarkisyanz's long-standing contribution was to introduce these ideas as part of the cultural landscape, raising the intellectual status of rural cultivators from a superstitious mass to custodians of a complex and sophisticated body of religious knowledge.

In doing so, Saya San and his lieutenants were recast as central figures of a religious reform movement, coherently organized along a belief system that represented much of what was considered to be "Burmese culture." Sarkisyanz repositioned the Rebellion narrative as an expression of long-standing Burmese millennial beliefs, rather than as an isolated incident within the recent history of the British in Burma. Movements of a similar nature had preceded Saya San's in 1839 and in 1858, with one individual claiming to be a *Setkya-min* (*cakkavartin*) and the other allegedly as *Metteya* (*Maitreya* Buddha).[27] A glimpse of Buddhism's many shapes in Burmese society, not merely the socioeconomic hardships of the depression, could be gleaned from the rebellion narrative. The mobilization of the countryside through Buddhist-defined images was a reflection of deeply entrenched beliefs that connected rural reformists in the twentieth century with precolonial intellectual currents. Saya San's choice to invoke familiar symbols of the monarchy and culturally significant images of a purified religion in his campaign was a predictable response so long as one recognized and could translate the vocabulary employed. More importantly, the terms for change, resistance, and social stability were derived from a much older, more widely accepted cultural language than the measures for reform that were emerging from urban-based nationalist groups. In many ways, Sarkisyanz's intervention was part of a larger epistemological project to construct and define Burmese identity through Buddhism.

While producing a more culturally sensitive and nuanced view of the Rebellion narrative, this explanation also helped to deepen, if not obfuscate, the Rebellion Ethnology's epistemological origins in the legal and ethnographical projects of the colonial administration. Sources that relied upon the official blue-book report were consulted, reintroducing its narrative structures and conventions into the discussion despite a courageous attempt to unpack its notable shortcomings. The image of the *minlaung* as merely a role to which aspirants to the throne would adopt in order to articulate delusions of grandeur was transformed by Sarkisyanz's vision into a much more sophisticated image of the *cakkavartin (Setya-min)* and in its ultimate form, the future Buddha Maitreya. The presentation of Burmese kingship as connected to the image of the Galon (Garuda) was diminished into a more pan-Buddhist figure whose background was considerably more complex than the simplistic notions that were originally articulated by Carey in 1914. The idea of a returning king was made to be more expressive of a tradition that led beyond Burma's cultural borders to the transnational field of the Buddhist world.

Saya San as Prophet

Fourteen years later, Michael Adas would pick up where Sarkisyanz left off; extending the millenarian explanation to other colonial revolts that included the Saya San Rebellion.[28] Whereas Sarkisyanz emphasized a Buddhist millenarian tradition specific to Burma, Adas sought to establish a formulaic pattern that occurred among several different cultural settings in a global context that all highlighted the importance and role of a prophetic figure in the organization of the Rebellion.[29] Repeating the identical narrative that was first delineated in the

OCBR, Adas reinforced the context that Sarkisyanz first suggested but added significantly more details available to him through official documents and sources not previously referred to in the earlier work.[30] In essence, both scholars appropriated the Rebellion Ethnology that made kingship the primary characteristic of the uprising but made it more complex, more sophisticated, and possibly more sympathetic to "indigenous culture" by casting millenarian Buddhism into the hopes and motivations of Burmese peasants. Adas argued that millenarian movements, ignored or misunderstood by colonial observers, were in fact "rational" if assessed within the cultural context that produced them. Clearly, the two scholars regarded Saya San as being "more than a mortal king," much more than the typical *minlaung* he was set up to be by colonial officials. Yet, their analysis of the Rebellion depended on the veracity of the conclusions of the report, that the Rebellion was about resurrecting the monarchy in the first place and that the facts and events leading toward this interpretation were supported by reliable evidence.[31] References to the growth of the *wunthanu athins* were subsumed within this enhanced ethnology, so that tax grievances, rising debt, forestry rights, and other reform issues were cast within a millenarian language of revolt that appeared to be more attractive to peasant representatives.[32] Where colonial administrators had linked the growth of village associations as a front to restore the monarchy of old, the millenarian interpretation expanded this view to demonstrate the sophisticated worldview of the peasant cultivator and other marginalized communities. Thus, the structure and content of the *OCBR* narrative provided scholars with a point of departure from which they could engage and interpret the narrative of the Saya San Rebellion.

The Rebellion Ethnology had now grown well beyond colonial Burma's geographical and cultural parameters, as it was conceived as just one example among many similar responses to European colonialism. No longer was the idea of a returning king the product of an unsophisticated, particular, and inherently traditional culture, but as a figure that embodied the reform ideals championed by rural and marginalized communities throughout the European colonialized world. The *minlaung* model was in fact a localized pattern of a far more universal language of conceptualizing, organizing, and articulating protest. The transformation of Saya San from a *minlaung* to a *cakkavartin* and now as a prophet, provided an image of the peasant leader that was not confined to Burma alone, he was now a global archetype forged through a combination of similar challenges, administrative policies, and economic conditions that were characteristic of the colonial project. Given this global viewpoint (and perhaps legitimacy), Saya San was no longer dismissed as a quack doctor or disgruntled rural activist, desperate to take advantage of gullible peasants in order to satisfy his own delusions of grandeur. Rather, he was understood by his fellow cultivators as a charismatic figure representing Burma's rich, dynamic, and ultimately politically conscious rural population, able to respond and mobilize dissent through a blueprint that exemplified its ultimately Buddhist foundations for understanding the world. While broadening the Rebellion's place in world history, *Prophets of Rebellion* also deepened the Rebellion Ethnology within the context of Burmese historiography, entrenching its characteristics as the structure for understanding resistance and political expression in rural Burma. In breadth and depth, Adas's seminal work intersects with and contributes to larger epistemological projects on peasant studies, resistance, agrarian studies, and world religions. Whereas colonial writers had often turned to ethnographic knowledge to explain notions of resistance, now scholars within the region were turning to rebellion to delineate "Southeast Asian Culture."

Rebellion as Religious Experience

The arrival of *The Cambridge History of Southeast Asian Studies* (1992) marked the Rebellion Ethnology's most sophisticated, refined, and influential rendering by situating Saya San and the movements associated with him within a pan-Southeast Asian religious framework. Unlike an early rendition that placed the Saya San Rebellion within the context of nation-building,[33] the *Cambridge* chapter on anticolonial responses sought to consider the role of religion as a vocabulary for resistance as well as a platform for organization, stressing not only a deep commitment to the study of indigenous mentalities, but the methodological call for more interdisciplinary scholarship within the ever-growing field of Southeast Asian Studies. Through the efforts of historian Reynaldo C. Ileto, religion was made the central focus for understanding resistance movements in the *Cambridge* history, following the methods and perspectives first presented in his pioneering book *Payson and Revolution: Popular Movements in the Philippines, 1840–1910*. In his contribution "Religion and Anti-colonial Movements," Ileto sought to address the deficiencies in the way popular movements had been discussed by "listening to them" on their "own terms" in order "to give them their due."[34] Echoing similar interventions by Ranajit Guha, Ileto urged readers to consider how religion could mean different things in different contexts while providing a framework for understanding peasant experiences. Within this discussion, millenarian movements were thought to be inherently connected to the more dominant cultural systems (such as Buddhism), but in localized forms that emphasized the agency and creativity of of subordinate, marginal, or subaltern communities in the region. Understanding these popular movements depended on one's ability to read and translate "the internal dynamics of the societies that produced them," suggesting that a key to understanding Southeast Asian culture was to decipher the cultural codes embedded within regional revolts.[35]

Whereas Cary's guidebook charts the predictability of Burmese pretender-kings emerging from time to time within a colonial context, Ileto presents a more nuanced picture of the same *minlaung* model back to the precolonial Burmese past, suggesting that Buddhist millennial ideas and notions of Burmese kingship had been traditionally intertwined, providing the throne with the terms and symbols required to express and maintain power. This was significant for the characteristics connected most closely to the Rebellion Ethnology were now being considered as crucial elements of a Burmese cultural vocabulary that did not rely on the grammar of rebellion for translation. References to the future golden era of *Maitreya* (or other prophetic figures), the reconstruction of symbols associated with the center (the throne), and the extraordinary powers of charismatic leaders were noted in

"Thai," "Vietnamese," and "Indonesian" examples as well, suggesting that the Burmese examples were indicative of a shared, *Southeast Asian* cultural matrix. From this fresh perspective, the indicators of rebellion that were originally documented by Cary were argued by Ileto to reflect much more than notions of resistance. They were, in fact, specific terms of a religious experience that could be utilized to explain change and articulate protest when deemed necessary. In other words, Burmese understandings of historical change, kingship, authority, healing, and time could be distilled from the narrative of the Saya San Rebellion. More importantly, these same characteristics could mark the contours of a regional socio-religious landscape as well.[36]

Within the Burmese context, marginalized figures such as the *weikza*, forest monks, and wandering *pongyi* were identified custodians of this religious vocabulary, often attracting followers to them through their abilities as counselors, healers, and spiritual negotiators between the more dominant religious doctrines and local practice. Like the *phuwiset* (individuals with extraordinary powers) of the Thai polities, the *nak sel* (holy men) of Vietnam, and the *resi* of the Javanese kingdoms, charismatic figures operating beyond formal sociopolitical institutions served as alternative sources of knowledge, guidance, and mediation in the villages and peripheries. These intermediators, as suggested by Ileto, provided rural communities with the leadership required if more militant action was required in times of distress.[37] At the same time, many of these marginal figures operated within the context of the center and its ideological context. In the case of Burma, the accessibility and dissemination of Buddhist texts (or collections) such as the *Anagatavamsa* (history of the future) to rural areas suggested that millenial ideas were as mainstream to cultivators as the beliefs in the potency of amulets, tattooing, and other medicinal forms. Expectations for a golden future associated with the advent of *Maitreya* was present as far back as classical Pagan times, present in donative inscriptions and possibly referred to in the prevalence of five-sided pagaodas.[38] In other words, features of the Rebellion Ethnology could be linked to precolonial worldviews, demonstrating not only the sophistication of these cultural attributes, but reconfiguring the way in which one thought about them. The *minlaung* model, which had been identified, categorized, and simplified by colonial administrators as indicative of traditional Burmese resistance culture was now liberated by that same exotic quality. Only this time these features were considered indicators of a shared, dynamic social system not needing to be qualified or compared with those ideologies eminating from urban centers. Rather than perceiving *minlaung* as figures of criminality, it was perhaps more useful to consider them as figures of folk Buddhism, connected to Burmese culture as much as *pongyi, weikza,* and *se sayas* (medicine men).[39] Rather than viewing these individuals, their symbols, and the actions of their followers within the context of protest, it might be better suited to consider their collective movement as one of many religious experiences in a rural Southeast Asian context or an "intense moment" in their lives.[40] In this manner, sanctifying rebellion was accomplished by infusing religion back into the Rebellion Ethnology, offering a direct link to one of the many "autonomous" Southeast Asian worldviews.

Autonomous History and the Rebellion Ethnology

For students interested in the study of indigenous worldviews, resistance, and peasants in Southeast Asia, the infusion of religion as a framework for studying rebellions such as Saya San's was an exciting prospect as it revealed that a regional "culture" could be detected and delineated through a careful reexamination of rural protest. Parallelling the methods of the Subaltern Studies "school," techniques and strategies for reading colonial sources were employed to sift the remnants of precolonial cultural forms from the pages of counter-insurgency narratives. In the case of the Saya San Rebellion (and perhaps other cases as well?), it meant accepting the authenticity, accuracy, and reliability of the Rebellion narrative's evidential foundation, which has an interesting, if not problematic, epistemology. Such a reading would require one to presume that the so-called facts pertaining to Saya San, the cohesive structure of the rebellion, and, most importantly, the prevalence of the *minlaung* model, were indeed in operation as recorded and registered by the official blue-book report, *The Origins and Causes of the Burma Rebellion (1930–1932)*. The possibility of a "religious explanation" for the Rebellion would indeed require one to overlook the legal circumstances surrounding the establishment of the Rebellion narrative, the questions surrounding the admissability of key sources, and the way in which knowledge about the Rebellion was first produced. Saya San's diary, the fundamental piece of material evidence supporting the entire Rebellion narrative, and the only real link between the precolonial traditions and the characteristics associated with the rebel leader, did not make a single reference to *Maitreya,* the *Setya-min,* or any of the specific ideas we associate with millenarian Buddhism.[41] More to the point, the diary's authenticity and admissibility were entered into the evidential record based on the testimony of a self-proclaimed handwriting expert unacquainted with the Burmese language. Rereading the descriptions contained within the diary through a lens of millenarianism may have raised interesting questions about Saya San's alleged identity as *the* returning king, but given the unconvincing authenticity of the diary, the entire *minlaung* connection to the Rebellion and its religious interpretations are rendered historically untenable. The murky origins of this counter-insurgency narrative and its transformation into a narrative of Southeast Asian resistance culture raise pressing questions about how we have viewed Saya San, the pursuit of "autonomous" Southeast Asian history, and the interpretation of peasant political activities in general.

We have long held to the idea that what might be identified as quintessentially "Southeast Asian" could be found by reversing, inverting, repositioning, or reinterpreting the narratives we inherited from predecessors in the colonial administration and in the academy. Following John Smail's important intervention, many scholars took to heart that, by reconsidering the manner in which we position our view, ask our questions, and stretch our periodization, we might uncover traces of a Southeast Asian past that lay between, among, and underneath more dominant narratives of elites, colonial officials, and nationalist scholars. To some extent, the career of the Saya San narrative could be seen to mirror these trends in the field in the way it was first conceived and later interpreted. Although he began as a personification of Burmese nostalgia for kingship, he was transformed into a peasant nationalist hero—but then returned by (outside) scholars to the realm of the traditional as a more complex figure that embodied not only the region's cultural attributes (Ileto) but global experiences as well (Adas). Studying this process of historical recovery has perhaps contributed to the ongoing discussion that the colonial foundations for the field are not as divorced from current knowledge as we might have hoped or intended it to be. While considering the possible role of folk religion in connection with anticolonial resistance is certainly important to pursue further, we should also be cognizant of how what we identify as "folk religion" came to be connected to protest movements in the first place. The role of the colonial surveyor, ethnographer, political officer, and judge are as much a part of this millenarian interpretation as the peasant communities it was meant to illustrate. The quest to understand and chart the notion of rebellion in Southeast Asia, like caste in India, has a colonial contribution to its historical construction that is important to recognize in our epistemological projects.[42]

In doing so, we may also begin to detect that different peasant communities in rural British Burma perceived and reacted to socioeconomic changes quite differently, but that they were perhaps not as isolated from each other and other urban-based communities as is suggested by some interpretations of the Saya San Rebellion. Rather than anchoring Saya San to the Rebellion Ethnology, perhaps he and figures excluded from "his" narrative might be seen as part of a larger process of political integration that was occurring throughout the early decades of the twentieth century. Following Patricia Herbert, the growth of new forms of political organization and expression had no doubt penetrated the countryside in the decades preceding the events of 1930–31, perhaps making the efforts of *wunthanu athins* less of a rebellion network and more the beginnings of an effort to integrate, appropriate, and coordinate rural concerns with policies generating from urban nationalists. At the same time, if we discard the cloak of the Rebellon Ethnology, what we also see are rural communities engaging urban-nationalist ideas and agendas in varying ways, some continuing to operate to alleviate local concerns, others using their newfound status to propel them above their neighboring competitors, whereas others rejected both nationalist and colonial administrator's attempts to control them. Clearly, the image of the Burmese peasant was much more differentiated, active, and adaptable than we might have previously held. Ironically, the fundamental characteristics of the Rebellion Ethnology are still alive and well in not only the way in which rebellion in contemporary Myanmar is discussed, but the manner in which memory is being utilized by both the State and its detractors.

Notes

1. See Peter Carey, *The Cultural Ecology of Early Nineteenth Century Java: Pangeran Dipanagara, A Case Study*, Singapore: 1974; Reynaldo C. Ileto, *Payson and Revolution* (Ateneo: Ateneo University Press, 1979); Ho Hue Tai, *Millenarianism and Peasant Politics in Vietnam* (Cambridge: Harvard University Press, 1983).

2. See comments in Victor Lieberman, *Strange Parallels: Southeast Asia in Global Context c. 800–1830* (Cambridge University Press, 2003), pp. 9–15, and Laurie Sears (ed.), *Autonomous Histories Particular Truths: Essays in Honor of John Smail* (Center for Southeast Asian Studies, monograph 11; Madison: University of Wisconsin Press, 1993). The genesis for the autonomous approach most likely began in the 1930s and 1940s, with some observers beginning to question the emphasis on external mechanisms marking the dynamism of the region's history. See J. C. van Leur's *Indonesian Trade and Society* (The Hague, 1955).

3. John Smail, "On the Possibility of Autonomous History of Modern Southeast Asia," *Journal of Southeast Asian History* 2, no. 2 (1961); C. V. Warren, *Burmese Interlude* (London: Skeffington, 1937) for an example of a scholar–official perspective of the rebellion. This work would be used by researchers as a source for the religious explanation of the Rebellion.

4. Donald S. Lopez (ed.), *Curators of the Buddha: The Study of Buddhism Under Colonialism* (Chicago: University of Chicago Press, 1995).

5. Oscar Salemink, "The Return of the Python God: Multiple Interpretations of a Millenarian Movement in Colonial Vietnam," in Peter Pels and Oscar Salemink (eds.), "Colonial Ethnographies," *History and Anthropology*, vol. 8, nos. 1–4, 1994, pp. 129–64.

6. For a thorough exploration of this theme, see Nicholas Tarling (ed.), *The Cambridge History of Southeast Asia*, vol. 2, ch. 4, "Religion and

Anti-colonial Movements" by Reynaldo C. Ileto, which also includes an annotated bibliography.

7. In addition to Tarling, see Emanual Sarkisyanz, *Buddhist Backgrounds for the Burmese Revolution* (The Hague, 1965), and Michael Adas, *Prophets of Rebellion: Millenarian Protest Movements against the European Colonial Order* (Durham: University of North Carolina Press, 1979).

8. See Sarkisyanz, *Buddhist Backgrounds to the Burmese Revolution*, pp. 150–53.

9. Though my research on Saya San diverges from Sarkiysanz's fine contribution, I consider his *Buddhist Backgrounds to the Burmese Revolution* to be one of the finest interventions in Burmese historiography as it significantly recasts Burmese colonial and postcolonial history within the context of Buddhist Buddhism, precisely the sort of perspective that John Smail champions. Ironically, it does not appear that Sarkisyanz was familiar with Smail's work at the time.

10. G. E. Harvey, *British Rule in Burma 1824–1942* (London: Faber & Faber, 1946), p. 73.

11. John Smail, "On the Possibility of an Autonomous History of Modern Southeast Asia," *Journal of Southeast Asian History*, 2, no. 2 (1961).

12. There is an ample record of precolonial millenarian beliefs that have been studied outside the framework of rebellion. Classical kingship in Pagan reveals belief in *Maitreya* Buddha, as often recorded in donative inscriptions (see Michael Aung-Thwin, 1985). Five-sided pagodas, such as the Dhammyazika, can only be found in ancient Pagan, which has been linked to the fifth Buddha of our world cycle (See Pierre Pichard, 1991). Several folk-Buddhist beliefs involving special medicine men/forest monks have been connected to the *Maitryea* tradition (see Mendelson, 1961), whereas stories of Buddhist saints, such as Shin Upago and Shin Male, are also connected to the future period of *Maitreya* (see John Strong, 1992). King Bodawpaya in the late eighteenth century was said to have claimed to be *Maitreya* but evidence does not support this account (see Steven Collins, 1998).

13. Donald S. Lopez (ed.), *Curators of the Buddha: The Study of Buddhism under Colonialism* (Chicago: University of Chicago Press, 1996).

14. Government of Burma, L/PJ/6/2020, BRGF, *Report on the Rebellion in Burma up to 3rd May, 1931*, command paper, 3900, (1931); *Origins and Causes of the Burma Rebellion (1930–1932)* (1934); *Report on Recent Rebellions in Burma*, Police Document, May 9 (1931); *The Rebellion in Burma, April 1931–March 1932*, September 13 (1931); *Causes of the Tharrawaddy Rebellion*, March 26 (1931).

15. Patricia Herbert, "The Hsaya San Rebellion: Reappraised," Centre of Southeast Asian Studies working paper (Melbourne: Monash University, 1982).

16. Union of Burma. *Taungthu Lethama Ayedawpon* [Account of the Peasants' Revolution], Rangoon, 1965.

17. E. Michael Mendelson, "A Messianic Buddhist Association in Upper Burma," *Bulletin of the School of Oriental and African Studies*, volume 24, 1961; "The King of the Weaving Mountain," *Journal of the Royal Central Asian Society*, 48 (July–October, 1961).

18. E. Michael Mendelson, "The King of the Weaving Mountain," *Journal of the Royal Central Asian Society*, 48 (July–October, 1961).

19. Ibid. pp. 230–31.

20. Mendelson, "A Messianic Buddhist Association in Upper Burma," pp. 568–71.

21. Ibid., p. 573.

22. Norman Cohn, *The Pursuit of the Millennium: Revolutionary Millenarians and Mystical Anarchists of the Middle Ages* (London: Secker & Warburg, 1957).

23. See Steven Collins, *Nirvana and Other Buddhist Felicities: Utopias of the Pali Imaginaire* (Cambridge: Cambridge University Press, 1998).

24. Sarkisyanz, *Buddhist Backgrounds*, p. 161. It is important to note that the citation for this association with the *Setkya-min* directs us to Maurice Collis's *Trials in Burma* (1938), a secondary source that relied on the *OCBR* for its narrative, raising questions about the Collis account reliability as a source and the claim that relies on it.

25. Sarkisyanz, pp. 150–51.

26. Ibid., p. 161.

27. Ibid., p. 155.

28. Michael Adas, *Prophets of Rebellion*, 1979.

29. Adas, pp. 92–121.

30. One such source, the "diary" of Saya San was cited to demonstrate his aspirations of kingship. This document, and the circumstances of it entering the evidential record, will be explored below.

31. Patricia Hebert, *The Hsaya San Rebellion 1930–1932 Reappraised* (1982), was the first to question this reading of the rebellion, suggesting that the evidence toward this "royal image" of Saya San deserves reconsidering. Based on the same body of evidence and narrative, she suggests persuasively that the Rebellion might be considered a "modern movement."

32. Adas, *Prophets of Rebellion*, pp. 75, 88–89.

33. David J. Steinburg (ed.), *In Search of Southeast Asia* (Honolulu: University of Hawaii Press, 1987).

34. Reynaldo C. Ileto, "Religion and Anti-Colonial Movements," in Nicholas Tarling (ed.) *The Cambridge History of Southeast Asia*, volume 2 (Cambridge: Cambridge University Press, 1992).

35. Ileto, pp. 198–99.

36. Ileto, pp. 199–213.

37. Ileto, pp. 200–201.

38. Michael A. Aung-Thwin, *Pagan: The Origins of Modern Burma* (Honolulu: University of Hawaii Press, 1985); Pierre Pichard, *The Pentagonal Monuments of Pagan* (Bangkok: White Lotus Publishers, 1991); Steven J. Collins, *Nirvana and Other Buddhist Felicities: Utopias of the Pali Imaginaire* (Cambridge: Cambridge University Press, 1998).

39. Ileto in fact follows Herbert's intervention that the Rebellion may not be as "traditional" as once held, suggesting that Saya San was familiar with this local vocabulary and harnessed it to fit the needs of a more modern political organization. In doing so, Saya San is regarded as continuing the localization process of new ideas and forms that penetrated the rural countryside in the 1920s and 1930s.

40. Though he may not have had Smail in mind when taking on this perspective (as he has intimated this to me in conversation), Ileto perhaps captures the closest we come to producing an autonomous history of regional resistance movements by considering the phenomenology of protest.

41. On the contrary, the descriptions of the coronation ceremony seem to pertain to a *gaing*-related ceremony, as first identified by Mendelson in the 1950s. See citation above.

42. Nicholas B. Dirks, *Castes of Mind: Colonialism and the Making of Modern India* (Princeton: Princeton University Press, 2001).

Chapter 8

REMEMBERING REBELLION
Museums, Monks, and the Military

The transformation of what early colonial administrators described as a local disturbance into what later scholars would deem a religious experience highlights the many ways in which the Saya San Rebellion was shaped by a variety of historical contexts and intellectual perspectives. Whether local in nature or representative of a wider pan-Southeast Asian worldview, the Rebellion narrative took different forms that often reflected ways in which particular institutions, individuals, and intellectual concerns produced notions of Burmese peasants, resistance, and other cultural forms we tend to associate with the region. Rebellion was constituted in ethnographic terms, linking anthropological projects to colonial counter-insurgency policies, but also revealing the connections between understandings of Burmese-ness with forms of peasant protest. Within this genealogy of rebellion, Burmese culture was identified as intrinsically responsible for the series of revolts associated with Saya San. Through counter-insurgency legal processes this ethnology was affirmed and authorized for documenting and preservation in the archive. Following Nicholas B. Dirks, Burmese culture enabled, and was enabled by, colonialism, affecting not only how resistance was melded to notions of "the Burmese peasant," but ultimately delineating key terms through which Southeast Asian culture would be understood. Rebellion had evolved

Ne Win and Galon veterans, 1960s

from "superstition, plain and simple" to a sophisticated example of religious life in peasant Southeast Asia.

The image of Saya San also changed according to these various interpretations of peasant revolt. His role in the rebellion steadily developed from a simple manifestation of the iconic pretender-king to the central protagonist of the movement. Just as the rebellion might be seen as reflecting different aspects of Burmese or Southeast Asian cultural traits, so too can Saya San be seen in corresponding epistemological forms—as a *minlaung,* a medicine man/ex-*pongyi,* the protonationalist, and as a Buddhist prophet/savior. For some he represents an unchanging, precolonial Burma, whereas for others he represents a new breed of political activist that was attuned to peasant concerns and thinking, but equally engaged with the strategies and techniques of urban political elites. Accompanying his shifting identity were certain basic elements of the Rebellion narrative that remained embedded with Saya San's story, most crucially his identity as a returning king and an embodiment of unchanging Burmese values. Yet from a third point of view, the figure of Saya San might also be seen as representing different stages of ethnohistorical knowledge production: (a) his "anthropological" profile as one of many faceless pretenders to the throne, (b) the "textual" phase within the context of counter-insurgency law, (c) his "historical" co-optation into national narratives and sites of memory, and (d) his eventual emancipation in the hands of sympathetic areas-specialists who ironically return him to an archetypal form representing regional worldviews and interdisciplinary sensibilities. Just as the narrative of the Rebellion developed, so too did it affect the contours of Saya San's persona and connection to rural politics. These multiple images of the main protagonist of the Rebellion also casts some light on the multiple narrators that were at work to inscribe him: the colonial ethnographer, the lawyer, and the scholar. The ensuing caricatures are as much connected to each other as they appear to be separated, each having been erected from the same evidential foundation (and often written against one another) in an attempt to embody particular political or intellectual perspectives deemed important to the writer. The career of the Saya San Rebellion reflects as much about its community of interpreters as it may reveal something about the worldview of Southeast Asian rural communities in the 1930s.

While scholars abroad have assured Saya San's place in Southeast Asian history as a messianic figure or as the paradigmatic rural activist, the shaping and anchoring of his contribution to the Burmese national narrative continues in a variety of ways in contemporary Myanmar. For many of these "home scholars," Saya San continues to hold an important, but somewhat uncertain place in the national story as depictions of his role in the anticolonial struggle continues to be the predominant paradigm. Although the range of interpretations that have characterized external scholarship are less frequently addressed within Burmese-language treatments of the Rebellion, local textbooks and official histories present Saya San sympathetically as a misguided, but ultimately compassionate and motivated peasant leader that sought to improve the livelihood of ordinary cultivators by appealing to their nostalgia for the monarchy and the familiarity of the precolonial past. In many ways, Carey's *minlaung* model continues to (indirectly) influence the way Saya San is remembered by Burmese today. More importantly, the Rebellion Ethnology and its depiction of Burmese political potential has also reappeared in much of the discourse on Myanmar's future.

Rebellion on Display

The former capital city of Yangon commemorates the importance of Saya San with a street and a memorial hall named after him. Public monuments for other political figures, like U Wisara and Aung San, have garnered attention as well, a reminder that the formation of the nation involved several types of individuals from the monkhood, educated elites, and peasant communities. Although Saya San has not been honored in Yangon with a monument of his own, he is given a special place within the Defence Services Museum, a fascinating site of memory where the history of the military and the nation are combined to form a single narrative detailing the emergence of the modern nation-state.

Strewn over a large hall, the history of Myanmar is reconstructed through the main historical exhibit consisting of paintings, photos, displays, and dioramas beginning with the monarchy and ending with the military's ascent to power. The narrative of the nation is presented in a linear fashion as a story of struggle and "nationalist spirit," with one display leading chronologically to the next, presenting the visitor with a visual account of the individuals and communities who contributed to the formation of the modern nation-state. Paintings reconstruct battles from the three Anglo-Burmese wars while galleries represent the pacification of the kingdom as a historical geography of resistance, with charts detailing the names of rebel leaders *(bohs)* and maps demarcating the locations of their movements within the boundaries of the contemporary state. Resistance "relics," such as shirts with cabalistic squares and a tall five-sided gallery featuring portraits and biographies of important fighters (including Bo Min Yaung, grandfather of Aung San) represent the last two hundred years as a period of unified resistance to internal and external influences. Upon reaching the early twentieth century, one is struck by the smoothness, clarity, and coherency of the story as images of nationalist groups such as the YMBA, GCBA, the Thakins, and other nationalist groups are placed side by side, unified by the trajectory of the narrative. Oddly enough, when the visitor approaches the 1920s and 1930s, Saya San is not included among other political figures like U Oktama, U Wisara, U Soe Thein, or any of the GCBA leaders. Greater emphasis is given to "the Thirty Comrades," the band of young students that were trained under the Japanese to form the Burmese Independence Army following the Japanese attacks on Pearl Harbor and Southeast Asia. One might think that Saya San has been stricken from the national narrative until coming upon a small display in the middle of the hall.

Adjacent to the main exhibit featuring the Burma Independence Army is a small enclosure with two display walls on opposite ends. One side is dedicated to the *Dobama Asiayone* (We Burmese) movement and other labor parties that were growing in number by the 1930s. The other side features a large painting of a battle scene (at Phar Swe Gyaw) on the central panel that serves as a backdrop for a bust of Saya San, flanked on two sides by panels showing photos of him at court, Galon members being tried under the Special Tribunal, and even a photo of the judges coming ashore from a boat. Enclosed by the three-paneled wall, the exhibit stands apart from the main story of the modern nation-state, the mirror image of the labor movement but disconnected with the dominant narrative of nationalist groups or other politicized monks who articulated reform through alternative approaches. At the same time, the exhibit is meant to demonstrate that peasants were clearly part of "the reemergence of nationalist spirit" even though they may have been separated by their choice of action. Clearly, notions of modernity contributed to how the national story was represented, with particular types of political expression appropriated for the metanarrative whereas others were left to the margins, suggesting that the Rebellion Ethnology was still very much present within contemporary understandings of the past. In many respects, Saya San's Rebellion is physically represented as an oddity, respected for its intentions but divorced from the main trajectory of the state. It could not be placed within the same story of the Burmese nation but it could not be ignored as well, since it was one of the few instances where rural communities found an opportunity to express themselves.

It also appeared anachronistic in that it occurred during a time when a new generation of educated elites was indeed articulating measures for political change in terms shared throughout the colonized world. By placing his exhibit outside the chronological and thematic trajectory of the other exhibits, Saya San seems to hold an uncertain place in the memory of the nation; he is considered part of the story but he does not seem to fit.

Three-and-half-hours' drive away from the Yangon city limits, one will find miles of green rice-padi fields with irrigation canals being attended to by groups of anonymous cultivators and the unbroken landscape, save for the occasional pagoda, village, or toll booth. Arriving in Tharrawaddy, one will come upon a large, red sign that proclaims it as *Saya San Town,* and further in, what looks like the original court house where his trial took place is flanked by a garden with a gilt statue of Saya San himself. One has to enter the fenced enclosure from the side, where small paths lead to the statue that stands nearly fifteen feet high from the ground, surrounded by flowers and other attractive fauna. If one looks closely, one section of the fence shows a Galon defeating the Naga, emblematic of the idea of the Rebellion that had been so deeply engraved into the memory of the revolt. The statue is a physical replica of a famous photo of Saya San that has him dressed in formal attire with a cane. But here he is cast looking eastward to where the Pegu Yoma lay in the horizon, and as the narrative holds it, where he built his palace on Alantaung. The infamous Tharrawaddy Prison is also nearby, about two miles from the monument, where many nameless detainees were locked up and executed during the counter-insurgency campaigns of the 1930s. Whereas the memory of Saya San idles uneasily in the narrative that is represented in Yangon's Defence Services Museum, in Tharrawaddy there is no conflicting narrative of the nation-state to contend with, no hint of political changes and processes that might conflict with the image of a simple peasant leader who would envision himself a king. Saya San is firmly rooted to the place and history of Tharrawaddy, having been returned to where his narrative first emerged.

The Return of Political Monks

When the world began to see the first images of monks marching on the streets in September 2007, many commentators abroad were immediately struck by what seemed to be a unified expression of political will from below. It was hard not to judge it as such, as the mass of saffron robes made it difficult to distinguish one monk from another, and for a good period of time there was no official statement from any of the marchers detailing the goals or issues that they were representing by their protest. There were some civilian participants as well, some carrying bullhorns and helping in the chanting of political slogans while others formed human rings surrounding the monks as they walked through the streets. Television reports and Internet exchanges presented footage of monks carrying *National League for Democracy* signs while other images of monks turning their donation bowls upside down (as a supposed symbol of refusing alms to government-linked supporters) added a particular political flavor to the coverage. One image that was repeated on Channel News Asia was of "a monk" with a green bandanna tied around his neck pumping his fist and holding a flag while he led a group of other equally committed monks. Though opposition parties in neighboring Bangkok and pro-democracy groups immediately offered explanations suggesting links with their own political causes, other more immediate explanations pointing to socioeconomic factors were also being circulated among the media. Some commentators linked recent fuel hikes and lack of social services to an overcrowding of monasteries, whereas other observers suggested that an incident involving the mistreatment of monks by government officials in a rural monastery sparked what was appearing to be unified demonstrations. Some foreign governments and United Nations officials opined that the marchers were calling for political change, and when a hundred monks or so did stop in front of the home of Aung San Suu Kyi, it confirmed for many that politics had everything to do with the activity on the streets of September.

When the government predictably stepped in to restore civil order, many anticipated the type of response that took place in 1988, wherein reportedly three thousand demonstrators were killed and many others were arrested or forced to flee. Although this was apparently not the case in 2007, the actions of riot police and military battalions sparked serious condemnation from ASEAN (Association of Southeast Asian Nations), the UN, and other nations regarding the manner in which the authorities reclaimed the streets. The majority of public statements in the media considered the demonstrations as a clear sign that people in Yangon and those in the countryside were not supportive of the current government policies, and although these political expressions were cast within rather ambiguous Buddhist terms, it was nonetheless perceived to be a call for reform and fundamental political change.

Commentators and pundits alike made little attempt to question just who these monks were, what were their grievances, where they originated, how long had they been in the monkhood, and the relationship between their respective monastery and the Sangha Council. Few ventured to consider the manner in which their actions were being classified, categorized, and connected to larger political agendas by those contesting the political legitimacy of the state. Monks, just like the rural peasant, were considered a homogeneous community, drawn to the life of austerity and meditation as an act of devotion and adherence to a calling that was central to Burmese identity. Even though it is well established that political activists in the 1920s and 1930s donned the robes and shaved their heads in order to appeal to particular sensibilities and articulate reform through Buddhist symbols, ideas, and principles, the monks of 2007 were deemed indistinguishable, uniform, and incapable of articulating their concerns in terms other than in the political language of democracy. Just as early nationalists sought to appropriate the growing dissent emerging from the countryside in the 1930s, so too did opposition groups, activists, and UN officials make claims on behalf of the monks on the streets. Local socioeconomic issues, inter-*Sangha* competition for patrons, and socioeconomic disparity between rural and urban classes were effaced in favor of interpreting the series of marches (that took place in other parts of the country as well) as a unified, coherent, democracy movement. Where British colonial officials had once turned to notions thought to be inherently "Burmese" to explain what was being defined as "rebellion," now activists, the media, politicians, and scholars were inscribing new ideas associated with democratic ideals upon Burmese monks to explain contemporary examples of protest, dissent, and other forms of political expression on the streets. This new explanation of Burmese resistance applied to the layperson as well. Despite a wide range of possible social identities stemming from religion, ethnicity, occupation, gender, networks of patron–clients, education, and class, "ordinary Burmese" were now being constructed as a unified community through their apparent appetite for democratic change, political reform, and condemnation of the government. As in the colonial past, Burmese continue to be defined by a culture of resistance—only this time it is toward their own government.

The Rebellion Ethnology Continues

While internationally acceptable forms of political expression and status have been assigned to Burmese monks and opposition groups, the same terms are not ascribed to the current government, even as it makes efforts to establish its own form of democratic institutions. Despite attempts to embrace some of the political terms, structures, and ideals espoused by many Western nations, the current government has been frequently described through some of the very cultural traits that were used to mark rural peasants in the 1930s. In short, familiar characteristics found in the Rebellion Ethnology persist in the discourse about contemporary Myanmar, only this time it is applied to the military government rather than to the rural masses, suggesting that the state is incapable of truly embracing and implementing the ideals and institutions of political governance that is considered legitimate to international observers and media critics.

Flawed economic policies aside, the manner in which developments in Myanmar are often discussed reveal the types of narrative conventions used to describe the political potential of Burmese peasants in the 1930s through the discourse of rebellion. Just as the *minlaung* model was applied to Saya San and his alleged lieutenants, so too are senior government officials often portrayed as making references to Burmese kingship and the royal ceremonies that often characterize such a figure. Sponsorship of particular monasteries and temples, patronage of religious festivals and relic tours, and the glorification of past kings through commemorative monuments seem to point to an obsession with the past and in particular to kings. Much ado was made about the recent erection of a statue of sixteenth-century King Bayinnaung, whose territorial expansion into then Siam and Cambodia was equated with the current government's frosty border relations with the Thais. Though the Thais also erected a statue of the king who reclaimed Siam from the occupying Burmese, the lack of political progress and the military's symbolic association with the Bayinnaung statue was directed toward the Burmese government.

When the Burmese authorities decided to relocate their capital to Upper Burma, a variety of interpretations immediately followed in the press, rekindling the Rebellion Ethnology. Fantastic stories that purported to explain the shift of the political center to paranoia, superstition, and astrology simply resurrected rather well-known colonial descriptions of the Burmese kings from the nineteenth century. Whereas certain cultural considerations may indeed have been at play, it was the overtly Orientalist portrayal of government officials as incapable of making rational decisions that reminds one of the types of images and language found in colonial-period gazetteers, reports, and histories. It did not help that images of three colossal statues of King Anawyatha, Bayinnaung, and Alaungpaya were built along the new capital's (Naypyidaw) parade route, as photos of the statues usually were taken with the current military leadership in the foreground—a less than subtle hint about the apparent nostalgia for monarchy and delusions of grandeur afflicting the leadership.

This is not to say that kingship is irrelevant to current political culture. To be sure, the three kings depicted also represent another idea that is important to the contemporary state: unification. Since independence in 1948, the new Burmese nation was plagued with civil war and real threats of separation, and only recently has it been able to bring many of these armed ethnic groups to the negotiating table in order to reinforce, redefine, and restructure the contours of the nation. The precolonial past certainly remains an important source for terms and symbols in the contemporary political scene, but it does not restrict the adoption, understanding, and ability to carry out reforms and initiatives that reflect the realities and challenges of the present. Mary Callahan's seminal research, among a few others, shows that the rise to prominence of the military, and its ability to sustain rule, were based on a range of historical circumstances and contexts that were particular to the post–World War II situation. Threats to the state are perceived, assessed, and acted upon within the context of contemporary warfare and risk management, not through the romantic images associated with past kings.

Yet, old ethnographies die hard. In early 2000, Karen twin boys were featured throughout the international media for the manner in which they were revered as leaders of God's Army, a small resistance group that was associated with the much larger Karen National Union. According to media interviews, the two boys were thought to be invulnerable, as they had allegedly survived a battle, though hopelessly outnumbered and outmaneuvered, unscathed. Subsequent stories focused on how the boys were perceived by their supporters, the nature of their fantastic powers, and the cultural meanings one could decipher from this unique and quintessentially different form of resistance occurring in the jungles of Myanmar. Yet the underlying implication persisting throughout the coverage was ultimately an unfortunate one. Though sympathetic to their cause, more enlightened audiences could not take these types of movements seriously as resistance in Myanmar seemed to be historically bound to traditional forms of political expression at best, and superstitious gullibility at worst. Burmese (or in this case Karen) were bound and constrained by their cultural beliefs as they had been in the 1930s.

BIBLIOGRAPHY

Indexes and Bibliographical Guides

Aung-Thwin, Michael. *Southeast Asian Research Tools: Burma*. Southeast Asian Paper no. 16, Part 3. Center for Southeast Asian Studies, Asian Studies Program, Honolulu: University of Hawaii Press, 1979.

Griffin, Andrew. *A Brief Guide to Sources for the Study of Burma in the India Office Records*. India Office Library and Records, 1979.

Herbert, Patricia M. *Burma*. World Bibliographical Series, volume 132, Oxford: Clio Press, 1991.

Shulman, Frank Joseph. *Burma: An Annotated Bibilographical Guide to International Doctoral Dissertation Research 1898–1985*. Lanham, MD: University Press of America, 1986.

Sims, John. *A List and Index of Parliamentary Papers Relating to India 1908–1947*. India Office Library and Records, London, 1981.

Government Publications and India Office Documents
L/PJ/6/2020–23

Appeal Judgment: Criminal Appeal No. 1121 of 1931, Special Tribunal Case No. 5. L/PJ/6/2022/, Burma Rebellion files, September 29, 1931.

Burma Criminal Law Amendment Act 1931. L/PJ/6/2021, Burma Rebellion files, July 6, 1931.

Burma Emergency Powers Ordinance 1931, L/PJ/6/2021, Burma Rebellion files, June 1, 1931.

Burma Legislative Council Proceedings. Volume XIX no. 1, February 12, 1931.

Burma Legislative Council Proceedings. Enclosure No. 3: Extract from the Proceedings of Council Relating to the Burma Criminal Law Amendment Bill, 1931, at a Meeting Held on the 14th February, 1931. L/PJ/6/2021, Burma Rebellion files.

Burma Rebellions Trials Bill 1931, L/PJ/6/2021, Burma Rebellion files, September 7, 1931.

Burma Rebellion Trials Ordinance 1931, L/PJ/6/2021, Burma Rebellion files, March 12, 1931.

The Burmese Situation by U Saw. Letter to W. Wedgwood Benn, Burma Rebellion files, L/PJ/6/2020, July 1931.

Causes of the Tharrawaddy Rebellion, Ralph Clarence Morris, deputy inspector-general of police for railways and C.I., Burma Rebellion files, L/PJ/6/2020, March 26, 1931.

Confidential. *Hints for the Guidance of Civil Officers in the Event of Outbreak of Disturbances in Burma.* B. S. Carey. Burma Rebellion files, L/PJ/6/2020, April 1931 (second reprint).

Confidential. *Note on the Growth of the Bengal Revolutionary Movement in Burma from 1922–1930.* No. 693W30, L/PJ/6/2021, Burma Rebellion files, December 15, 1930.

Confidential. *Police Letter No. 429C30,* Burma Rebellion files, L/PJ/6/2020, January 5, 1931.

Confidential. *Police Letter No. 429C30,* Burma Rebellion files, L/PJ/6/2020, January 12, 1931.

Confidential. *The Rebellion in Burma, April 1931–March 1932.* Burma Rebellion files, L/PJ/6/2020, September 13, 1932.

Copies of Telegrams [Secret]. Government of India, Home Department, to secretary of state for India, repeating telegram from Burma.

7:50 A.M., December 24, 1930, L/PJ/6/2020. Burma Rebellion files.

9:20 P.M., December 24, 1930, L/PJ/6/2020. Burma Rebellion files.

5:30 P.M., December 25, 1930, L/PJ/6/2020. Burma Rebellion files.

6:00 A.M., December 27, 1930, L/PJ/6/2020. Burma Rebellion files.

3:45 P.M., December 29, 1930, L/PJ/6/2020. Burma Rebellion files.

5:15 P.M., December 30, 1930, L/PJ/6/2020. Burma Rebellion files.

8:00 P.M., December 31, 1930, L/PJ/6/2020. Burma Rebellion files.

5:45 P.M., January 1, 1931, L/PJ/6/2020. Burma Rebellion files.

6:15 A.M., January 2, 1931, L/PJ/6/2020. Burma Rebellion files.

1:30 P.M., January 4, 1931, L/PJ/6/2020. Burma Rebellion files.
7:00 P.M., January 6, 1931, L/PJ/6/2020. Burma Rebellion files.
5:35 P.M., January 8, 1931, L/PJ/6/2020. Burma Rebellion files.
Extract from the Proceedings of the Government of Burma in the Police Department, No. 386C31. "Report by the Commissioner, Federated Shan States, on the Recent Rising in the Shan States," L/PJ/6/2020, Burma Rebellion files, August 20, 1931.
Judgment Order: Criminal Appeal No. 1121 of 1931, Special Tribunal Case No. 5. L/PJ/6/2022, Burma Rebellion files, October 11, 1931.
Judgment Summary: Special Tribunal Case No. 4 of 1931, King Emperor v. Saya San and Others. August 28, 1931, L/PJ/6/2022, Burma Rebellion files, October 19, 1931.
Judgment Summary: Special Tribunal Case No. 5 of 1931, King Emperor v. Saya San. August 28, 1931, L/PJ/6/2022, Burma Rebellion files, September 29 1931.
The Origins and Causes of the Burma Rebellion (1930–1932), The Burma Rebellion Files, L/PJ/6/2020, 1934.
Press Communiqué. Copy of letter no. 429C30, May 17, 1931. From the government of Burma to the government of India Home Department, L/PJ/6/2020, Burma Rebellion files.
Private Letter: Edward Thompson to the Secretary of State for India. January 2, 1931. L/PJ/6/2020, Burma Rebellion files.
Report on the Rebellion in Burma Up to 3rd May, 1931. Communique Issued by the Government of Burma, command paper 3900, June 1931.
Report on Recent Rebellions in Burma. Police document, Burma Rebellion files, L/PJ/6/2020, May 9, 1931.
The Tharrawaddy Outbreak. Copy of letter no. C30, December 29, 1930. From the government of Burma to the government of India Home Department, L/PJ/6/2020, Burma Rebellion files.

Burmese Language Sources, Books and Articles

An observer. "On the top of Ah Lan Mountain, The Original Place of the Peasants' Revolution." *Forward Magazine* 6, no. 7, March 1965.
Bamaw Tin Aung. *History of Myanmar in Colonial Period.* N.d.

Dagon Shwe Mhya. *The Record of 1930 Revolution*. U Myat Soe. Yangon: Sarpay Beikman, n.d.

Hla Kyaw (Mawlamyaing) U. "Galon Saya San Whom I Knew." *O Way Journal,* March 1970.

Kyaw Mya Than. *Saya San in the Death House.* N.d.

Kyee Maung. "A Peasant Leader Who Fought for the Revolution Till He Died." *Shumawa Magazine* 17, no. 202, March 1964.

Kyi Nyunt (Chit Kyi Yae). "The Right Attitude of Morris Collis and Today Peasants' Victory." *Myanmar Newspaper,* March 1971.

Maung Maung (Kyauk Se). "Saya San Peasants' Revolution." *People's Journal,* no. 6, March 1969.

Maung Maung Kyi. "Saya San in Yamanya." *Myawaddy Magazine* 13, no. 5, March,1965.

Min Yu Wai. "Saya San, Peasant and Galon Leader." *Ngwe Tar Yee Magazine,* March 1966.

Myanmar Encyclopedia. Volume 4. Third edition. Yangon: Sarpay Beikman Press, 1975.

Myint Naing, Tekkatho. "The Last News of Saya San." *Myawaddy Magazine* 24, no. 9, July 1976.

Myint Swe. "Books from Galon Revolution." *Myawaddy Magazine* 18, no.5, March 1970.

———. "The Four Verses Composed by Galon Saya San Just Before He Was Hanged." *Myawaddy Magazine* 21, no. 5, March, 1973.

———. "The Fund for Galon Saya San." *Ngwe Tar Yee Magazine,* March 1969.

———. "Saya San's Explanation Letter." *Ngwe Tar Yee Magazine,* no. 117, March 1970.

Nay Win, Maung. "Peasants Revolution and the Patriotic Poet's Blessing Poem." *The Daily Mirror,* March 1993.

Thumana Maung. "The Place where Saya San and his Followers Stayed." *O Way Journal,* no. 38, March 1970.

Tin Nwe Maung. "Galon Saya San and the Peasants' Army." *The Working People's Daily,* March 1993.

Saw Shwe Bo. "From Ah Lan Mountain to Pawam Camp in the Shan State." *Forward Magazine,* March 1969.

Saya Myint. "Saya San Revolution." *Myawaddy Magazine,* March 1959.

Sein Sein. "The Burial Site of Saya San is Now Revealed." *Shudaung Journal,* no. 1, March 1969.

Sin Phyu Kyun Aung Thein. *Galon Saya San.* Yangon: Bagan Publishing House.

Soe Shein. "The Record of 1292 Peasants' Revolutionary." *Ngwe Tar Yee Magazine*, March 1969.

Win Pe, Monywa. "Peasant Rebel Galon Saya San Who Fought the Colonial Government." *The Daily Mirror*, March 1973.

Books and Articles

Adas, Michael. "Bandits, Monks, and Pretender Kings: Patterns of Peasant Resistance and Protest in Colonial Burma, 1826–1941," in Robert P. Weller and Scott E. Guggenheim, eds., *Power and Protest in the Countryside*. Durham: Duke University Press, 1982.

———. *The Burma Delta: Economic Development and Social Change on an Asian Rice Frontier 1852–1941*. Madison: University of Wisconsin Press, 1974.

———. "Comment" in Nicholas B. Dirks (ed.), *Colonialism and Culture*. Ann Arbor: University of Michigan, 1992, 127–34.

———. "From Avoidance to Confrontation: Peasant Protest in Precolonial and Colonial Southeast Asia," in Nicholas B. Dirks, ed. *Colonialism and Culture*. Comparative Studies in Society and History Book Series. Ann Arbor: University of Michigan Press, 1992.

———. "Immigrant Asians and the Economic Impact of European Imperialism: The Role of South Indian Chettiars in British Burma." *Journal of Asian Studies*, XXXIII, 1974, pp. 385–401.

———. *Machines as the Measure of Men: Science, Technology, and Ideology of European Dominance*. Ithaca: Cornell University Press, 1989.

———. *Prophets of Rebellion: Millenarian Protest Movements against the European Colonial Order*. Chapel Hill: University of North Carolina Press, 1979.

Alexander, H.R., ed. "The Pacification of Upper Burma: A Vernacular History (by Maung Tha Aung and Maung Mya Din)." *Journal of Burma Research Society*, 31, 1941, 80–1936.

Amin, Shahid. *Events, Metaphor, Memory: Chauri Chaura, 1922–1992*. Berkeley: University of California Press, 1995.

Anderson, Benedict. *Imagined Communities: Reflections on the Origins and Spread of Nationalism*, London: Verso, 1983.

Anderson, Clare. *Legible Bodies: Race, Criminality and Colonialism in South Asia*. Oxford: Berg, 2004.

Arnold, David. *Colonizing the Body: State Medicine and Epidemic Disease in Nineteenth Century India*. Berkeley: University of California Press, 1993.

Ashcroft, Bill, Gareth Griffiths, and Helen Tiffin. *The Empire Writes Back: Theory and Practice in Post-colonial Literatures*. Second edition. London: Routledge, 2002.

Aung-Thwin, Michael. "The British 'Pacification' of Burma: Order without Meaning." *Journal of Southeast Asian Studies*, 16, no. 2, 1985.

———. *Myth and History in the Historiography of Early Burma: Paradigms, Primary Sources, and Prejudices*. Athens: Ohio University Center for International Studies Monographs in International Studies, Southeast Asia Series, no. 102, Athens, 1998.

———. *Pagan: Origins of Modern Burma*. Honolulu: University of Hawaii Press, 1985.

———. "Spirals in Early Burmese and Southeast Asian History." *Journal of Interdisciplinary History*, 21, no.4, 1991, 572–602.

Axel, Brian (ed.). *From the Margins: Historical Anthropology and Its Futures*. Durham: Duke University Press, 2002.

Badgely, John H. "Burma: The Nexus of Socialism and Two Political Traditions." *Asian Survey*, III, 2, 1963, 89–95.

Barnard, Timothy P. (ed.). *Contesting Malayness: Malay Identity across Boundaries*. Singapore, NUS Press, 2004.

Bell, Catherine. *Ritual: Perspectives and Dimensions*. New York: Oxford University Press, 1997.

———. *Ritual Theory, Ritual Practice*. New York: Oxford University Press, 1992.

Benda, Harry. "Peasant Movements in Colonial Southeast Asia." *Continuity and Change in Southeast Asia*. New Haven: Yale University Press, 1972.

Benton, Lauren. *Law and Colonial Cultures: Legal Regimes in World History 1400–1900*. Cambridge: Cambridge University Press, 2002.

Blouin, Francis X., Jr., and William G. Rosenberg, eds. *Archives, Documentation, and Institutions of Social Memory: Essays from the Sawyer Seminar*. Ann Arbor: University of Michigan Press, 2006.

Breckenridge, Carol A., and Peter van der Veer, eds. *Orientalism and the Postcolonial Predicament*. Philadelphia: University of Pennsylvania Press, 1993.

Brohm, John F. "Burmese Religion and the Burmese Religious Revival," Ph.D. dissertation, Cornell University, 1957.

Burger, Mark T., "Decolonization, Modernisation, and Nation-Building: Political Development Theory and the Appeal of Communism in Southeast Asia, 1945–1975." *Journal of Southeast Asian Studies*, 34, no. 3, 2003, 421–48.

Cady, John F. *A History of Modern Burma*. Ithaca: Cornell University Press, 1958.
Carey, Peter. *The Cultural Ecology of Early Nineteenth Century Java: Pangeran Dipangara. A Case Study*. Singapore, 1974.
Charney, Michael. *A History of Modern Burma*. Cambridge: Cambridge University Press, 2009.
Chatterjee, Partha. *Nationalist Thought and the Colonial World: A Derivative Discourse*. Minneapolis: University of Minnesota Press, 1986.
———. *A Princely Imposter? The Strange and Universal History of the Kumar of Bhawal*. Princeton: Princeton University Press, 2002.
Chaturvedi, Vinayak. *Peasant Pasts: History and Memory in Western India*, Berkeley: University of California Press, 2007.
Chit Maung. "The Real Origins and Causes of the Burma Rebellion." *Thu Lou Lu* (by Ma Ma Lei), Rangoon, 1953.
———. *The Predicament of Culture: Twentieth Century Ethnography, Literature, and Art*. Cambridge: Harvard University Press, 1988.
Clifford, James. *Routes: Travel and Translation in the Late Twentieth Century*. Cambridge, Harvard University Press, 1997.
Cohn, Bernard S. *An Anthropologist among the Historians and Other Essays*. Oxford: Oxford University Press, 1990.
———. *Colonialism and Its Forms of Knowledge: The British in India*. Princeton: Princeton University Press, 1996.
Cohn, Norman. *The Pursuit of the Millennium*. London: Secker & Warburg, 1957.
Collins, Steven. *Nirvana and Other Buddhist Felicities: Utopias of the Pali Imaginaire*. Cambridge: Cambridge University Press, 1998.
Comaroff, Jean, and John Comaroff, *Of Revelation and Revolution: Christianity, Colonialism, and Consciousness in South Africa*, vol. 1. Chicago: University of Chicago Press, 1993.
Cooper, Frederick, and Ann Laura Stoler. *Tensions of Empire: Colonial Cultures in a Bourgeois World*. Berkeley: University of California Press, 1997.
Crosthwaite, Sir Charles. *The Pacification of Burma*. London: E. Arnold, 1912.
Dautremer, Joseph. *Burma Under British Rule*. London: Fisher Unwin, 1913.
Desai, Walter Sadgun. *History of the British Residency in Burma (1828–40)*. Rangoon: University of Rangoon, 1939.
———. "The Rebellion of Prince Tharrawaddy and the Deposition

of Bagyidaw, King of Burma, 1837." *Journal of Burma Research Society* XXV, 1935, 109–120.

Dirks, Nicholas B. *Castes of Mind: Colonialism and the Making of Modern India*. Princeton: Princeton University Press, 2001.

———. *Colonialism and Culture*. Ann Arbor: University of Michigan Press, 1992.

———. "Introduction: Colonialism and Culture," in Nicholas Dirks (ed.), *Colonialism and Culture*. Ann Arbor: University of Michigan Press, 1992, 1–26.

Donnison, F. S. V. *Public Administration in Burma*. London, 1953.

Dunn, Charles W. *Studies in the History of Tharrawaddy*. Rangoon, 1957.

Edney, Matthew H. *Mapping an Empire: The Geographical Construction of British India, 1765–1843*. Chicago: University of Chicago Press, 1997.

Edwards, Penny. *Cambodge: The Cultivation of a Nation, 1860–1945*. Honolulu: University of Hawaii Press, 2007.

Fabian, Johannes. *Language and Colonial Power*. Berkeley: University of California Press, 1986.

Florida, Nancy K. *Writing the Past Inscribing the Future: History as Prophecy in Colonial Java*. Durham: Duke University Press, 1995.

Foster, Anne L. "Alienation and Cooperation: European, Southeast Asian, and American Perceptions of Anti-colonial Rebellion, 1919–1937." Dissertation, Cornell University, 1995.

Foucault, Michel. *The Archaeology of Knowledge: The Discourse on Language*. New York: Pantheon, 1992.

———. *The Order of Things: An Archaeology of the Human Sciences*. Translated by Alan Sheridan. New York: Vintage, 1970.

———. *Power/Knowledge: Selected Interviews and Other Writings 1972–1977*. New York: Pantheon, 1980.

Furnivall, John S. *The Fashioning of Leviathan: The Beginnings of British Rule in Burma*. An occasional paper of the Department of Anthropology, Research School of Pacific Studies. Canberra: Australian National University, 1991.

———. *Colonial Policy and Practice: A Comparative Study of Burma and Netherlands India*. New York: New York University Press, 1956.

———. "Communism and Nationalism in Burma." *Far Eastern Survey*, XVIII, 1949, 193–97.

———. *An Introduction to the Political Economy of Burma*. Rangoon: Burma Book Club, 1938.

Ghosh, Parmimal. *Brave Men of the Hills: Resistance and Rebellion in Burma*. London: Hurst, 2000.
Grantham, S. G. *Studies in the History of Tharrawaddy*. Cambridge: Cambridge University Press, 1920.
Guha, Ramachandra. *The Unquiet Woods: Ecological Change and Peasant Resistance in the Himalaya*. Berkeley: University of California Press, 1989.
Guha, Ranajit. *Elementary Aspects of Peasant Insurgency in Colonial India*. New Delhi: Oxford University Press, 1983.
———. *Dominance without Hegemony: History and Power in Colonial India*. Cambridge: Harvard University Press, 1997.
———. "On the Prose of Counter-Insurgency," in Ranajit Guha (ed.), *Subaltern Studies II*. Delhi, 1983, 1–42.
———. "On Some Aspects of the Historiography of Colonial India," in Ranajit Guha (ed.), *Subaltern Studies I*. Delhi, 1983, 1–8.
Hall, Catherine. *Cultures of Empire—A Reader: Colonizers in Britain and the Empire in the Nineteenth and Twentieth Centuries*. New York: Routledge, 2000.
Gwynn, Sir Charles William. *Imperial Policing*. London: Macmillan, 1934.
Hall, Daniel George Edward. *Burma*. London: Hutchinson's University Library, 1950.
Hardiman, David. *The Coming of the Devi: Adivasi Assertion in Western India*. Oxford: Oxford University Press, 1987.
Harvey, Godfrey Eric. *British Rule in Burma 1824–1942*. London: Faber and Faber, 1946.
———. *History of Burma from the Earliest Times to 10 March 1824, the Beginning of the English Conquest*. London, 1925.
Haynes, Douglas E. *Rhetoric and Ritual in Colonial India: The Shaping of a Public Culture in Surat City, 1852–1928*. Berkeley: University of California Press, 1991.
Herbert, Patricia. *The Hsaya San Rebellion (1930–1932) Reappraised*. Centre of Southeast Asian Studies, working papers No. 27. Melbourne: Monash University, 1982.
Hla Aung. "The Effect of Anglo–Indian Legislation on Burmese Customary Law," in David C. Buxbaum, ed., *Family Law and Customary Law in Asia: A Contemporary Legal Perspective*. The Hague: Martinus Nijhoff, 1968, 67–88.
Hla Baw. "Superstitions of Burmese Criminals." *Journal of the Burma Research Society*, 30, 1940, 376–83.

Ho Hue Tai. *Millenarianism and Peasant Politics in Vietnam*. Cambridge: Harvard University Press, 1983.

Htin Aung. *The Stricken Peacock: Anglo–Burmese Relations 1752–1948*, The Hague, 1965.

———. *A History of Burma*. New York and London: Columbia University Press, 1967.

Ileto, Reynaldo Clemena. *Pasyon and Revolution: Popular Movements in the Phillippines, 1840–1910*. Manila: Ateneo de Manila University Press, 1979.

Innes, Charles. "The Separation of Burma." *Asiatic Review*, XXX, 1934, 193–215.

Ireland, Alleyne. *The Province of Burma*. New York: Houghton Mifflin, 1907.

Koenig, William J. *The Burmese Polity, 1752–1819: Politics, Administration, and Social Organization in the Early Kon-baung Period*. Michigan Papers on South and Southeast Asia no. 34, Center for South and Southeast Asia Studies. Ann Arbor: University of Michigan, 1990.

Kyaw Thet. "U Htaung Bo's Rebellion." *Journal of the Burma Research Society*, XXVI, 1936.

Kyin Yi. *The Dobama Movement in Burma 1930–1938*. Ithaca: Cornell University Press, 1988.

Leach, E. R. *Political Systems of Highland Burma*. London, 1954.

Leach, F. Burton. *The Future of Burma*. Rangoon: British Burma Press, 1936.

LeBar, Frank M., Gerald C. Hickey, and John K. Musgrave. *Ethnic Groups of Mainland Southeast Asia*. Human Relations Area Files. New Haven, 1964.

Lieberman, Victor, ed. *Beyond Binary Histories: Re-imagining Eurasia to c. 1830*. Ann Arbor: University of Michigan Press, 1999.

———. *Burmese Administrative Cycles*. Princeton: Princeton University Press, 1984.

———. *Strange Parallels: Southeast Asia in Global Context, 800–1830*. Cambridge: Cambridge University Press, 2003.

Lopez, David (ed.). *Curators of the Buddha: The Study of Buddhism under Colonialism*. Chicago: University of Chicago Press, 1995.

Maung Ba Han. *A Legal History of India and Burma*. Rangoon, 1952.

Maung Maung U. *Burmese Nationalist Movements*. Edinburgh: Kiscadale, 1989.

———. *From Sangha to Laity*. Manohar: Australia National University Monographs on South Asia, no.4, 1980.

Maung Maung Pye. *Burma in the Crucible*. Rangoon: Khittaya Publishing, 1952.

Maung Tin Aung. *The Stricken Peacock: Anglo–Burmese Relations, 1752–1948*. The Hague, 1965.

May, Glenn Anthony. *Inventing a Hero: The Posthumus Re-creation of Andres Bonifacio*. Madison: University of Wisconsin Center for Southeast Asian Studies, 1996.

Memmi, Albert. *The Colonizer and the Colonized*. Boston: Beacon Press, 1965.

Mendelson, Michael E. *Sangha and State in Burma*, Ithaca: Cornell University Press, 1975.

———. "The King of the Weaving Mountain." *Royal Central Asian Society Journal* 48, 1961, 229–37.

———. "A Messianic Buddhist Association in Upper Burma." *Bulletin of the School of Oriental and African Studies*, 24, 1961, 560–80.

Merry, Sally Engle. *Colonizing Hawai'i: The Cultural Power of Law*. Princeton: Princeton University Press, 2000.

Metcalf, Thomas R. *Imperial Connections: Indian in the Indian Ocean Arena, 1860–1920*. Berkeley: University of California Press, 2007.

Mills, J. A. "Burmese Peasant Response to British Provincial Rule 1852–1885," in D. B. Miller, ed., *Peasant and Politics*. Melbourne: Edward Arnold, 1978, 77–104.

Moscotti, Albert D. *British Policy and the Nationalist Movement in Burma 1917–1937*. Honolulu: University of Hawaii Press, Asian Studies Program no. 11, 1974.

Ni Ni Myint. *Burma's Struggle against British Imperialism 1885–1895*. Rangoon: University Press, 1983.

Nisbet, John. *Burma Under British Rule and Before*. London: Archibald Constable and Co., vol. I–II, 1901.

Orwell, George. *Burmese Days*, London: Harcourt Brace, 1962 (original 1934).

Pels, Peter, and Oscar Salemink, eds. *Colonial Subjects: Essays on the Practical History of Anthropology*. Ann Arbor: University of Michigan Press, 2000.

Pemberton, John. *On the Subject of Java*. Ithaca: Cornell University, 1994.

Pollack, Oliver B. "The Saya San Rebellion (1930–1932): Buddhism, Anti-colonialism, and Nationalism in Burma." *Indo-British Review*, 15, no. 1, 1988, 67–76.

Prakash, Gyan. "Subaltern Studies as Postcolonial Criticism." *American Historical Review* 99, no. 5, 1994, 1475–90.

Pye, Lucian W. *Politics, Personality, and Nation-Building: Burma's Search for Identity*. New Haven: Yale University Press, 1962.

Rabinowitz, Peter J. *Before Reading: Narrative Conventions and the Politics of Interpretation*. Ithaca: Cornell University Press, 1987.

Rafael, Vicente L. *Contracting Colonialism: Translation and Christian Conversion in Tagalog Society under Early Spanish Rule*. Third edition. Durham: Duke University Press, 2003.

Rafael, Vincente L., ed. *Figures of Criminality in Indonesia, the Philippines, and Colonial Vietnam*. Ithaca: Southeast Asia Program Publications, Cornell University, 1999.

Rosen, Lawrence. *Law as Culture: An Invitation*. Princeton: Princeton University Press, 2006.

Said, Edward W. *Orientalism*. New York: Vintage, 1979.

———. *Culture and Imperialism*. New York: Vintage Books, 1996.

Salemink, Oscar. "The Return of the Python God: Multiple Interpretations of a Millenarian Movement in Colonial Vietnam," in Peter Pels and Oscar Salemink (eds.), "Colonial Ethnographies." History and Anthropology 8, nos. 1–4, 1994, 129–64.

Sarat, Austin, and Thomas R. Kearns. "Editorial Introduction" in Sarat and Kearns (eds.), *The Rhetoric of Law*. Ann Arbor: University of Michigan Press, 1996, 1–28.

———. "Writing History and Registering Memory in Legal Decisions and Legal Practices: An Introduction," in Sarat and Kearns (eds.), *History, Memory, and the Law*. Ann Arbor: University of Michigan Press, 1999, 1–24.

———, eds. *History, Memory and the Law*. Ann Arbor: University of Michigan Press, 1999.

———, eds. *Law in the Domains of Culture*. Ann Arbor: University of Michigan, 1998.

———, eds. *Law's Violence*. Ann Arbor: University of Michigan Press, 1995.

———, eds. *The Rhetoric of Law*. Ann Arbor: University of Michigan Press, 1996.

Sarkisyanz, Emanuel. *Buddhist Backgrounds of the Burma Revolution*. The Hague: M. Nijhoff, 1965.

Sathyamurthy, T. V. "Indian Peasant Historiography: A Critical Perspective on Ranajit Guha's Work." *Journal of Peasant Studies* 18, no. 1, 1990, 92–144.

Saya San. *Let-hkanu-zu-kyan*. Moulmein: Myanmar taing thadin-za pon-hneik-taik, 1927.

———. *Weik-za theik-pan in-got-taya-kyan.* Nat-talin: Pyinna alin-bya, n.d.
Scott, James C. *The Art of Not Being Governed: An Anarchist History of Mainland Southeast Asia.* New Haven: Yale University Press, 2009.
———. *The Moral Economy of the Peasant: Rebellion and Subsistence in Southeast Asia.* New Haven and London: Yale University Press, 1976.
———. *Weapons of the Weak: Everyday Forms of Peasant Resistance.* New Haven and London: Yale University Press, 1985.
Scott, Sir James G. *The Burman: His Life and Notions.* New York: W. W. Norton, 1963 (original 1882).
Sears, Laurie J. "The Contingency of Autonomous History," in Laurie J. Sears, ed., *Autonomous Histories, Particular Truths: Essays in Honor of John Smail.* Madison: University of Wisconsin, Center for Southeast Asian Studies 11, 1993, 3–35.
Singha, Radhika. *A Despotism of Law: Crime and Justice in Early Colonial India.* Delhi: Oxford University Press, 1998.
Smith, Donald E. *Religion and Politics in Burma.* Princeton: Princeton University Press, 1965.
Solomon, Robert L. "Saya San and the Burmese Rebellion." *Modern Asian Studies*, 3, no. 3, 1969, 209–23.
Spiro, Melford. *Burmese Supernaturalism.* Englewood Cliffs: Prentice Hall, 1967.
———. *Buddhism and Society: A Great Tradition and Its Vicissitudes.* New York: Harper & Row, 1970.
Starr, June, and Jane F. Collier (eds.), *History and Power in the Study of Law: New Directions in Legal Anthropology.* Ithaca: Cornell University, 1987.
Steinberg, David I. *Burma: A Socialist Nation of Southeast Asia.* Boulder: Westview Press, 1982.
———, ed. *In Search of Southeast Asia.* Honolulu: University of Hawaii Press, 1987.
Stoler, Ann Laura. "'In Cold Blood': Hierarchies of Credibility and the Politics of Colonial Narratives." *Representations,* 37, 1992, 151–89.
———. "Sexual Affronts and Racial Frontiers: European Identities and the Cultural Politics of Exclusion in Colonial Asia," in Frederick Cooper and Ann Laura Stoler, eds., *Tensions of Empire.* Berkeley: University of California Press, 1997, 198–237.
———, and Frederick Cooper. "Between Metropole and Colony: Rethinking a Research Agenda," in Ann Stoler and Frederick

Cooper (eds.), *Tensions of Empire: Colonial Cultures in a Bourgeois World*. Berkeley: University of California Press, 1997, 1–58.

Tai, Hue-Tam Ho Tai. *Millenarianism and Peasant Politics in Vietnam*. Cambridge: Harvard University Press, 1983.

Tarling, Nicholas. *The Cambridge History of Southeast Asia*, volume 2. Cambridge: Cambridge University Press, 1992.

Taylor, Robert H. "The Burmese Concepts of Revolution," in Mark Hobart and Robert H. Taylor, eds., *Context Meaning and Power in Southeast Asia*. Ithaca: Cornell University Southeast Asia Program, 1986, pp.79–92.

———. "Politics in Late Colonial Burma: The Case of U Saw." *Modern Asian Studies*, 10, 2, 1976, 161–94.

———. *An Underdeveloped State: The Study of Modern Burma Politics*. Melbourne: Monash University, Centre for Southeast Asian Studies (working paper no. 28), 1983.

Thompson, John Seaburg. "Marxism in Burma," in Frank N. Trager, ed., *Marxism in Southeast Asia: A Study of Four Countries*. Stanford: Stanford University Press, 1959.

Tinker, Hugh. *The Foundations of Local Self-government in India, Pakistan, and Burma*. London: Athlone, 1954.

Trager, Frank N. *Burma: From Kingdom to Republic; A Historical and Political Analysis*. New York: Praeger, 1966.

———. *Furnivall of Burma: An Annotated Bibliography of the Works of John S. Furnivall*. New Haven: Yale University Press, Southeast Asian Studies (bibliography series no. 8), 1963.

Trautmann, Thomas. *Aryans and British India*. Berkeley: University of California, 1997.

Turton, Andrew and ShigeharuTanabe, eds. *History and Peasant Consciousness in South East Asia*. Osaka National Museum of Ethnology, Senri Ethnological Studies no. 13, 1984.

Von der Mehden, Fred R. *Religion and Nationalism in Southeast Asia: Burma, Indonesia, and the Philippines*. Madison: University of Wisconsin Press, 1968.

Winichakul, Thongchai. *Siam Mapped: A History of the Geo-body of a Nation*. Honolulu: University of Hawaii Press, 1994.

———. "Writing at the Interstices: Southeast Asian Historians and Postnational Histories in Southeast Asia" in Abu Talib Ahmad and Tan Liok Ee (eds.), *New Terrains in Southeast Asian History*. Athens: Ohio University Press, 2003, 3–29.

Wood, Conrad. *The Moplah Rebellion and Its Genesis*. New Delhi: Peoples Publishing House 1987.
Woodman, Dorothy. *The Making of Burma*. London: Cresset Press, 1962.
Yang, Anand A., ed. *Crime and Criminality in British India*. Association for Asian Studies no. XLII. Tucson: University of Arizona Press, 1985.
Young, Robert. *White Mythologies: Writing History and the West*. London: Routledge, 1990.
Zinoman, Peter. *The Colonial Bastille: A History of Imprisonment in Vietnam, 1862–1940*. Berkeley: University of California Press, 2001.

Memoirs and Autobiographies

Ba Maw. *Breakthrough in Burma: Memoirs of a Revolution*. New Haven: Yale University Press, 1968.
Ba U. *My Burma*. New York: Taplinger Publishing, 1958.
Collis, Maurice. *Trials in Burma*. London: Faber and Faber, 1938.
Gwynn, Sir Charles William. *Imperial Policing*. London: Macmillan, 1936.
Mi Mi Khaing. *Burmese Family*. Bloomington: Indiana University Press, 1962.
Warren, C. V. *Burmese Interlude*. Plymouth: Skeffington and Son, 1937.
White, A. J. S. *The Burma of AJ; Memoirs of A. J. S. White*. London: British Association for Cemeteries in South Asia, 1991.
White, Herbert Thirkell. *A Civil Servant in Burma*. London: Edward Arnold, 1913.

INDEX

Adas, Michael, 24, 25, 171, 172, 195, 204, 205, 211
Alantaung, 59, 60, 64, 68, 117, 210, 221
Alaungpaya, 3, 10, 225
Amulet, 2, 55, 56, 57, 67, 79, 97, 109, 111, 140, 150, 156, 162, 187, 208
Anagatavamsa, 208
Andaman Islands, 14
Anglo-Burmese War, 27
  First, 11
  Third, 12
Annexation, 2, 11, 12, 50, 53
Anticolonial, 2, 11, 25, 38, 39, 148, 167, 169, 170, 176, 192, 194, 198, 206, 207, 211, 218
ASEAN, 223
Arakan, 11, 14
Area-studies, 9, 28, 192, 193, 195, 196, 198
Athin, 6, 16, 67, 119, 144, 149, 151, 152
  Wunthanu, 7, 17, 18, 26, 116, 130, 143, 144, 145, 146, 148, 149, 150, 153, 154, 174, 182, 205
Aung Hla, 6, 108, 110, 149, 153
Aung San, 219
Aung San Suu Kyi, 222
Ava, 10, 11

Ba Maw, 8, 111, 112, 114, 117
Ba U, U, 123, 178
Baguley, J. M., 117, 119
Bandit, 8, 11, 12, 14, 18, 68, 140
Bengal, 80, 81, 87, 88, 90, 92, 94
  Criminal Law Amendment Act, 78, 79, 81, 90
  Government, 89
  Revolutionaries, 47, 81, 87, 89, 90, 92, 94, 95
  Revolutionary Assoc., 92, 94, 97
  Revolutionary Party, 80, 81, 84, 88, 89, 92
  Terrorists, 80, 84, 87, 88, 91
Bengali, 91, 92, 95, 96, 98, 99
Blue Book Report, 36, 38, 61, 71, 112, 118, 133, 141, 142, 161, 163, 178, 200, 204, 209
Bo, 6, 155
  Aung Pe, 6
  Aung Shwe, 6
  Min Aung, 200
  Min Yaung, 219
  Taungbyat, 155
Bose, Rash Bihari, 88
British, 1, 2, 6, 8–16, 20, 22, 24, 27, 31–33, 38, 48, 50, 52, 53, 55–58, 60, 66, 68, 69, 77, 78, 88, 89, 96, 116–20, 122, 123, 130, 132, 143, 150, 157, 160, 162, 164–66, 168–71, 173, 176–78, 180, 181, 193, 195, 197, 198, 202, 203, 211, 223
  Administration, 53, 60, 89, 157
  Authorities, 12, 88, 118
  Burma, 1, 12, 14–16, 20, 24, 32, 38, 78, 143, 160, 162, 176, 178, 211
  India, 2, 11–14, 77
Buddha, 65, 199
  Future, 3, 23, 170, 171, 195, 200, 201, 202, 204
  Gotoma, 199, 202
  Maitreya, 23, 194, 199–204, 207, 208, 210
  Metteya, 170, 194, 203
Buddhism, 22, 57, 147, 148, 167–71, 183, 191, 193–95, 197–205, 207, 209, 210
Buddhist, 2–4, 7, 10, 12, 16, 20, 22–24, 55, 68, 89, 147, 151, 167, 170, 171, 194–97, 199–204, 206–8, 217, 223
Hindu-Buddhist, 3
Burma Criminal Law Amendment Ordinance, 79, 86, 87, 90, 91, 99

Burma Criminal Law Amendment Act, 81
The Burma Delta, 24, 166
Burma Leglislative Council, 8, 14, 19, 78, 84, 91, 93, 94
Burma Rebellion General File, 33, 58, 69, 76, 113, 161, 196
Burma Rebellion Trials Ordinance, 79, 82, 85, 86, 97, 99, 110, 112
Burma Rifles, 62
Burmese Culture, 13, 14, 34, 36, 52, 55, 57, 97, 98, 99, 109, 122, 126, 131, 132, 139, 152, 157, 171, 173, 180, 181, 183, 197, 203, 209, 216
Burmese-ness, 216

Cady, John F., 21, 164, 165, 167, 179
Cakkavartin, 10, 23, 170, 195, 201, 202, 203, 204, 206
Capitation tax. *See* Tax
Carey, Bertram S., 52–54, 57, 61, 197, 204 ("Cary," 207, 208)
Causes of the Tharrawaddy Rebellion, 66, 69, 76, 77, 144, 145
Chittagong, 92
Colonialism, 23, 25, 28–31, 56, 69, 132, 167, 169, 171, 192, 194, 205, 216
Coronation, 2, 10, 125, 126, 178, 198, 200, 202
Counter-insurgency, 2, 8, 9, 31, 33, 34, 36, 39, 48, 50, 60, 66, 71, 76–79, 86–89, 93, 95–99, 106–8, 112, 115, 116, 128, 131, 132, 139, 141, 142, 146, 148, 151, 153, 160, 181, 196, 209, 210, 216, 217, 221
    Law, 31, 33, 36, 39, 79, 115, 116, 128, 132, 142, 153, 217
Court, 2
    Factionalism, 9
    Konbaung, 11
Crime, 18, 31, 52, 82, 93
Criminalization, 68, 87, 96, 98, 130

Dacoit, 12, 80, 88, 90
    Dacoity, 69, 140, 143
Dedaye, 149, 153
Delhi, 1, 19
Democracy, 222, 223
Dirks, Nicholas B., 216

Eggar, Arthur, 111, 112
Emergency Powers, 8, 33, 35, 77, 95, 97
Epistemology, 32, 39, 115, 123, 209
Ethnology, 10, 31, 34–39, 47, 51–57, 59, 62–64, 66, 67, 70, 71, 76, 78, 79, 80, 86, 87, 96, 107–10, 115, 119, 121, 122, 129, 132, 133, 139, 140, 143, 146, 148, 150, 152, 156, 161, 189, 192, 195–98, 200, 201, 204–9, 211, 212, 216, 218, 220, 224, 225
    Rebellion, 10, 34–38, 52–54, 56–59, 64, 66, 67, 70, 71, 76, 79, 80, 86, 87, 96, 107, 109–11, 115, 119, 122, 133, 139, 140, 143, 146, 148, 149, 150, 152, 156, 161, 180, 192, 195–98, 200, 201, 204–9, 211, 212, 218, 220, 224, 225
Execution, 85, 139

15th Punjabis, 62

Gaing, 23, 52, 149, 199–201
Galon, 6, 65, 67, 68, 116–26, 130, 131, 144, 145, 150, 151, 155, 157, 179, 204, 217, 220, 221
Garuda, 2, 3, 6, 39, 65, 67, 116, 122, 150, 204
Genealogy, 38, 70, 113, 216
General Council of Burmese Associations 4, 6, 16, 17, 26, 88, 89, 94, 98, 120, 144, 145, 147–50, 155, 156, 219, 220
General Council of Sangha Sammeggi (GCSS), 17, 144, 145, 147, 148, 156
Ghosal, 127, 128
Ghose, Rash Bihari, 89
God's Army, 226
Governor, 10, 84, 95
    Acting, 1
    General of India, 85, 89, 90, 91

Hall, D. G. E., 21, 162–64
Han Tha, U, 149, 154
Harvey, G. E., 21, 57, 162–64, 176
Headmen, 1, 2, 12, 61, 62, 156
Henzada, 6, 117
Historiography, 21, 28, 161, 165, 176, 177, 206

Healing, 4, 13, 150, 208
Herbert, Patricia, 26, 27, 133, 174, 175, 196, 211
Heritage, 3, 37, 192

Identity, 16, 20 22, 28, 29, 33, 37, 39, 54, 63, 125, 150, 155, 160, 161, 171, 193, 201, 204, 210, 217, 223, 224
India, 2, 8, 11–14, 16–18, 21, 31, 32, 47, 50, 56, 57, 59, 61, 63, 64, 66, 76–82, 84–88, 90–92, 118, 129, 143, 165, 193, 211
Indian Civil Service, 12, 13
Indian Penal Code, 18, 80–82, 85, 93, 97
Insein, 6, 127
Invulnerability, 51, 130, 150, 180
Irrawaddy
   Delta (region), 1, 2 (as Lower Burma Delta), 11, 19 (as delta region)
   River, 48
   Valley, 13

Judges, 9, 82, 83, 113, 116, 121, 131, 132, 156, 220

Karen National Union, 226
King, 2, 3, 9, 10, 12, 35, 39, 48–51, 54, 55, 59, 60, 65, 68,76, 80, 81, 85, 93, 94, 106, 111, 116, 117, 122, 125, 130, 144, 149–54, 174, 179, 195, 198, 201, 202, 204, 205, 210, 217, 221, 225
Kingship, 2, 10, 26, 35, 39, 56, 57, 60, 63, 64, 68, 69, 71, 76, 87, 98, 106, 113, 115, 122, 125, 130, 132, 142, 143, 143, 149–51, 157, 165, 169, 170, 173, 178, 194, 196–99, 202, 204, 205, 207, 208, 211, 225
Konbaung Dynasty, 3–4, 11 (about Konbaung, 10), 12 (king), 54, 136, 198
Knowledge production
   33, 38, 56, 58, 129, 131, 217

Law, 8, 14, 31, 33, 35–39, 58, 79, 86, 89, 92–94, 97, 106, 107, 109, 115, 116, 129, 131–33, 142, 153, 196, 217
Legislation, 8, 14, 18, 35, 70, 77–82, 84–90, 93–96, 98, 99, 107, 196
Letpada, 117

London, 1, 19, 21, 47, 48, 61, 67, 78, 79, 81, 82, 84, 91, 96, 110, 131, 141, 161, 165
Lower Burma, 2, 4, 7, 10

Mandalay, 2, 11, 52, 57
Maung Gyi, Joseph, 1, 91 (as Maung Gyi, 92, 93)
Maymyo, 62
Memory, 33, 36, 51, 54, 56–61, 64, 68, 69, 115, 116, 198, 212, 218, 219, 221
Military, 6, 8, 12, 18, 47, 53, 59, 61, 82, 107, 140, 179, 216, 219, 223–26
Millenarian, 3, 23–25, 52, 170–73, 191, 193, 194, 196, 198, 201, 202, 204, 205, 207, 210, 211
Millenarianism, 25, 26, 39, 169–71, 180, 194–96, 201, 210
Minlaung, 3, 35, 54, 55, 57–59, 63, 64, 71, 76, 77, 87, 89, 96, 98, 99, 106, 108, 110, 116, 129, 140, 142, 144, 149, 150, 194, 196, 197, 202, 204–7, 209, 210, 217, 218
Monarchy, 2, 11, 12, 17, 26, 35, 50, 51, 53–60, 64, 65, 67, 68, 96, 98, 99, 106, 116, 125, 143, 144, 148, 149,151–53, 168, 171, 194, 198, 203, 205, 218, 219
Monk, 7, 8, 11, 12, 17, 47, 51, 55, 69, 78, 88, 89, 96–98, 146–48, 151, 152, 156, 163, 167, 193, 208, 216, 219, 220, 222–24. *See also* Sangha
Morris, Ralph Clarence, 66–69, 77, 181, 182
Moscotti, Albert D., 177–79

Naga, 3, 6, 67, 68, 122, 123, 125, 126, 150, 208, 221
Narrative, 2, 8, 9, 20–22, 25, 27, 28, 31–39, 47, 48, 50, 54, 64, 66, 68, 70, 77, 78–80, 83, 86, 87, 111–16, 119, 121, 128–31, 133, 139, 141, 142, 144, 146, 149, 152, 153, 157, 158, 160, 161, 164, 168, 171, 172, 175–82, 191–93, 195, 196, 198, 201–5, 208–11, 214, 216, 221, 224
Nat, 111, 180, 199, 200
Nationalism, 20, 23, 28, 147, 148, 165, 167–70, 175, 182

Nationalist, 3, 4, 9, 17, 18, 20–22, 32, 52,
   60, 63, 65–69, 96, 118, 130, 141,
   143, 145, 146, 148–50, 155, 156,
   164–68, 170, 172, 175–77, 192,
   195, 197, 198, 202, 204, 210–12,
   217, 219, 220, 223
Naypyidaw, 225
New Delhi, 6, 11, 12, 47, 48, 59, 61, 67, 77,
   78, 79, 80, 81, 82, 84, 85, 86, 110,
   131, 141, 161

Oaths, 2, 51, 69, 120, 150–52, 162, 179, 180
Origins and Causes of the Burma Rebellion
   1930–1932, 58, 83, 133, 141, 142,
   145, 150, 157, 160–63, 173, 177,
   178, 180, 181, 201, 203, 210
Oktama, U, 88, 89, 96, 98, 145, 147, 156
   as U Ottama, 17, 98, 99, 220
Opposition, 67, 84, 85, 88, 93, 94, 95
   Groups, Movements, 12, 223, 224
   Parties, 67, 80, 222

Paddy/Padi, 2, 144, 167, 221
Pagoda, 48, 126, 221
Palace, 2, 6, 48, 49, 59, 60, 63, 64, 65, 68,
   157, 202, 221
Patron, 10, 223
Patron-Client, 10, 155, 224
Patronage, 10, 12, 19, 80, 147, 203, 225
Peasant, 2–4, 9, 17, 19–21, 23–25, 27–29,
   31, 32, 34, 35, 52, 53, 55–57, 60,
   67–69, 71, 77, 78, 87, 96, 106, 110,
   116, 117, 125, 129, 130, 132, 141,
   143, 144, 148, 149, 154, 158, 166,
   169, 170, 172–75, 177, 182, 191–
   98, 201, 202, 205–7, 209, 210–12,
   216–21, 223, 224
Peasantry, 2, 32, 60, 77, 125, 130, 165, 175
Pegu, 6, 10
   Yoma, 48, 221
Phashwegyaw, 1, 61, 220
Police, 1, 6, 7, 11, 19, 47, 54, 61–63, 78, 92,
   110, 132, 164, 223
Pongyi, 7, 55, 144, 148, 151, 152, 167, 197,
   208, 209
Pretender (king), 3, 21, 47, 55, 57, 63, 64,
   68, 75, 76, 94, 96, 106, 111, 129,
   132, 197, 207, 217
Production of knowledge. *See* Knowledge
   production

Prophet, 3, (25), 52, 58, 171, 172, 204, 206,
   207, 217
Protest, 11, 14, 16, 25, 27–29, 33, 37, 56,
   60, 98, 130, 158, 164, 165, 170–72,
   175, 185, 206, 208, 209, 211, 216,
   222, 224
Pyapon, 6, 93

Rangoon, 1, 14, 16, 47, 48, 59, 61, 62, 77,
   78, 80, 81, 84, 85, 87, 88, 90, 92, 95,
   97, 129, 149
Officials/authorities, 1, 6, 8, 47, 54, 59,
   61, 70, 79, 80, 81, 82, 83, 84, 86, 90,
   94, 97, 106, 110, 130, 131, 141, 160,
   181
University, 17
Rebellion, 3, 6–10, 12, 13, 18–28, 32–39,
   47–71, 76–80, 82–91, 94–99,
   106–25, 128–33, 139–46, 148–54,
   156–58, 160–83, 191–212, 216–21,
   224, 225
Religion, 2, 10, 16, 17, 20, 25, 37, 55, 106,
   168, 170, 171, 173, 179, 191–99,
   201-3, 206, 207, 209, 211, 224
Revolt, 1, 9, 11, 19, 20, 23, 24, 27, 47, 48,
   52, 54, 56, 60, 69, 122, 123, 131,
   152, 162, 164, 166, 167, 170, 172,
   173, 174, 180, 181, 191, 192, 193,
   194, 195, 198, 201, 204, 205, 207,
   216, 217, 221
Resistance Ethnology. *See* Ethnology,
   Rebellion
Rice, 4, 27, 48, 221
   Economy, 1, 24

Sandanti Galon Organisation
Sangha, 17, 22, 23, 167, 168, 170, 177,
   299, 223
Sarkiyanz, Emanuel (listed as both E.
   Manuel and Emanuel), 23, 24,
   170, 171, 172, 195, 201, 202, 203,
   204, 205
Saw, U, 8, 14, 19
Saya Sa, 117, 149, 154
Saya San, 2–6, 8–10, 19–28, 32–39, 48,
   51–54, 59–61, 64–71, 77, 78,
   80–81, 83, 84, 88, 89, 94, 95, 98,
   106–22, 124–33, 139, 140, 144,
   145, 149–55, 157, 158, 161, 162,

164, 165, 167–78, 180, 181, 183,
    191–205, 208–11, 216–21, 225
Scott, James C., 24, 166
Se Saya, 4, 209
September 2007, 222
Setkya-min, 170, 180, 200, 202, 203. *See also
    Cakkavartin*
Shan , 65
    State, 2, 6, 139, 151
Shwebo, 13
    District 3, 62
Shwenakwin (village), 117, 120, 149
Singapore, 88
Soe Thein, GCBA, 65, 89, 94, 120, 144,
    146, 155, 156
Southeast Asian, 3, 9, 10, 28, 32, 34, 35, 38,
    39, 60, 133, 166, 169, 173, 191–96,
    209, 210, 218
    Culture, 20, 25, 28, 37, 39, 168, 170,
    191, 196, 206–8, 210, 216, 217
    Worldview, 33, 192, 193, 196, 216
Southeast Asian studies, 25, 29, 37, 38, 39,
    166, 168, 169, 195, 207
Special Rebellion Tribunal, 8, 36, 71, 86,
    98, 106, 107, 109, 110, 112, 115,
    121, 129, 131, 141, 149
Subaltern studies, 31, 34, 58, 209
Superstition, 21–23, 39, 57, 60, 145, 146,
    157, 163, 167, 171, 173, 176, 191,
    192, 195, 216, 225

Tattoo, 2, 3, 6, 7, 14, 39, 51, 55, 56, 63, 65,
    67, 69, 78, 79, 87, 88, 96, 97, 98,
    109, 111, 119, 122, 123, 124, 125,
    130, 140, 145, 147, 150
Taungnyogale village, 126
Taxes, 2, 6, 17, 144, 149, 163, 167 (as
    taxation), 205
    Capitation, 6, 69, 120, 123

Collection of, 1
Collectors, 4
Thathameda, 6
Tenasserim, 11
Tharrawaddy, 1, 2, 6, 8, 13, 14, 19, 35,
    36, 47–52, 55, 59, 61–64, 66–71,
    76–78, 80, 85, 87, 88, 91, 93, 94, 96,
    110, 117, 124, 140, 133, 145, 153,
    154, 163, 164, 178, 221
Thayetmyo, 6, 7
Thebaw, King, 12, 14
Throne, 9, 10, 12, 21, 35, 52, 54, 56, 59, 68,
    94, 129, 152, 153, 200, 202, 204,
    207, 217
Thupannaka Galuna Raja, 65, 120, 122,
    150, 178. As *Thupannaka Galuna
    Raja*, 150
Trial, 8, 36, 67, 69, 78, 79, 81, 83, 85, 87,
    90, 93, 106, 110, 111–18, 123, 125,
    126, 128–33, 149, 150, 153, 156,
    178, 181, 221
Twin(s), 226

University, 87, 147
    Rangoon, 17
Upper Burma, 3, 10,11, 52, 55, 57, 62,
    139, 225

Vishnu, 3

Weikza, 199–201, 208, 209
Wisara, U, 17, 147, 219, 220
Wunthanu, 65, 149, 153, 154
    Athin. *See under Athin*

Yandabo, Treaty of, 11
Young Men's Buddhist Association, 16,
    147, 219

Index 247

www.ingramcontent.com/pod-product-compliance
Lightning Source LLC
Chambersburg PA
CBHW031239290426
44109CB00012B/361